OUT *of* BOUNDS

OUT *of* BOUNDS

COMING OUT OF SEXUAL ABUSE, ADDICTION, AND MY LIFE OF LIES IN THE NFL CLOSET

❖❖

ROY SIMMONS

with DAMON DIMARCO

in collaboration with
DAVID FISHER *and* JIMMY HESTER

CARROLL & GRAF PUBLISHERS
NEW YORK

OUT OF BOUNDS
Coming Out of Sexual Abuse, Addiction,
and My Life of Lies in the NFL Closet

Published by
Carroll & Graf Publishers
An Imprint of Avalon Publishing Group Inc.
245 West 17th Street, 11th Floor
New York, NY 10011

AVALON
publishing group incorporated

ISBN-10: 0-7867-1681-9
ISBN-13: 978-0-78671-681-4

Book design by Pauline Neuwirth

Printed in the United States of America
Distributed by Publishers Group West

Dedicated to the memory of
my grandmother, Lou Smith Simmons.
If there's anything good about me,
it came from you, Grandma.

And to all the women in my life
who paid for my maturing process
with the currency of their affections.

To Sheila, Roz, my loving mother Norma,
and my dear daughter Kara, especially.

Thank you.

OUT *of* BOUNDS

1

San Francisco, California, January 1993

I MET THIS guy named Mike in East Palo Alto. He was a fast-talking Cuban dude built squat like a sparkplug with wide shoulders and big hips. Mike liked to use his hands a lot when he talked. He'd cut the air in front of his face with kung fu zigzags every time he used a verb. Watching Mike talk was like watching somebody go through a contortion. The dude was totally wired.

He had skin as black as charcoal and this huge-ass smile glowing white in the middle of his face. His front teeth were buck, like a beaver and, now that I think about it, that's just what Mike was really like: a Cubano beaver. Busy, busy, busy—dance, dance, dance. If that dude got himself a flat tail and some tree trunks I bet he could dam up a river in no time flat. Mike could be industrious.

I found this energy attractive, which is why I did him. I'm pretty sure we didn't go all the way, though—maybe we did. I know I probably wanted to. But doing it and wanting to isn't the same thing. My recollections of back then can get kinda blurry.

Mike had a Winnebago. He kept a shitload of crack balled up in a lump of wax paper on the kitchenette counter. We stopped by the Winnebago and smoked the crack. Pretty soon my head was spinning very fast.

We smoked and drank and smoked some more. I was feeling that particular way so I blew him a second time; why not? Mike had really good shit, he deserved some kind of reward for that. When the shit was all gone, though, I was really sad. I looked at Mike and said, "Damn."

But Mike didn't feel sad. He just sort of shrugged. He looked at me and said, "Aw, thas awright, bro. I know where we can get *lots* more."

❖

MIKE HAD A real close, personal connection with some folks who ran an exchange. They'd trade anything you handed them for drugs.

"Anything at all?" I asked.

"Sure, man. Cars. Computers. Clothes. Anything."

"You get a fair price?"

"Bro," Mike said, and he took a step back from me with his hands held up to his shoulders to show me he was sincere. "Would I fuck with *you*? Why on earth would I fuck with *you*?"

That was good enough for me. We jumped in my friend Gladys's car and headed out on the highway. My apartment in San Mateo was twenty minutes away. It was broiling hot outside—you could see the heat waves coming up off the asphalt ahead of you—and the air conditioner was broken in Gladys' car. We kept the windows rolled down and the radio turned up, shouting over the wind. Classic R&B from 101 point something.

When we got to my apartment, we ransacked the place. All the little things went: my clock, my jewelry, some table lamps. We jumped back in the car and drove to East Palo Alto, where we made the exchange with this guy who worked out of the back of an appliance store. Mike handled the transaction. All the shit I'd gathered up bought us a little less than four grams of rock. I was hoping for more. But we took what we had back to the Winnebago and started smoking again.

By now I was royally fucked up. Mike wasn't as bad off as I was, though. Looking back now, it's real clear to me: he kept himself sharp so he could play me like a fool.

❖

WHEN THE CRACK was gone we went back to my apartment again. This time I grabbed my Sony 32-inch TV set out of the living room. I also took my stereo system, a Sony amp, double tape deck, stereo tuner, modified amp unit, CD player, and turntable. It was all top-of-the-line equipment that had cost me thousands of dollars when I bought it—I figured it was worth a lot of crack. But I wanted more. I ducked into my roommate's bedroom and grabbed my roommate Thomas's 27-inch TV, too.

Grabbing Thomas's property started two voices arguing in the back of my head. These voices were both very agitated. They screamed at me. The first voice said, *No! Stop! Roy, you stupid sonovabitch! What the fuck do you think you're doing? Thomas is your friend.* But the second voice was louder. The second voice shouted the first voice down, and the second voice said, *Fuck it, man. Do it. Buy the crack. Smoke it. It'll be all right. You'll make it all work out somehow. Meantime, do what you gotta do.*

I followed the second voice.

The second voice had some other things to say. For instance, the second voice said it was sorry if I was disappointed in myself, but what other kind of behavior could anyone expect from a good-for-nothing loser addict who'd done nothing but bring heartache and suffering to everyone who'd ever loved him throughout the entire course of his life? The second voice had evidence to present on behalf of this opinion. First, I'd brought a beautiful baby daughter into the world and promptly abandoned her. Second, I'd lied to my daughter's mother—I'd cheated on her, with men. Third, I'd kept my chemical addictions under wrap for so long that I couldn't stand before another human being on earth, lowly or grand, without having to put on some kind of emotional mask. I was dishonest. I was untrustworthy. I lied. I stole. I manipulated.

The second voice was very gentle indeed. It told me that sometimes this can be a person's role in life. We find ourselves cast as the bringer of destruction, heartache, fear, and evil to the world. It's nothing personal. It's just destiny. Fate. We don't have any choice but to play the parts we're given in life. Try not to judge things too much.

We went back to East Palo Alto.

❖

ON OUR THIRD trip back to San Mateo we started to get real serious. Mike borrowed a big white station wagon from one of his friends so we could load up more items in one trip. Then he called up some people and gave them my address over the phone.

"Be there in, like, half an hour, Bro. Bring a truck." When we arrived at the apartment, these men had already arrived. They were loading every item in my apartment into the back of a cube van. My stuff, Thomas's stuff. It didn't matter. Everything went. The refrigerator, the microwave oven, the lightbulbs, the fixtures, the furniture. By this point a refrigerator, a microwave, lightbulbs, fixtures and furniture weren't important anymore. But crack was *very* important.

I watched them walk Thomas's antique grandfather clock out the front door and struggle to put it on the truck. One of the loading guys said, "Don't scratch it, man, that looks like some really good shit." It was. Thomas and his family had had that clock in their family since the beginning of the nineteenth century. It was the finest thing he owned, and he loved it. It worked beautifully, too; gave off a chime every hour. The tone of the chime was beautiful, too; rich and dark like the wood of the clock itself. *Dong! Dong! Dong!*

The loading man said, "Watch the base, heave it up now." And that's just what they did. They heaved the clock up into the back of the truck where it disappeared from my sight, and I never saw it again. Mike came around the side of the house, paused for a second to eyeball the work, and clapped me on the shoulder. Then he handed me a lit splif and I took a good hit from it.

The loading crew kept working for a long time.

❖

ONE OF THE guys from the cube van finally ambled over and said, "That's it." Mike said, "Okay," and I felt myself nodding. It's like I wasn't in charge of my body, though. I was just sort of *inhabiting* my body and going along for the ride. My eyes weren't my own, they were just a couple of windshields that I looked out of while all this was going on. There was no steering wheel in the cab of this machine. I could observe everything that happened to me, but I couldn't control my actions.

The loading men jumped into the cab of their cube van and the driver stuck his arm out the window. He waved at Mike. Mike waved back.

Then the van pulled out of the apartment complex parking lot and was gone. Mike clapped me on the shoulder again and said, "You ready?" Again I nodded. "Good," said Mike. "Now we go pick up the payoff." We climbed into the station wagon—Mike was driving—and headed back toward East Palo Alto where the crack was waiting.

❖

We never got there. The cops pulled us over on Highway 82. Apparently they'd noticed a couple of black guys tooling through the white side of town in a station wagon jam-packed with all sorts of electrical appliances sticking out the side windows. This made them suspicious.

A cop with dark sunglasses stuck his head in the driver's side window and asked Mike for his license and registration. Mike didn't have a license and the station wagon wasn't his; he couldn't find the registration. The cops were not pleased. They were pretty cold to begin with and they got even more unfriendly when they checked in with radio dispatch and found out that there was a warrant out for Mike's arrest. This was news to me, but then . . . it sort of fit.

The cops asked Mike to please get out of the station wagon, which he did. Then they put him in the back of their cruiser and made sure he was handcuffed to the convict bar before they turned their attention to me.

The officer who'd leaned in the driver's side window came around to my side of the car and said, "Sir, may I see your driver's license please?"

I said, "Yes." But really I was thinking something like this:

Oh mister officer, sir! I'm scared outta my britches here. But—in a way? Thank you. Thank you for stopping me! Man, you wouldn't believe the day I've been having! I did some very bad things today and I think it's time that somebody like you came along and helped me put on the brakes. This shit's getting way too intense for me. It's getting too hard just to maintain. *So here's my license and could I ask a favor of you? What do you think . . . could you lock me up, too?*

They didn't arrest me. Don't ask me why. Shit, man, anybody could see I was higher than Sputnik. My hands shook so bad when I handed the policeman my license, I almost dropped it. In the station wagon's rearview mirror, my eyes had that bugged-out, pinpoint-pupils look worn by only the most extreme drug abusers. My face was bathed in sweat. My shirt was stuck to my body. Yeah, it was hot out that day but somehow I didn't think that would fool the cops. But it did. Or maybe they just didn't know what to do with me in the first place. They let me go.

A close call like that should have been enough to scare me straight right there on the spot. It didn't. After that, things got worse.

❖

HINDSIGHT IS 20/20. Looking back, I know what I should've done. Shots like that are easy to call after the play's been run and your quarterback is lying on the turf buried under twelve hundred pounds of defensive linemen. I should have been *sensible*. I should have used my brain and thought the situation through, figured out the right thing to do and stuck to it like glue. I should've sucked it up, admitted defeat, and started a new campaign to clean up the mess I'd made.

To wit, when the cops let me go, I should have driven that fucking station wagon back to my apartment in San Mateo and started refurnishing it. Didn't matter how. I could have bought yard sale furniture or scrounged up the raggedy shit folks sometimes threw out in the city dumpsters. Armchairs, sofabeds, easy chairs—the battered, cigarette-burned items with broken springs and frayed hems that college students leave out on the curb for the trashmen at the end of a semester.

Anything would have helped. Anything at all. I would still have to explain the whole deal to Thomas when he got home, and that would suck. But at least he'd have something to sit on while I poured out my heart to him and begged him to forgive me. *I admit it, I relapsed. I totally fucked up. You have every right in the world to hate me. But I'm gonna fix it, I promise. I'll dedicate my life to fixing it.*

Like I said, I know what I should have done looking back. But I didn't do it. Instead, I drove the station wagon to a filling station across the highway from my apartment. I parked it out in the far corner of the parking lot, got out, and sat down on a curb where I put my head in my hands and tried to focus on breathing for the next thirty or forty minutes. To any passerby, I must've looked like just another stoned-out crackhead watching the world go by.

❖

I GUESS I wasn't really your average stoned-out crackhead, though. In fairness to myself, most crackheads can't say they ever played professional football. They can't say they played in a Super Bowl, can't say they were ever picked in an NFL draft or did battle with the Pittsburgh Steelers' defensive line in front of 75,000 screaming fans. They can't say they've been on national television, under the bright lights, playing tag with the big men, making huge salaries, and working out endorsement deals with international sportswear companies. I had my *up* time. The average crackhead never knows anything but *down*. I had my up time and I chose to do nothing with it. I let it slip away like I'd let go of everything else in my life. My fiancée. My child. My family. Myself.

Sitting there on that curb at the filling station, I remember wondering, *Oh, baby! How you gonna get outta* this *shit? Thomas is gonna come home and Thomas is gonna kill you. He's got every right in the world—no jury in this land would convict him.* I also remember thinking, *How much lower do you have to go, Roy? When is this cycle of abuse gonna end?* Finally, I thought, *Maybe—just maybe—things would've been different if I'd come out of the closet earlier.*

It made no sense to me, none of it. I raised my head up and looked around. The sky was pinking and purpling over with dusk and I could see tall towers of twinkling lights way off in the distance, out by the water. They looked beautiful against the rose background of the sky. I heard the cry of seagulls and realized that where I was sitting was very close to the water. Close enough for a quick trip. An easy out. That's when I figured that the best damn thing in the world for me to do would be to go to those lights, climb out over the water, and throw myself off the Golden Gate Bridge.

❖

So THAT'S WHAT I did, but first I went into the filling station and bought some beer, just to keep myself steady. I climbed back into the driver's seat of the station wagon, popped the beer, turned the key in the ignition, and started driving. I was still incredibly high, blasting down Highway 5. The windows were still open and the air blowing past my face felt cooler than it had before, more inviting. The radio was still on and the Four Tops were singing. It took me half an hour to get to the bridge.

❖

I'VE ALWAYS LOVED the Golden Gate. When I was sober, I used to take long, meditative walks across it; they were very therapeutic. Sometimes I'd look down at the water rushing past and wonder what it'd be like to jump in, imagining it in that morbid way that people do when things don't really seem to make much sense. I'd read an article once in the *San Francisco Chronicle* that said nearly a thousand people had jumped from the Golden Gate since it was built. Only a handful survived. From that high up, a body hits the water doing 75 miles per hour. A trip like that's not like jumping into a lake or a pool or the ocean. The surface of the water acts like concrete when you hit it going that fast. Your body doesn't break the surface, the surface breaks you. The handful of people who survived jumping off the Golden Gate almost always kept their lives due to the fact that they hit the water feet first and at such a small angle that their organs were crushed and their bones snapped like toothpicks. They suffered massive internal injuries, but they survived.

I didn't want to survive, though. Right then I wanted to hit that water head fucking first. Do it once and do it right. For once in my life, I wanted to do something right.

❖

I PULLED OVER into a parking lot on the Marin County side of the bridge and got out of the car. I closed the door behind me and locked it. I wasn't thinking of coming back, but there was still a boom box and either a washer or a dryer—one of them, I can't remember which—tied down in the back of the station wagon. My notion was to keep them secure. I started jogging up the walkway of the bridge, and I knew from experience that I'd have a little over a half mile to go before I reached the optimal jumping point, the apex. It didn't take me long. Time was, I could run a half mile in two minutes and some pocket change. I love to run. I've always loved to run.

❖

IT WAS A cool, clear night around 8 p.m. A soft breeze was blowing across San Francisco Bay. The smell of the water filled my sinuses, the briny perfume of the ocean. The cars whizzed past me on the road, but none of them noticed me. People go out jogging on that bridge all the time. It's completely normal. It's a wonderful experience.

Back then, they didn't even have a safety fence up to keep folks from jumping. So all I had to do when I reached the apex of the bridge was hop the rail. After that there were some other barriers and obstacles to crawl under, but within moments I was right out over the water looking straight down 220 feet to where the water churned below. All I had to do was turn around. Spread my arms. Fall backward and let gravity take its course. A moment of weightlessness and that would be it. I'd finally be out of my misery.

I found my mark, got into position, closed my eyes, and prepared to let go.

❖

MY GRANDMA LOU saved me that night. She'd been dead since 1981, but death was no matter to Grandma Lou. She was a strong black woman—tough as nails—and just before I let go of that rail and killed myself, her voice popped into my head. She spoke clearly to me, as if she was standing right next to me, and she was angry.

"Roy," she said. "People who commit suicide go straight to hell." And even though I didn't turn out to be much of a Christian, I had enough of one in me at the time to stop what I was doing and give some serious thought to the situation I was in.

I had knowledge of my grandmother's views on suicide because someone close to my family had killed herself when I was twelve years old. Our next-door neighbor, Gloria, shot her brains out with a pistol one afternoon. I came home from school that day and found the whole neighborhood out on the front lawn of Gloria's house. There were police cars parked down the street with their red and blue lights flashing silently and an ambulance with some paramedics leaning against it looking bored.

Apparently, Gloria had been depressed. Her man was cheating on her again and they'd had an argument of some sort. She told him that if he wasn't going to be hers—all hers—she'd rather kill herself than continue living. He hadn't thought she was serious.

Grandma Lou moved to intercept me before I became one of the bystanders milling around. She didn't say anything when we met, she just took me by the hand and led me back toward our own little one-story house in the middle of the row at 2419 Burroughs Street. She took me right up the four sagging steps, through the screen door that used to bang shut with a loud clap behind you every time you passed through it, right into the kitchen, where she sat me down on a stool and started frying chicken for my dinner. She seemed unusually drawn.

When I asked Grandma what had happened, she shook her head and told me, "That Gloria just sent herself straight to hell, Roy. That's what happens to people who kill themselves. They go straight to hell 'cause they got no faith." At the time, I didn't really understand any of this. I didn't understand the concept of hell—I got that it was nasty, but the details were vague—and I didn't understand why Gloria would choose to *send* herself to such a place. She'd always seemed like such a sensible woman. Sure, she had a tendency to get a little sad now and then. Sometimes she cried for no apparent reason that I could see, and other times I'd avoided her because she could get so downright bleak. But she seemed way too practical a person to just up and send herself to hell. I mean, who'd want to go and do a thing like that?

I asked Grandma Lou this same question and she put it like this: "An idiot would, Roy. A person got no faith in God would want to do that."

Or someone like me, trying to jump off a bridge. I almost turned out to be an idiot, too. Just like Gloria.

Hearing Grandma Lou's voice in my head out there on the bridge was like a slap in the face. *A person got no faith in God would try and kill himself. An idiot would try it.* That's not to say that I didn't consider myself an idiot. If the truth be told, I myself had considered things that were much worse than that. But the thought of having Grandma Lou disapprove of me was too much to bear. She'd raised me all by herself when my own father made it clear that he was a drunkard, too, just like Grandma Lou's husband back in Statesboro. She took me in as her own when my mother had to head north in order to look for real work—work that paid, work with a salary that allowed you to put food in your children's bellies instead of sitting around watching them starve.

Death was one thing; I respected death. But it couldn't hold a candle to the way Grandma Lou looked when she frowned. So I hopped my ass back over that rail and ran back down the length of that bridge—all the way back to my car. I noticed that my hands were shaking again when I got in and locked them on the steering wheel. Then I drove myself very slowly back to the gas station across from my apartment.

Back in the parking lot, I sat down on that same stretch of curb and put my head in my hands again. I couldn't believe what I'd almost done. Guilt and pain and confusion welled up in me like I was gonna be sick. Instead, I started to cry. I cried so hard that I nearly choked the breath from my own lungs. I rocked back and forth in agony.

Killing myself wasn't the answer. I knew that now. All the same, if I *wasn't* going to kill myself, I knew I needed some serious help. So I went to the pay phone across the street and called 911.

When the operator picked up, I told him, "I've done a lotta drugs and I feel like hurting myself." He said: "Where are you? What is your name?" I slurred my name and other information and tried to offer directions to the filling station. None of what I said sounded right to me, but I guess the operator was satisfied with what I'd told him cause the last thing I remember hearing is him saying, "I know where you are. Stay right there. Whatever you do, don't move."

You got it, man. You got it.

I sat back down, put my head in my hands, and waited.

The ambulance arrived in twenty minutes. A pair of paramedics got out and walked over to me; I was still sitting on the curb, rocking back and forth. They asked me my name, so I gave them my ID. They took my blood pressure and checked my reflexes and shined this little flashlight in my eyes. I could see their conclusion written all over their faces. *This guy is out there, man, he is really gone.* One of them kept looking at me with this wary, suspicious expression. He kept his distance from me as if I might leap up at any moment and take a huge bite out of his neck. Even if I were capable of doing that then, I didn't. I was too tired and confused.

The paramedics strapped me to a board, loaded me into the back of the ambulance, and took me to a hospital. I hate hospitals. I was there for two days before I tried to escape and some large men in white coats physically restrained me. It was a tough job. I hadn't played pro ball in over nine years but I still had my size, I still had my strength, and I still knew how to take a man down fast with quick blows thrown from my shoulders, elbows, and arms. I think I put three of them on the floor before they stuck the needle in my arm. The world began to fade out quick, like a TV set blowing a tube. The picture got fuzzy. Then gray. Then gone. After that, for a while, I remember nothing at all.

2

Savannah, Georgia, October 1967

He stood straight and tall, a towering man at 6'3"—muscular, handsome, and broad-shouldered; he was forty years old. He had short, dark hair, brown eyes, and a fine, little moustache—perfectly trimmed—with short, perfectly trimmed sideburns. Whenever I got near him, the musky smell of Old Spice floated off him and wrapped me up in a cloud of cologne. The scent made my head dizzy, making me wonder if all men who took care of themselves smelled liked that. No one had ever taught me such things. There were no men in my life; I barely knew my father.

Sometimes I'd watch this man with the perfectly trimmed sideburns bounce down the stoop of his house in the early-morning hours, clean-shaven, smiling, and ready for work. Man, he could rock that municipal uniform he wore. It was ironed crisp. Razor-sharp creases stood out in the shirtsleeves and pants. The whole outfit was fitted to his body. Perfect.

When he spoke, he spoke deliberately. He shaped his vowels perfectly, round and full, with no trace at all of a Southern twang. To hear him talk, you'd think he was some sort of Ivy League professor or a poet or a preacher, even. But no—he was just Travis. Travis the Neighbor. I was eleven years old when he raped me.

My mother, Norma, was always away while I was growing up. She worked in a factory up north, the only place she could get a job. Sometimes she did part-time housecleaning work in New York and New Jersey, too—anything she could to make enough cash to send back down to Savannah. There wasn't much of an economy in that part of

Georgia back then. We were very poor. Grandma Lou worked as a housekeeper and nanny for a wealthy Jewish family who lived nearby, and barely made enough to make ends meet what with so many mouths to feed under her one roof.

For a long time I only knew my mother from the quick conversations we'd have from time to time over the phone.

"When you coming back, Mama?"

"Soon, baby. Real soon. I'm making good money up here. I'm gonna buy you a new pair of Converse sneakers."

She sent us money whenever she could. She sent me sneakers and some other clothes, too. From time to time she'd visit us, taking the train or the bus or whatever means was most affordable. She always came home for Christmas.

My father lived nearby but was never really part of the equation. So my early years were about me, my brother Larry, my sister Catherine, and my younger cousin Jimmy all living under the single roof of Grandma Lou's one-story roadhouse on a dirt road called Burroughs Street on the west side of Savannah, Georgia. It was a small, simple place. We didn't have much room to spare, so Larry and I shared a bedroom; we slept in separate beds. The front of the house touched the sidewalk—there was no front yard. From the sidewalk, you walked up four rickety steps up to the front porch. The screen door was the only way in or out. When I was real young, I remember we didn't have indoor plumbing, just an outhouse slouching off in the far corner of the backyard. In the summer time it stank like hell, and there were flies. Grandma Lou's house wasn't much to look at, but it was ours.

We made a good home for ourselves there. I'm not talking about the house, now; I'm talking about the home we created for each other as a family. Larry and I got along real well even though I was two years younger than he was and much, much bigger. I hear that a lot of brothers fight with each other growing up, but no, not me and Larry. We ended up liking each other a lot. Just as well, too. I might have been bigger, but Larry was compact and quick. He could pack a wallop when he wanted to.

Catherine and I got on well, too. She introduced me to all of her girlfriends, and that was cool. The truth of the matter is, I grew up in the company of women. I found out that I could fit into a girl's world as easily as I fit into the world of boys. I'd go from playing touch football on the dirt road outside our house to playing Suzie Homemaker Oven with the neighborhood girls, Allison and Sharon Cole. Boys or girls. One way was just as good as the other to me.

Grandma Lou kept us all in line, kept us together as a unit, kept us a family. She worked her behind off as a housekeeper to make sure there was always a roof over our heads and the lights were turned on. There was usually enough food in the kitchen, too. She did traditional things like cook breakfast for us on Sunday mornings. And if you didn't feel like going to church with her, she'd come into your room with a belt and start beating on anything she saw. She'd holler, "Up! Get up!" And lemme tell you: when this happened, you got up.

One time I guess I felt myself bigger than I was. I'd spent the afternoon running all over the neighborhood doing jobs for elderly folks, which was something I'd do for extra spending money. I was wearing a pair of Converse sneakers my mother'd just sent down from up north, and I had just sat down on a corner of my bed, completely exhausted. I was taking my sneakers off when Grandma Lou came in and asked me to run down to the store and bring back some milk.

I said, "I don't feel like it."

Bad move. That old woman could move like a cobra. Before I saw it coming, she grabbed up one of my sneakers and smacked me across the thigh with the sole. The hard rubber base of the sneaker hit me so hard, it opened a cut. My thigh popped open like a can of spaghetti and started bleeding. I was speechless. It wasn't so much the pain as it was that I didn't know a sneaker could do something like that. But I guess that new rubber sole just grabbed the skin and pulled it back till it stretched open and burst.

Grandma Lou stopped the moment she saw blood. She dropped the sneaker like *okay, I'm done with that now* and calmly said, "Come here. Let me look at that." This time I did exactly what she said. She put one of her home remedies on the cut and that was that. I still have a scar to this day. I guess the moral of this story—the thing about Grandma

Lou—she never apologized, didn't feel like she had to. To her mind, I had mouthed off to her and she was just doing her job. She was keeping us in line.

Travis and his wife Ellen lived in a big house in the neighborhood. Ellen called me up on a hot Saturday afternoon in October. She asked if I could come over and clean their house. 'Course I said yes.

For an eleven-year-old kid, I made pretty good money doing odd jobs around the neighborhood. I could clean a house till the doorknobs shined and the windows glowed. I could mow your lawn fast and tight, make it look like a professional landscaper had done the job. And if you sent me down to the laundromat to pick up your clothes, you never had to count your change 'cause everybody in the neighborhood knew that I never took without asking. I was honest. I was reliable. I was Roy Simmons, Junior Entrepreneur. I was the neighborhood angel.

'Course, it was Grandma Lou who taught me everything I knew about working. I remember one time when I was real small, she took me aside and told me to stand up straight, like a respectable young man. I did just like she asked. Then she spent a few moments brushing lint off my clothes and squaring my shoulders. Out of the blue, she asked me, "Roy, would you like to know the secret to success in life?"

I told her I did, and she said: "It's simple. You got to take care of people—all people—as if they was your very own. You treat their property and you treat their souls as if they was the ones that God gave to *you* Himself. If you do this, if you treat people like they was your very own—can you guess what happens?" I honestly could not. "They become a part of you," said Grandma Lou. "They become an extension of your spirit." Man, I loved the woman. She was right. She was oh, so right.

I liked cleaning Travis and Ellen's house because, for one thing, Ellen and my mother were friendly. When Mama was home, she and Ellen'd spend summer evenings together on each other's front porches, whiling the nights away with gossip and cocktails. Ellen was a generous woman by nature. She'd had a couple children with a different man, and now that they were all grown and moved away, she and Travis had no children of their own. This meant she was always spoiling me with fresh-baked cookies and little bits of extra money here and there.

When I got to the Neighbor's house that Saturday afternoon in October, Ellen pinched my ears and thanked me for coming. She told me she had errands to run but since I'd cleaned their place before, she said I could work alone, I knew what to do. "I left your money on the dresser in the bedroom," she said. "Take it when you leave. Travis's home today, he'll probably be asleep." Then she patted me on the head and left. I went to work.

Travis was often home when I worked, but he never said much to me. Our relationship consisted mostly of silent acknowledgement of the other person's presence. It was almost like we were developing our own brand of sign language when we were around one another. This time, though, he was in the bedroom, as Ellen had said. I could hear the TV on, so I set about my work, I started vacuuming. I'd almost finished the hallway carpet when Travis came out of the bedroom and bumped into me from behind on his way toward the kitchen. He didn't say a word, so I thought it was an accident and I kept on vacuuming. It was no accident.

Travis returned from the kitchen a few minutes later and went right back into the bedroom, where I saw him lay himself back down and sort of lean up against the headboard. He saw me glancing through the doorway at him and he said, "Roy. Come in here." I said, "Yes, sir." I shut off the vacuum and went inside.

It was dark in the bedroom. The blinds were closed and the curtains were drawn. I couldn't see Travis's face real well at first, but as I got closer I noticed that his eyes were red and wandering. He was breathing heavy. There was a sour smell coming off his tongue—no spicy cologne today, no municipal uniform with crisp, neat lines. Travis looked like he'd been dragged through an alley after a cat fight. He'd been drinking something heavy.

He said, "Turn around." I had no idea what he wanted so I wasn't nervous when he said that. I just stood there, confused. So Travis got out of bed and walked over to me. He turned me around and pulled down my pants. Then he bent me over the bed. I remember clench-ing the duvet in my fists. I remember being confused. I didn't know exactly what was happening to me, but I was sure it wasn't good. I felt uncomfortable. I felt ashamed. My mind was racing with all sorts of thoughts, but the one I recall standing out clearest in my mind was this: *Please, God, tell me that this shit's not happening to me.*

I felt a sharp sting. Then like a tearing. After that, my body and my mind went numb. The last thought I remember was, *What is he doing to me?*

It lasted ten or fifteen minutes maybe, I don't know. That's my best guess, but really, you could say the whole thing lasted a lifetime. I guess there's ample evidence to support that. Finally, it was over. Travis said: "There's the money for cleaning." He pointed to the dresser. Ellen had left me $15. I didn't look at him. I took the money and left.

It was dark outside. I walked home real fast. There was an awful, throbbing feeling in my behind but, apart from that, I was still numb all over. My mind was still a blank.

I walked into my house like I was walking through a dream—felt like I was floating, like I wasn't really in my body anymore. I passed by the archway to the living room and saw Grandma Lou. She looked up from the couch where she was watching professional wrestling on the TV and smiled at me. I smiled back. I said hello. She said hello back. I've learned since then that this is the way people act when crazy shit happens to them and they have no way of explaining it or figuring it out or fixing it or fighting back. We try to act normal. Looking back, I think I was in shock.

On Saturday nights Grandma Lou sat around watching TV with her quart of Colt .45 Malt Liquor. She loved to watch professional wrestling, really got into it, too. She'd lean forward on the edge of the couch almost to the point where she was about to fall off. And when something excit-ing happened, she'd leap to her feet shouting, "Thas right! Go on now! Kick his ass!" That's what I heard her say as I left her in the living room that night. As I moved down the hallway toward my bedroom, I heard her yell out, "Thas right! Go on now! Stomp him good!"

In my bedroom, I took off my clothes and something caught my eye.

Blood stains on the crotch of my Fruit of the Looms. Without thinking, I balled the underwear up in my fist, opened the flip-up hatch to the hamper behind my bedroom door, and shoved the shorts down deep in the pile of dirty laundry. That's when the numbness I'd felt since the rape finally broke like a fleeing fever and the fear hit me hard, slamming into my face like a giant fist, making me want to double over at the waist and vomit.

I took a bath and nearly scrubbed my skin off because I felt so dirty. The rest of the night was all about me walking through the house like a ghost, restless, settling nowhere. I was completely paranoid. *What did I do wrong? Does anyone know? What will they say when they find out? Grandma Lou? My brother Larry? My sister Catherine? Cousin Jimmy? The neighbors? What will I say when they ask? Should I say, 'I'm sorry'? I guess I should say, 'I'm sorry'* . . .

I thought the whole thing was my fault. I ended up staying inside that night and watching TV after Grandma Lou had gone to bed. I don't remember what I saw. My mind was moving too fast, flipping quickly through its own series of pictures.

The next day my grandmother discovered my bloody drawers and asked me if I felt sick. I told her I was fine, but nothing I said could convince her. She took me into the dining room and made me take my pants off. She bent me over in almost the exact same manner as Travis had and took a look at my butt. My humiliation was now complete. Grandma Lou didn't say anything, but her hands were shaking when she tapped me on the shoulder and told me to get dressed again. When I had my pants on, she asked me, "Roy, what happened? Did someone do something to you?" Her voice was shaking, too, now.

"No," I said. "Nothing."

She gave me that look. "Roy, are you telling me the truth?" She knew. I could tell by the look in her eyes that she knew.

"Yes, ma'am." No, ma'am. I just couldn't find the words. Where would I begin? How could I apologize? I didn't mean to make Travis angry or whatever he was—I'm sorry—honestly, I didn't mean it. It's all my fault.

"Roy, I want you to tell me exactly what happened to you."

"Nothing, Grandma. Honest. Nothing at all. I feel fine." That might have been my first big lie, maybe even the one that created all the others, I don't know.

Ellen didn't call back for a while and somehow I got the feeling that she'd spoken to my grandmother or somebody. They knew. I became certain of that. People knew. *Everybody* knew. Or at least it was Ellen and grandmother, me and Travis—our own little private club with our own little terrible secret. Man, was I ever confused. I remember wishing I had a father to talk to.

My father's name was Rudolph Harris. He was a bricklayer who drove cement trucks for a construction company. He never lived with us. He and Mama never married and they split up not long after I was born. My father would stop by our house every now and then to give my grandmother money. He had money for us kids, too—fifty cents here, a dollar there. Back in the '60s, that was a lot of money for Savannah, Georgia. I loved getting money, but I always used to think, *Why isn't he here with us? What's wrong with us that Daddy's not here?*

Rudolph and my mother had two kids together, first Larry, then me. My sister Catherine was my mother's daughter by a different man; Catherine's father was a man by the name of Curtis Winn. Later on my mother had two more kids, Ricky and Latwan, with a man named James Purdie. Then she had my brother Gary with a man named Johnny Briggam. And Rudolph had my half-brother Stevie with a woman named Miss Gloria, plus six more kids with other women.

As I got older, maybe thirteen or fourteen years old, I'd make a habit of hunting Rudolph down every two weeks or so. It wasn't hard to do. He used to go to the same place every day after he got off work and I'd stop by 'cause I knew he'd give me money. I'd wait outside the bar and ask the men coming out. "Is my daddy in there?"

"Who's your daddy, son?"

"Rudolph Harris. Would you tell him I'm outside?"

He'd come out, all right. He was a compact, quick little man—you could see where Larry got it from—with lighter skin than my dark cocoa tone and a high, muttering voice. He was a Gullah/Geechee, which meant that his people were West African blacks who'd been enslaved along the South Carolina/Georgia rim. You can always tell a Geechee by the way they talk. They talk fast, like Uncle Remus from the Br'er Rabbit tales—he spoke Geechee. The dialect twists different bits of African grammar and pronunciation into English phrases, mostly because the Gullah/Geechee were often left alone by their white masters on plantation islands where their ancestral culture could be retained.

Rudolph was always warm and friendly when he greeted me outside the bar but I could tell he wanted me to go away so he could go back inside and continue his drinking. He'd say, "Well, now! Who now! Howzaa, howzaa mah big boy?" He called me a big boy even when I was small.

"Fine," I'd say. "Can I have some money?"

"Why, sure," he'd say. "Yeah, yeah. Uh huh, uh huh! Why, sure." He'd dig in his pocket and haul out some change for me. After that came the part where we indulged each other in a few sentences of polite conversation. This became our ritual. We practiced it many, many times over the years until, eventually, it got to the point where my daddy and I could do it in no time flat.

Although Rudolph never married my mother, he did marry one of my mother's friends, a woman named Miss Gloria. This confused me. I felt that if my daddy should be with any woman, he should be with my mother. In high school, she was the head majorette in the school marching band; Rudolph had been captain of the football team. I figured that qualified them to be a big love story with a happy ending. I was wrong.

Mama and alcohol were fast friends. Everyone knew it; she never bothered to hide her drinking ways. She loved her gin and she loved her vodka. When she came home from up north, she often went out all night to clubs with her cousins and sisters, but she drank every day even if she never left the house. She had a great sense of humor, though. She'd do this thing where she made a face by sticking her tongue way out, rolling her eyes and screaming, "Bulley Bulley!" It never failed to crack us all up. And for the most part she was fine in the afternoons. But sometimes, in the evenings, she'd get real mean and start cursing. It was the alcohol.

All in all, Mama could be a handful. But still, I always wondered, *Why aren't she and my daddy together?* I'll probably never know the answer to that question. Rudolph is dead now and my mother refuses to talk about it.

❖

I WAS IN a lot of pain those first few days after the rape. I felt as if I had this huge weight on my shoulders and it was pressing straight down, crushing the breath out of me, crushing me to death. Grandma Lou's tacit understanding of the situation wasn't enough to satisfy my sense of outraged confusion, I had to tell someone what had happened. But who?

My mother had a first cousin who lived two blocks away. She was three or four years older than Mama—5'9" and built stout, like a dump truck. Her name was Catherine, but everyone called her Big Cat. This woman was a force of nature. Big Cat was fearless. She brooked bullshit from nobody. People in my family still talk about the time she got into an argument with her husband and cut him up with a knife, sliced him right across the arm, deep enough to hit bone. Eventually they divorced. Another time she did the same thing to her boyfriend, only this time she hit his neck.

I trusted Cat. I spent a lot of time over at her place, too, mostly to eat her food. At eleven years old I was already beginning to show signs of the giant I'd become, and that kind of growth requires a serious fuel intake if it's going to sustain itself. Cat's immense talent for cooking fit the equation perfectly. Lord, that woman was always at the stove, and she cooked real down-home Southern-style soul food, too, everything a growing boy loved to eat and eat and eat. Her specialty was deviled crabs with dirty rice and collard greens, but I'd still pay good money to this day just to lick the crumbs off one of her plates.

A few days after the rape, I was in Cat's kitchen eating a sandwich at the counter. It was five or six at night. I think she'd already got word of what had happened. Though she never came right out and said that, I'm confident she knew because I distinctly remember how Cat kept her teeth clenched whenever she talked to me that day, like she had a butterfly trapped in her mouth and didn't want to let it out. I'd never seen her do that before.

She wasn't looking me in the eye, either; that was new. She just kept her head down over the stove and stirred her saucepans. She didn't say a word. This was not Big Cat behavior at all; Big Cat was not a quiet woman, another reason I feel certain saying she had an inkling of what had happened.

I didn't decide to tell her what had happened, it just sort of came out on its own. One moment I was standing there chewing on my sandwich, wondering how Cat always did such interesting tricks with mayonnaise. The next moment I said, "I was cleaning Ellen's house. Travis called me into the bedroom. He pulled down my pants and put his thing in." I couldn't help myself, I started to cry when I said that. These great big sobs gurgled up from my gut like bubbles breaking open from deep under water. And that's when Big Cat went crazy.

She dropped her spoon in the frying pan and rushed over to me. Reaching out with her massive arms, she crushed me to her breast, and for a second I couldn't breathe. That woman had ample breasts. "Oh, Roy, Roy, Roy!" she said. I think she was crying, too. "It's all right, Roy, it's all right. That dirty old bastard. We'll get him, baby, we'll get him. It's gonna be all right."

But it wasn't.

Travis was a respected man in our community. I guess my family figured that if the whole thing boiled down to Travis's word against mine—in front of the police, say, before a court of law, or even in the church—my word would lose. Plus, like I said, there was no man in my household to take this fight where it needed to go. We weren't educated folks. We were proud, but we were poor. This sort of thing was completely out of our sphere. I'm not offering that as an excuse for the fact that no one in my family stood up and became my champion. I'm just telling you how things were.

Nowadays I've had time to think over what happened. I've speculated about what kind of action I would have taken if somebody had touched *my* kid like that, or *any* child for that matter. Although I'm unclear as to the specific actions I'd have taken, I can guarantee you that whoever did the touching wouldn't have lived to tell about what I'd done to him. I'd have had that bastard's head on a platter.

But things were different back in '67. Things were very different, indeed. Remember, this was the era when daughters who got pregnant out of wedlock were sent away to live with distant relatives so as not to disgrace their families. The irony of it all is that moves like that never really hid the problem—everybody in the community knew what it meant when a young girl went away to live with, say, an aunt and uncle or her grandparents. Still, it was enough to sweep the matter under the carpet so people didn't have to look at it right out in the open. That was very important in our community back then: the appearance of propriety. The upshot of it all was that nobody did a goddamn thing about my rape. Travis the Neighbor got off scot-free and everybody sort of went about their business, trying as best we could to get back to life as we'd known it before it all happened. It was easier said than done.

Cat wouldn't let it lie. A day or two after I told her what happened, she came by our house. She used to do that a lot, come over and sit on the front porch and drink Burnett's gin. She'd unwind. Laugh it up with Grandma Lou. Talk shit. Talk about life. That night, she'd got a few drinks in her when all of a sudden she stood up and screamed toward Travis's house at the top of her lungs: "DIRTY! OLD! BASTARD!"

I didn't stick around to see what happened next. My worst nightmares were coming true: people would hear, people would know. Cat's shout didn't make me feel any better at all. In fact, I was suddenly overwhelmed with guilt and terror and shame and anger. So I jumped off the stoop and hauled ass for Camp Park, which was a playground about a mile away. I stayed there for over an hour drawing shapes with a stick in the sandbox which I quickly erased so that no one would see that I'd been there.

When I got home later on, Big Cat was gone. Grandma Lou was in the living room again, watching her wrestling. She looked up at me as I came in the door. Our eyes met but this time we didn't say hello. We didn't say anything at all. Some sort of silent understanding passed between us. We were beaten. It was over; I felt it in my bones. After that, nothing was ever said inside the house about what had happened. Not a peep was heard about Travis, and that was fine by me. That was fine by me. I just wanted the whole damn thing to go away.

Cat wouldn't let the issue drop, though. Every time I saw her, she'd bring up the topic and say: "He had no right to do what he did to you, Roy. No right." To which I remember thinking, *Okay. All right. I believe that. Sort of.* The sheer mental force that woman must have exerted to hold herself back from going right over to Travis's house and cutting his throat like she'd cut her beau must have driven that woman crazy. It had a much different effect on me, though; in the end it just got more and more confused. Because if what Cat said was true, if the Neighbor really hadn't had a right to do what he'd done to me, how come nobody had defended me?

I'm forty-nine years old now and that question still haunts me to this day. I've learned to forgive my family for what they did or didn't do. There's no sense holding on to such bad feelings. But I'm left to wonder, *Is that why things turned out the way they did? What would have happened if someone had come to my rescue? What kind of life would I have led if someone had shown up during that dark time and made such a wrong thing right?*

As time went on, I grew to despise Travis. But the situation was very complicated, because at the same time I hated him I felt this confusing sort of *attraction* to him. Don't ask me why. Maybe a part of me saw him as the person I'd sensed I was missing all along growing up. Maybe a part of me saw him as . . . *Daddy.*

❖

A FEW WEEKS later, Big Cat dropped another bombshell on me. She told me I'd been molested by my step-grandfather when I was five years old, although I had no memory whatsoever of that molestation. I remember hearing the news and feeling really dumb. My step-grandfather's name was Willy White. He was Grandma Lou's boyfriend, the man she stayed with when she'd first arrived in Savannah after fleeing Statesboro back in the 1930s.

Grandma Lou's farm in Statesboro turned a profit even during the

Great Depression. She had several hired hands on her payroll, plus a horse and buggy during an era when that was a real symbol of affluence. She'd been very devoted to her husband, Leroy, my mother's father, but the sonovabitch apparently had a real bad drinking problem. He used to beat Grandma Lou to within an inch of her life. Finally she'd figured enough was enough. She packed up whatever clothes and belongings she could carry on her back, took my mother's tiny hand, and beat it out of Statesboro. They wound up in Savannah where Grandma Lou had kin, and that's how I came to be born there.

I met Leroy once in my early childhood and promptly forgot him. Or maybe it's best to say that I didn't care to remember him. I figured I knew all I needed to about Leroy's drinking ways and crazy fists from the stories Grandma Lou and my mother used to tell. My memories of Willy White are much kinder than the image I hold in my mind of Grandpa Leroy. I think that, all in all, Willy White made a much better grandfather to me than Leroy ever could have. My memories of Willy White are loving and good.

When Cat told me what he'd done, I thought, *Willy molested me? How could that be? I barely remember the man, and what I do recall is all about ice cream cones and piggyback rides and silly old man jokes like, 'Hey, kiddo! Pull my finger!' How could a sweet old dude like that be the same kind of man as Travis? He wouldn't ever think to molest a poor defenseless child.*

Or would he? Did he?

After Cat told me this news, I wracked my brain, but no, I couldn't remember Willy ever touching me the wrong way. The only recollection I had that came close was being in bed with ol' Willy, but that was only natural. He used to have his own place around the corner from the house I grew up in with Grandma Lou; Larry and I used to stay over there from time to time when we were very young. Willie's place wasn't big, so all three of us slept in the same bed. I was the youngest so I used to sleep between Larry and Willy.

I said, "Cat, I don't remember nothing about Willy touching me." The very act of mentioning it seemed like an act of betrayal to this nice old man whom I'd loved dearly, like my own flesh and blood. But Cat said she was sure it had happened. She wouldn't say how she knew, but she said she was sure. I set about wracking my brain some more, but try as I did, I just couldn't conceive of Willy doing something like that.

He'd always been there for us, giving us attention, joking and laughing with me and Larry, watching TV programs with us. He used to carry Larry in his arms and put me on his back when we walked back and forth from his house to ours. Willy was an usher at the United Methodist Church—I remember that, too. He used to hum church tunes all the time with this big smile on his face. And he used to bring us cups of ice cream, bags of chips, and fresh-baked donuts. He was the first man I ever trusted. He left his mark on me. I loved Willy. He died when I was seven and I was heartbroken.

I remember going into his bedroom those first few days after the funeral. How empty it suddenly felt. I remember looking in his closet and seeing all his suits hanging in neat rows with the shoes laid out below them on the floor. Everything felt quiet and still, like his clothes were waiting for him to return. And I started to cry. Because I missed Willy. He'd always been like a . . . well, like a father to me.

"He touched you," said Cat. "Believe me, he did." I never asked why I didn't remember, or why she had waited so long to tell me. Try as I did to prod Cat into telling, each time I asked her about how she'd come to know all this, she just shook her head and gave me this cryptic little grunt. Then she'd turn her back to me and keep right on cooking.

3

TRAVIS AVOIDED ME for about a month after the rape and I began to feel hurt and angry over his lack of attention. The cheerful, fun-loving kid I'd been before October of '67 had started to change into someone else, a quiet boy who glanced around a lot to make sure no one was looking at him the wrong way. I think I actually figured that someone might be able to tell I'd been touched by Travis just by looking at me. Paranoia crept in, and I carried the heavy feelings of my shame and my guilt and my confusion around with me like a hump on my back. What confused me the most, though, was this crazy expectation I felt toward the next time Ellen would call. Part of me wanted to go back inside that big house. Part of me wanted Travis to see me vacuuming the hallway floor outside his bedroom. Part of me wanted him to bump into me from behind again. I wanted his attention. I wanted his love. I'd never had a man give me that before.

One day I was at the market picking up packages for my mother and I saw Travis coming down one of the aisles with his cart. I called out to him. I said, "Travis! Hey, Travis!" You should have seen him jump. When he saw who I was, he looked at me like I was crazy. Who knows? Maybe I was. It felt good to have him look at me, though. Even if Travis didn't seem particularly happy to see me—even if he looked positively horrified—I liked having him look at me, anyway.

Soon after that, the phone rang one evening. It was him. He said, "I want you to come over. I have some things for you to do." He was slurring his words so bad I knew he was drunk as hell. Again, I immediately felt conflicted. Part of me knew I should tell him to go fuck himself right there and slam down the phone. Or tell someone he wanted to rape me again. I should have called my mother up north in whatever town she was working in. Or my grandmother. Or Big Cat. At the very least, I should have been too petrified to speak. But I didn't do any of that. Instead, I said, "Okay." Because part of me wanted it to happen again, as crazy as that sounds. I went over to his house and told myself with every step that I was just going for the money. *The money . . . the money . . . the money . . .*

I knocked on the door and he called out from inside, "Come in." He'd left the door unlocked. His wife wasn't home. I met him in the foyer and we looked each other over for a moment. I asked him, "What do you want me to do?"

He said, "I want you to drive me somewhere." Which was strange because I was only eleven years old, I didn't have a driver's license. But he made it clear he wanted me to use his car and this got me all excited. *Hell*, I thought. *This ain't no problem. I can drive. I've had experience.* And this, in fact, was true. My aunt's boyfriend, Roy Thrasher, used to sit me on his lap and let me drive around the parking lot at Hagan's supermarket. *Hell*, I thought. *Roy taught me everything I need to know. Driving is easy.*

I said, "Okay. Let's go." The Neighbor smiled and grabbed my ass. Then he reached in his pocket and pulled out his car keys. He handed them to me and said, "Come on." Then he staggered out the front door and I followed him.

Travis's dark green Chevy was parked in front of the house. I got behind the wheel and Travis went around to the other side. He pulled the passenger side door open, but he didn't sit down. It was more like he poured himself into the seat.

There were no cars parked in front of Travis's Chevy so I was able to pull straight out. *Like I said. Driving is easy.* But when I got to the intersection of 40th and Burroughs, there were cars parked on both sides of the street and I had to make a tight right hand turn. That changed everything.

I made the turn and . . . BOOM! My left fender hit a parked car and dented the shit out of it. I knew that car, too. It was owned by the Baileys, this nice elderly couple who lived up the street from me. I remember thinking, *Oh God, they're gonna haul my ass to jail!*

I glanced over at Travis but he seemed completely unconcerned. He saw me looking at him and just gave this little sort of shrug. He waved one of his hands as if to say, *Whatever.* And that was it; he never said a word but slumped down in the passenger seat and mumbled directions, which I followed. After a few moments of being scared and concerned about the Baileys' car, I shrugged it off, too. I figured, *Well, if Travis isn't concerned, I guess it'll be all right.*

Apparently I was more skilled at making lefthand turns and that was good—the remainder of the trip was all lefts from there on out. Left onto W, left onto Broad. After that it was a straight shot down the road—two, maybe two and a half miles—to the place Travis had in mind, a hotel parking lot which we made without further collision.

Travis showed me where to park and said, "Wait in the car." Then he pulled the handle and shoved his door open, staggered out, and disappeared inside the hotel office. I waited, feeling a mixture of excitement and dread and something else that might've been shame. I don't think I even took my hands off the steering wheel. My fingers were locked on it like vise grips.

A few minutes later Travis came back to get me. He had a set of keys, and we drove around back to the room he'd rented.

The room was small and gray, dimly lit by standing lamps in the corners. There was one bed in the center of the room with a wobbly nightstand, and a cheap plywood TV cabinet with a TV inside. Travis coughed and burped and staggered into the bathroom, closing the door behind him. I saw the light go on underneath the door and heard water running. He was in there for some time. I wasn't afraid. I put the TV on and sat down on the bed to watch some program. I don't remember what it was.

When Travis came out again, he looked a little more focused. Maybe he'd thrown water on his face. His eyes looked a little sharper. He told me to lie down on the bed, so I did. Then he lay down on top of me and started humping me through his clothes and mine. His weight was massive on top of me; it crushed the breath from my lungs but I didn't struggle. I didn't say a word. This went on for a while until, the next thing I knew, Travis lay still and started snoring.

I rolled him off me, which was tough to do since he was so much bigger than I was. Then I reached into his back pocket and slid out his wallet. I took $60 and dropped the wallet on the bedside table. Then I used the phone in the room to call the Milton Cab Company; a car arrived about ten minutes later. I paid the cab driver with some of the money I'd found in Travis's wallet and made it home by 10:30 that night.

I should've been home much earlier, since Grandma Lou always wanted me in the house by the time the street lights came on. She was too busy watching professional wrestling to notice me sneaking back into the house, though. This time I didn't bother trying to make eye contact with her on my way toward my bedroom. We'd done that twice already since the rape, and on neither occasion had it resulted in any positive outcome. When I got to my bedroom, I stripped off all my clothes. This time, I didn't take a bath. And that was that: my second time with Travis. It hadn't been nearly as bad as the first. It also wouldn't be the last.

❖

LOOKING BACK, THIS relationship I had with Travis—if you really want to call it *a relationship*—well, that was probably the beginning of my lifelong tendency to keep secrets. As I continued to grow up after the rape, I found that I could withhold more and more of myself from the people I knew. I got real good at it, too; for instance, I know for a fact that only a handful of people ever suspected I was developing these *other tendencies*. On the outside I was still the same old sweet, loveable kid who liked to run errands for the old folks in the neighborhood. I was intelligent, polite, and eager to please. On the inside, though, I was something else entirely. A different person altogether.

To me, I am and always have been Roy Simmons. Labels are for people trying to define me—that's *their* problem. The only insight I can offer into my sexuality is that I did exactly what everybody else around me did when I was growing up: when I came into my sexual maturity, I went with the flow, and for me the flow moved naturally to boys *and* girls. I found out soon enough that I liked dick and pussy in almost equal measure—you don't need a *label* to enjoy either one. A label is for the outsider trying to look in. To me, playing with dick and playing with pussy seem like natural ways of showing my appreciation for a person I'm attracted to. That's all I know about my sexuality, and all I care to. The rest is politics.

People who say that sex is wrong are just trying to oversimplify a complex issue. Or maybe they're just afraid of something they don't understand. I want to communicate exactly what sex means in my life, regardless of my race, whatever other problems I may have as a person, or what team I played football for in the NFL. To me, sex is a part of life. It's a gift from God. Lord knows, the world is full of more pressing issues that deserve humanity's attention than, *What's your sexual preference?* Whenever people ask me that, I start to think: *With all the shit that's going on in the world right now, who really cares about who's zooming who?*

But to be perfectly honest with you, I'd have to admit that even before my run-ins with Travis I'd had some indications I was different. For instance, I used to love running. I was a running fool. Everywhere I went, I never walked—I ran. Heaven for me was jumping off the top step of the front porch of my house so I could start running. To me, running put me in my own little world. And I liked it there. I liked that world a lot. It had simple rules I could understand. Well, one day I was running in a yard across the street from mine and this boy maybe two years older than me grabbed my ass. I was shocked and puzzled. I have to confess that something about that touch automatically registered in my brain. I had a thought like, *Oooh, that shit felt good!* and I was only nine or ten years old when that happened.

As it turned out, that touch was no accident. The boy who grabbed me? I had him five years later. He was my first sexual experience after the rape. His name was Wayne and I knew him from the community pool, where we used to see each other in the summertime. I'd be lying if I said he was a handsome guy, but he was tall, maybe 5'11", very smart, and very athletic. He played sports—basketball in junior high, baseball and basketball in high school.

I remember the first time I saw his dick. We were both changing in the locker room at school and I caught sight of it dangling like a thick black snake between his legs. I was like, "God*damn*!" It was beautiful and it was huge. Wayne glanced up and saw me staring. He smiled at me and I smiled back. That was all we needed to do.

We headed into the big communal shower room and stood next to each other under the nozzles. There were guys lined up behind us, but no one paid any attention to what we were doing. Wayne started playing with his dick and it got a little hard. I took a few peeks, and some of my peeks were obvious. Wayne noticed them, of course; he didn't seem to mind at all. In fact, he pointed his dick at me a few times while he stroked it, just so I could see. We shut off the water, got dressed, and went outside. There was no conversation between us. Didn't need to be.

He asked, "Is there someplace we could go?" Hell yes, there was. The Exxon station.

We decided to play it like this: Wayne would wait around the corner of the gas station while I got the key to the bathroom. Then I'd unlock the door, go inside, and wait for Wayne to knock. It was a simple plan.

I remember feeling very calm as I asked for the key. The gas station attendant handed it to me without looking up from his newspaper. I went around back and opened the washroom door. It was real nice in there, not like some other places where they let all the filth and the slime accumulate. Someone took real good care of that washroom. Kept it ready, kept it clean.

I closed the door behind me. It didn't take long. Wayne knocked a few minutes later and I let him in. He wasted no time, he pulled down his jeans. He was wearing boxers. Then he just sort of stood in front of me and waited.

I tried sitting on the toilet at first, but that didn't work, it was a bad angle. So I dropped to my knees instead. I pulled his dick out of his shorts—it was almost all hard at that point—I put it in my mouth and I started to suck. It was my first blow job and I was so excited! While I was sucking Wayne's dick, I pulled out my own and jerked off.

He came. I spit it out. I came. It felt good. Then Wayne washed his dick in the sink and left. I stayed in the bathroom for a minute before returning the key to the gas station attendant. Again, he didn't look up from his paper. I said, "Thank you." And I left. It was easy.

❖

So Wayne was the first. And then there was Stick. Honestly, though, I never really thought of Stick as a lover. He was more like a fuck buddy. We were on the same JV basketball team—Stick was an excellent basketball player—and just like it'd been with Wayne, the whole thing began with eye contact and a smile. After that, my relationship with Stick happened automatically, like we were puppets on a stage and somebody else was above us both, pulling the strings and making us dance.

Stick was a little older than me, and once he got his driver's license, he'd call up my house and say, "Wanna go out?"

"Sure, man." He'd cruise by in his father's old Ford and pick me up. I'd jump off the top stoop step and run out to meet him while Grandma Lou and my sister Catherine waved good-bye to us from the front porch.

He was smooth and aggressive, ol' Stick was, 6'2", maybe 200 pounds. Light coffee-with-cream skin and big Bette Davis eyes. Later on, Stick became an auto mechanic, and that was good, that was fitting—he was very good with his hands. He had a nice, comfortable dick and he introduced me to it the first time by asking out of the blue, "Yo, man. Can you suck this for me?" He pulled it out while we were driving. I looked at it. Wasn't as big as Wayne's but—damn, it looked good. I didn't say anything. I just got to work. Like I said, it wasn't love. We were just friends.

We probably saw each other maybe twice a week. Stick started fucking me in seventh or eighth grade. I was always a little nervous about getting caught, but Stick knew just what to do. He introduced me to the old house next to the elementary school. At one point, it'd been the rectory where the town preacher used to live. Now it was all boarded up and nobody went there. Nobody but me and Stick.

He knew just how to work it. It was too risky tying to go through the front entrance on Victory Drive, but nobody noticed if you went around back and slipped in one of the first-story windows. Stick had gone in ahead of us and laid out some blankets on the floor of one of the upstairs rooms for our first time. After that, we fucked all the time in the preacher's house. But if that location didn't work for one reason or another, on any given day we could use a secluded section in a local park as backup.

Stick fucked me, I never fucked him. I was always the "bitch" in that relationship, though I didn't know it at the time. This was way before I understood what gay sex was or meant. I didn't know about tops or bottoms or roles or expectations. All I knew is that Stick was good fun.

We saw each other off and on for years. Even after I went off to college—even while I was playing football for the NFL—I'd still come home to Savannah and meet Stick and we'd fuck around like no time had passed at all. He had a few girlfriends in high school, but that never mattered to me. Eventually he had a wife and kids. Still didn't matter. With Stick, I just wanted the sex. I'm pretty sure he felt the same way. He was living in the closet, too. It's not a lifestyle that typically revolves around commitment or attachments.

After Wayne and Stick came Gerald. I met Gerald through his sisters, who were friends of mine from elementary school. It's funny. I used to go visit them at their house all the time I was growing up but I never met Gerald until the tenth grade or so. I don't know how we missed each other all those years. Gerald was in the same grade as me even though he was two years older.

That Gerald was something! Everybody in school knew him and loved him. His skin was cocoa chocolate, but he had white features, and Lord, he was handsome! He sang in the school chorus and his voice was so pure, so rich, so textured, so true. He could charm the heavenly choir of angels with a song. He could sing the stars into alignment when he wanted to.

His personality was magical, too. He had energy levels off the charts. Charisma? Off the charts. When we got together we were pure dynamite! We'd eat lunch together and start up one of our routines—in seconds flat, we'd have the whole table rolling! The whole cafeteria!

Gerald was bisexual and then some. Nothing mattered to him, he held no prejudices. He liked boys and he liked girls. He liked whites and he liked blacks. No distinction of race, creed, or color ever seemed to register with him. He hung out with, and slept with, and befriended whoever he wanted, whenever he wanted.

I suppose the one common denominator of all the people I met through Gerald was this: they were definitely into drugs. Alcohol, pills, acid, you name it. These folks ate drugs like they were candy.

Gerald and his friends didn't experiment with drugs. They'd gone way beyond that into hardcore usage. I'm not sure where they got all their shit, but they certainly had access to lots of it. It was all a big introduction to me, a totally new frontier. We drank a lot of Taylor port, and cases and cases of Boone's Farm Apple Wine. Every now and then we had some pot and some pills, some uppers, some downers, some Valium, some quaaludes. And acid. Lots and lots of acid.

I tended to be pretty cautious with my overall chemical consumption, but Gerald and his friends would literally try anything once. For instance, if you had a bottle of prescription medication on you, Gerald would want to eat some; he didn't care what it was for. I remember him taking a bottle off a friend of ours one time and getting this crazy look in his eyes. "Hmmmmm," he said, like a spider watching a fly land on its web. "What's this, now?" I pleaded with him, "No, man. Don't do it. Please. That's not safe." He didn't care. In a few seconds he'd popped the top off the bottle and swallowed a handful of pills, washing them down with big swallows of wine. I couldn't believe he had done that.

Gerald was also really fond of drinking mushroom juice. I didn't know what that was, so I asked him. And he said: "Mushrooms? They're great, man. You pick them out in the cow pastures. Then you brew them up in water like you're making tea and you drink it. Gets you higher than the moon." I'd never heard of such a thing and I wasn't willing to try it. "That's okay," Gerald said. "Probably not a good idea for you anyway, Roy. You gotta be real careful with mushrooms. Weird shit can happen if you pick the wrong ones."

Weird shit? I asked him, "Weird shit like what?"

"Well, for starters . . . they can kill you."

❖

Now I NEED to say something about Sheila, 'cause she was the love of my life. The female love of my life, that is. We knew each other from almost the very beginning. I met this beautiful little girl in the third grade. Back then she was so pretty that I couldn't get up the nerve to go over and talk to her. I pretty much wasted that whole year just staring at her from the back of the classroom. I didn't really start talking to Sheila until the fourth grade. I should've done it sooner. She turned out to be so cool.

In childhood, we all had very different personalities than the ones we ended up with as adults. I was known as the Candy Man 'cause I had this routine where I used to go to the store every morning before school started and buy these things called Twisters for my friends. These days I guess you'd call them Jolly Ranchers. Those things were so sweet! They came in all different flavors, too. You'd better believe those candies made me a popular kid.

I was also known for being real smart. Real smart and real fast. I used to always be the one to finish a class assignment first and hand it in. That way I'd have more time to run my mouth off—I was a real talker. It got so that every marking period, Grandma Lou would open up a report card that said, "Roy Simmons—good student, talks too much."

Sheila wasn't like that. Sheila was quiet. She hardly said a word, but you could tell she was awful smart. You could tell she saw everything that went on around her—and I do mean *everything*. But she never judged it. She never chose sides. She just went about her business and had a smile ready for anybody who came up to her, anybody at all. Even at a young age, she was like a magnet for other children. She was a lot like me in that she got along well with practically anybody. Sheila had that rare talent where she could made friends about as easy as she breathed. That's a rare and special quality in a person.

She was real tall with long braids, pink lips, and beautiful brown eyes. She definitely cut a figure. She took good care with the way she dressed so she always looked put together, like a fashion model. I used to pull her hair on the playground a lot just to show her I appreciated her. And I know I wanted to sneak in a kiss every now and then, but after the first time I tried that, Sheila started to ignore me completely.

I got real persistent with Sheila, though. I started doing all sorts of little things to attract her attention. Sometimes I'd go out of my way to carry her books and walk her home. One time I hit her with one of my shoes in class, just like Grandma Lou had done to me. It seemed like a good idea at the time, much better than how it played itself out. The teacher made me stand up in class and turn around, and she paddled my behind in front of everybody. I cried.

It wasn't till junior high school that I started having thoughts about what it might be like to touch Sheila. In the ninth Grade we became boyfriend and girlfriend, and we kept that up all through high school. She became the head majorette of the high school band. I was captain of the football team. Sound familiar? Just like my mom and my dad.

Sometimes I spent time with Gerald on the weekends, sometimes I spent time with Sheila. Sometimes I went out with Sheila and met up with Gerald later on, or there were moments I'd pull it the other way round—hang out with Gerald and meet up with Sheila later. Sheila knew Gerald and Gerald knew Sheila. They liked each other so it was an easy trick to pull off. But Sheila had no idea what Gerald and I sometimes did together behind closed doors. No one did; that was our secret. By this point, the need to keep my homosexual activities a secret was as clear to me as my desire to sleep with men. So I did both.

We started sneaking over to the gay clubs in downtown Savannah, for instance. Most of the guys who hung out there were white so we tended to stick out a bit, but not much. The clientele had other interests. They were in those places primarily to drink and dance and pick up guys. Color definitely wasn't on the radar. Gerald and I never picked anyone up. Not in the beginning, anyway. In the beginning, we were just exploring.

We explored each other, too. One night Gerald and I were at his place having a drink and I don't know what exactly happened. Either I grabbed him or he grabbed me, that's the physics of it, but it's not like we actually wanted each other. It's more like he knew what was going on with me, I knew what was going on with him, and we both respected that. It wasn't passion. It was more like something that needed to be done. So we fucked. And that was that.

Don't get me wrong. I liked Gerald, but I could have done without the sex. Sex with Gerald was never that big a thing with me. On the other hand, Gerald had practically fallen in love. He used to babble over and over again, "I love you, dude. Y'hear me? I *love* you." To which I'd say, "Man, shut the fuck up! Don't tell me that! Please!" I just didn't feel comfortable having him think of me in that way. In fact, it used to make me downright mad when he said shit like that. I said, "Just be cool, huh? Just be my friend."

As it turned out, we got with each other off and on. Eventually, I broke it off. But then I'd have a little relapse and we'd hook right up again, until the next time I came to my senses and broke it off. And went back again. Broke it off. And went back. And so on. Basically, with Gerald, when I felt like it I would. Despite the fact that he always wanted our relationship to be something a little more than it was, Gerald turned out to be a steady friend. In fact, years later, he would help me exact my revenge on Travis.

❖

IT HAPPENED LIKE this: in 1979 I was twenty-two years old and I'd just started playing football for the New York Giants. During the off season, I came home to Savannah to visit family and friends. Naturally, I hooked up with Gerald and we went out on a whirlwind tour of our old stomping grounds. One night we found ourselves drinking Taylor port at this gay club called Sey Hey. I looked up and noticed who was sitting across the bar. Short hair. Neat moustache. Perfectly trimmed side burns. I couldn't believe my eyes. It was like we were in a time warp. The man didn't seem to have aged a bit.

"Damn!" I said. "There's Travis."

Gerald asked, "Who's Travis?" So I told him what happened when I was eleven. And Gerald got furious. "That fucking bastard! We need to *get* his ass!"

"What should we do?"

"First let's get that motherfucker drunk."

It sounded like a plan. So I got up, steadied myself a little, and went over to confront the Neighbor. I wasn't prepared for what happened next.

"Travis? Hey."

"Roy? Roy?!"

"Yeah."

"Jesus, what the hell are you doing here?"

So we went through all that, and gradually we got around toward talking about the big elephant in the room. I had no idea how to broach the subject but Travis actually brought up the rape before I did. Apparently, he'd been carrying the guilt of it around with him all those years. He bowled me over when he said, "Look, I apologize for what I did." For sure I hadn't been expecting *that*. It threw me off balance, and the next thing I knew I was inviting Travis back to our table and introducing him to Gerald. They said their hellos and Gerald kept ordering rounds. Travis was drinking some sort of dark liquor. We stayed another hour, then Gerald was ready. He said, "Let's go back to my place." He only lived two miles away.

Travis had this look on his face like he'd just won the lottery. He smiled so big I thought his face would crack. He said, "Okay."

We separated in the parking lot outside the club. I got into Gerald's car and Travis got into his. We drove out on the highway with Travis following us back to Gerald's place.

Gerald was so excited he was bouncing up and down in the seat. "We gonna fuck him. We gonna *fuck* him! Let's get him! Let's get that bitch! Show him what it feels like!" Now, Gerald had a real skinny dick that was twelve inches long, so we used to call him Snake. Travis didn't know what he was in for. I wanted it to happen, too. I looked out the window and watched all the headlights whizzing by us in the darkness. I said, "Okay."

When we got to Gerald's place, he started the party off right by hoisting the mattress out of his bedroom and laying it out on the living room floor. Then he made us a round of drinks and started playing loud

music over the stereo. It wasn't long before all three of us were dancing and singing and very drunk. Clothes started coming off. Touches
were exchanged.

I was in the kitchen fixing another round of drinks when I heard
Gerald crack the sliding doors open. I turned around and saw him
stick his head into the kitchen. He winked at me. I got the message: he
wanted me to watch what happened next. So I did. I put my eyes up to
the crack in the sliding doors and saw Gerald and Travis kissing each
other. Then Gerald said, "I'm gonna fuck you like you fucked Roy."
And that's precisely what he did.

Travis flipped over and Gerald started fucking him from behind. I
couldn't believe what I was seeing. My dick got hard. The scene was
hot. One of Travis's legs was kicked forward up by his hands like he
was doing a hurdler's stretch. The other trailed out behind him, underneath Gerald's body. Travis started moaning, "Aaaaah! Aaaaah, man!
Aaaaah, shit!" They went at it for about twenty minutes. When Gerald
finished, he came into the kitchen and we high-fived each other. Then
it was my fucking turn.

It was as much passion as it was revenge. Not just mine, either. Travis
was definitely into it. He kept yelling, "Fuck me, man! Fuck me!" For
a split second, I had flashbacks of the rape. I felt paranoid and afraid.
My head started to grow hot like it was on fire and ready to burst. But
the feeling passed just as quickly as it came and I heard a voice shouting
out, loud and strong, a man's voice, not the voice of a child. It was my
own voice, and I was saying, "I got you, man, I *got* you! Here we are,
motherfucker. I'm fucking YOU now!" After that I just let myself go.
I looked up and saw Gerald smiling at me from the kitchen. Somehow
I knew right then that part of my life had come full circle. The wound
had closed, and that was something. But that wasn't the end. The scars
are still there. I still carry them with me; I'll carry them for the rest of
my life. Some marks can never be erased.

Travis fell asleep later to the muted sounds of the TV. Gerald and
I went to bed in his room. When I woke up the next morning, Travis
was gone, and that was fine by me. I didn't want to see him again.

What would we say to one another? Whatever feelings I'd built up around him—the confusion, the fear, the longing—it was all gone. Or so I thought. I never saw him again and never wanted to. I had bigger fish to fry.

4

SHEILA AND I started getting pretty close in our junior year of high school, close enough that she started inviting me over for dinner. I'd catch the three-dollar Milton's cab that brought me across town from my doorway to hers; Sheila's aunt and mother kept house together.

The first time I was over, I was so nervous I could barely speak. I needn't have been. Retha seemed to sense I was having a hard time and took me under her wing. As it turned out, she was as easy to be around as her daughter. What really captured my heart though was that Retha could be all that and still cook so well! Lord, that woman could set a table! She laid out a full Southern spread: chicken with gravy, rice and corn bread, macaroni and cheese, and collard greens done up in pepper and vinegar. She had homemade desserts, too: angel food cake, apple pie and ice cream, and ice cream. Retha pulled out all the stops in her kitchen to celebrate my friendship with her daughter. She believed what every woman back then believed: the way to a man's heart is through what they always said it was.

Later that night, Sheila's mother and aunt went to bed early, saying good-night with little smiles. Left to our own devices, Sheila and I watched TV until we couldn't stand the ruse anymore and began making out. Nothing too crazy, just a little tongue-kissing and maybe some light foreplay. We were young. It was fun.

Sheila used to visit family in Richmond Hill, Georgia, during the summers, and when she did that, she used to hang around with this other boy named Tracey. I hated Tracey. I hated his name, I hated the town he grew up in, and hated his family because they were his people. Every fall Sheila'd come back to school with this starry-eyed, gaga look all over her face. We'd sit down to talk and reconnect, but all I ever heard coming out of her mouth was, "Tracey *thinks* this," and "Tracey likes to do it like *that*." Tracey, Tracey!" I was like, "Who *is* this stupid sonovabitch? I don't even know what he looks like and he's kicking my ass."

We weathered it. By the twelfth grade, Sheila and I were talking on the phone every night for hours. When we got our licenses, she'd sometimes drive over to my house in the Ford Fairlane she'd bought with money she'd saved working jobs after school. There were more dinners at her mother's house, more tiny little nods from her mother and aunt before going to bed early, more making out, though still nothing too heavy. In the twelfth grade, I took the plunge and went to a jewelry store to buy her a little ring. Again, nothing too heavy. Not like we were engaged or anything. I just wanted her to have something that let her know how much I cared for her, that was all. She went crazy when she saw it.

We didn't have sex in high school. I refused to do that, I was saving her for marriage. I realize this may sound strange to some people. Here I was fucking Stick or Gerald on some nights, some nights having them both, but Sheila was different. Sheila was my girl. In my head I had this vision of my girl dressed up all pretty in white on our wedding day. I wanted that, I dreamed of that. In my vision, she was all mine for eternity and she was most definitely a virgin when I slipped that ring on her finger.

I don't think many people will understand this at all. It's tough to explain. But that role was very important for me to play. Of course I knew I was a lowdown dirty dog, but not with Sheila. With Sheila, I was all those things that a black man tries to be for his woman. Those were big shoes I wanted to fill. My father and mother hadn't done it right. Travis and Ellen hadn't done it right—obviously not, I guess, when you think about it. Very few black couples I saw were making it work but I was game. Sheila and I talked about having ten kids. We had plans.

Deep down I think what most young black men want—maybe most young men, period—is to strut. When you strut, you're shouting to the world that you've successfully overcome some major hurdle in your life, or you're about to. You feel like the world just got a little bit smaller and you got a little bit bigger. It's a great feeling, maybe the best feeling on earth. For a lot of guys, being with a woman is part of that. In the culture I grew up in, being the "man" in a family was very, very important, more so when, like me, your father was absent. Loving that family, providing for that family, guiding that family through its challenges—that was the ideal to which the black people I grew up with aspired. Of course none of us really made it—that's beside the point. The point is that's what we were shooting for. That's the goal we had in mind. Virgin wives. Loving kids. Good job. Nice neighbors. Cookouts on the weekend. All of it.

Sheila and I went to the senior prom together at the Savannah Jewish Alliance Center. This was a big night for us, since we both knew what had happened to the last man in my family who'd been captain of the football team and taken the head band majorette to the prom. Retha took so many pictures that night, I suspected she was gathering material for a wedding album. Larry got into the act, too. He worked out one of his great schemes so that Sheila and I could be truly alone for the first time in luxury and comfort. He gave me his '75 Lincoln Town Car for the evening and rented a hotel room for me—"For later," he said, and he leered at me. "You two can get into anything you want at the hotel. Anything at all." I said thank-you because I knew his gift was thoughtful, but it also made me a little uncomfortable.

We danced our asses off at the prom. It was a great time, but all night I was too shy to tell Sheila about the hotel room. After the prom, I asked her if she'd like to go for a walk through Savannah, and she said yes. I took her down to the docks by the river. It was very romantic with the lights twinkling on the shorelines. We found a secluded spot and fooled around for a while. Then I noticed it was getting late and I didn't want to get Retha upset, so I took Sheila home. We parked outside her house and kissed good night. Then I watched her walk up the steps of her front porch. She turned and waved to me before going inside. I waved back. And that was it.

I drove back to the hotel and checked in. It was a nice room. Nicer than the one Travis had shown me. I turned on the TV and sat on the bed drinking apple wine that Gerald had put into a flask for me. I don't remember what was on TV; I wasn't really watching. Then I lay back and fell asleep. The next morning I gave Larry back his car and I thanked him again. He said, "Sure, bro. How'd the night go?" I told him it had been beautiful. Just beautiful.

❖

ABOUT THIS TIME, football was starting to become the focus of my life. I was always an athletic kid in high school. I sort of had to be. By the tenth grade I was 6'3" and 240 pounds. My rapid growth spurt taught me some very important life lessons, but maybe the most important of all was this: when you're as big as I was at age sixteen, you'd damn well better get your ass into a sport so you can find some way of channeling all that energy into something educational and constructive. If you don't, you'll have to deal with the many frightening possibilities related to what that energy will do if left unsupervised. I'd seen other boys like me get into trouble and I wasn't going to be a part of all that.

My size and strength didn't translate well at first to football. Even though nobody could tackle me, I guess my spirit was more like a floppy old puppy dog instead of the killer bear that the coaches seemed to want me to be. I didn't do things in the ways they'd come to expect. When I ran track, I'd sprint out the anchor leg for the 440 relay in my pair of Converse All-Stars and I could still beat all the kids who had the fancy running shoes. They tell me I looked like the world's biggest goofball. I probably was. But I was also the world's *fastest* goofball and that was something to be proud of. All those early days of leaping off the front porch steps of Grandma Lou's house had sure prepared me for the 100-yard dash and the sprint medley.

I also threw shot put and discus. I put a lot of goofball energy into those, too, until one day I wasn't doing my spin just right and Coach Lewis hauled back and slapped the shit out of me with the back of his hand. He said, "Roy, you gotta *focus*! You ain't never gonna go nowhere in this world 'less you get to work and *focus*!" How right he was. Looking back, I wish I had listened.

I was scared as hell the first time I played organized football. I wasn't so sure I wanted to get hit, number one. Plus Larry and my half-brother Stevie were both starting running backs on the school team, so I had the pressure of living up to the family name. I soon found out that Larry and Stevie were supportive enough; they didn't have much advice to offer since they were running backs and I was pretty clearly going to be tapped as a guard. I also soon found out that while I didn't particularly like *getting* hit, I was relatively okay with the idea of *hitting* people. In fact, I did pretty well at that. Not in an overly violent sort of way; I was never the kind of lineman who screams like an animal before charging you like a rhino with the aim of hurting you. But hitting someone in the right way, the way the rules said it could be done, I found very appealing. And I was good at it.

The team tried me out as a defensive tackle. I wasn't very good at first. Mostly I had a tough time with the footwork. A word to the wise: without footwork, you might as well stay in the locker room because you have no business being out on a football field. I couldn't master the art of getting my feet under me when I tried to project my weight forward; I ended up falling on my face a lot when I tried to block enemy players. I couldn't hit with my shoulders, and that was bad because you can only take so many shots with your head before the your whole field of vision starts to get a little blurry. And my hands got in the way all the time; I ended up dinging my fingers on other players' pads. In short, I was a mess.

Luckily, the team captain back then was also a defensive tackle, a very kind guy named Ulsum. I guess he saw how hard I was trying, and he took pity on me, because the next thing I knew Ulsum was staying late with me after practice every night. He showed me how to hit right on the practice dummies. We ran through a lot of drills and I started to improve. As it turns out, I started for the team in my sophomore year.

❖

THE HEAD COACH for the football team was Carl Middleton. He was short, neat, and well-spoken. A gentle guy, too. He was the kind of coach you *wanted* to play for because he gave a hundred and ten percent of himself to his players, both on and off the field. When Coach Middleton saw that I didn't have a decent pair of cleats, he went out and bought me one with his own money. He was that kind of man. Finally, I had a real father figure, a grown man who believed in me and wanted to see my talent shine. No wonder I did so well in football.

I recall that Coach Carter was tougher to convince than Coach Middleton. Coach Carter was the defensive line coach, and I felt like he made a point of ignoring me my first few months on the team. I wasn't deterred; I just kept practicing harder. He didn't seem to notice me at all freshman year. Then Coach Middleton pulled me off the defensive line to see how I'd work on offense. Wouldn't you know it, that move was like pulling a square peg from a round hole and putting it where it fits. Offense was where I was meant to be. I started leading the offensive line and Coach Carter suddenly became my greatest advocate.

I kept working my ass off—freshman year, sophomore year. By the time the team met for summer practice at the start of my junior year, I could play the game from both sides and really play it well. My versatility made me a secret weapon against other teams. It confused the hell out of our competition when I'd start the first quarter as a nose guard or tackle for the defensive line, then switch off to offensive guard or tackle for the second, then back to defense for the third, and so on. One time we kicked the asses of our local rival team and Coach Carter hunted me down in the locker room after the game. "Simmons," he said, "keep it up, boy. I ain't never seen nobody play both ways before. You're going places, boy. Keep on it."

Play both ways. If he only knew.

❖

I PUT IN a lot of summer-school work in high school. It was Grandma Lou's idea—a way of keeping me out of trouble, she said—and for the most part it worked really well. But I put in so *much* summer-school work that I was offered the opportunity to graduate high school a year early. I declined. I'd just made co-captain of the football team my junior year. I knew that if I came back to play as a senior, I'd be made captain, and I wanted that very much. I wanted it for me and I wanted it for Sheila.

I guess it's not entirely immodest of me to say that I was a kid who liked to work hard. Didn't matter whether it was on the gridiron or pulling weeds in an elderly neighbor's garden, which was something I still did in my spare time. For the most part, too, I did everything with a smile on my face, but that's not to say that I didn't have my occasional moments of piss and vinegar. One of them happened during my senior year when a man named Russell Ellington took over Coach Carter's position as head football coach. Ellington came up from the basketball team and I could tell right away that he didn't know what he was doing. There's no such thing as a full court press on the gridiron, but there is such a thing as a flea-flicker dropback with a halfwing push. Ellington was speaking another language entirely, one that none of us on the football team understood or appreciated. It didn't take long for the two of us to establish that we were never meant to get along.

One day at practice Coach Ellington really yanked my chain by calling a play that everyone knew wasn't going to work. We tried to tell him, but he just yelled at us like we were soldiers in the army or something. "Pipe down and run that play!" His attitude was so rude that I got mad and said, "Fuck this. I don't need this. To hell with it, I'm not going to practice." I didn't report to the field the next day. Russell Ellington was not amused. He left the practice field and came hunting for me, right up to the front door of my house.

I was home alone when he came around. My bedroom was right next to the house's front door, so I definitely heard it when Coach Ellington pounded up the rickety stoop steps and hammered on the door with his fist. He yelled, "Dammit, Simmons! I know you're in there!" I threw myself under the window and crouched there, waiting. I didn't say a word! Just waited. "Simmons, I'm gonna tell you this right fucking now! You want to go to college? You better bring your ass to practice!"

This was actually a pretty ample threat. By the start of my senior year it was pretty apparent to anyone who knew anything about the local sports scene that I'd have my pick of college football scholarships. Worse players than me had worked out excellent deals to play for all sorts of colleges across the country, so football wasn't just a hobby for me anymore. It was a way out of the life that most black folks were condemned to live back then in Savannah, without jobs, education, or opportunity. I was destined for better things. I knew it and Coach Ellington knew it. Which is why he tried to hit me right where I lived. "Simmons, you get your ass down to that field right now, goddammit, or you won't go no-fucking-where! No college, no way, nohow!" That was the last thing he said. He waited around for a while and left. For a long time, I didn't move a muscle.

That might have been the first time I ever considered turning pro. Sitting there wedged under my bedroom window, I realized that I must really have some kind of special talent if I'd managed to piss off Russell Ellington so bad. I didn't end up going to practice that day. But I did the day after, and Russell Ellington confronted me in the locker room. I was sitting on the bench talking to some friends when he rounded the bend and glared at them. They mumbled good-byes and left in a hurry. Ellington turned his head and stared at me for a moment. He glanced over his shoulder to make sure we were alone. Then he looked at me real hard and said: "Simmons, goddammit. I swear to you. If you ever try that shit again, I'll kill your ass dead. We *need* you here."

College ball, here I come.

❖

WITH THE EXCEPTION of that one day I cut practice, I kicked ass my senior year. I made MVP and All-City at football, but that was just the tip of the iceberg as far as my talents were concerned; I also made All-Kitchen. I was a proud member of FHA, the Future Homemakers of America, which meant that while the rest of the football team was making bird houses in wood shop, I took Home Economics and made cookies.

A couple of my teammates hassled me one time about how only fags take Home Ec. I made it very clear that inappropriate comments such as that would not be tolerated. I only said it once and that was all they needed—they listened real good. They damn well had to. Back then I was bigger and faster than anybody else on the team. I was the team captain, too, which meant that I could deal out laps around the field if I felt one of my players was underperforming or simply in need of a good ass-whooping. I also really enjoyed discovering the proper technique to make a chocolate soufflé rise. That was a pleasure I wasn't going to let anyone's callousness rob me of. So I put my foot down once and never had to deal with it again.

Home Ec class was my haven and my renewal. We had this beautiful classroom space with three working kitchen dinettes complete with ranges, ovens, dining tables, and chairs. Man, you should have seen the way the FHA kept those dinettes hopping. The ovens were hot and humming. The scent from the oven was always delicious fresh-baked cornbread or Carolina hush puppies or sweet rolls you could tear open with your fingers while they were still hot, and cram into your mouth. It was heaven! One time, we made dinner for the principal, whose name was Mister Otis J. Brock. Hoooo, was he surprised! We trotted out a full-course meal. There was spinach sautéed with garlic, scalloped potatoes, and the best damned baked chicken you ever ate. We washed it all down with pitchers of good ol' southern sweet tea and a nice strawberry shortcake for dessert.

I just loved Home Ec class. Our teacher was Miss Genie Blake, and I never once heard her open her mouth to me without using the words, "Young man." She used to say to me, "Young man? Why are your elbows on the table? Didn't your momma raise your right?" Or: "Young man! You're late to class. This is the second time this marking period. One more time and you and I will have words."

Gerald was in my Home Ec class, too. True to form, we used to tell jokes and cut up and make everybody laugh until we hurt, all in the middle of making a tasty soufflé.

Miss Blake also taught us how to sew. I made my first pair of pants in her class. I liked sewing so much I started having dreams about going to college to be a high-fashion designer. I even made a beautiful pair of black and white nylon pants in Home Ec class. They were perfectly stitched, but I made a tiny mistake with the measurements so I couldn't get them on over my thighs. I had really big thighs back then, 33½ inches around. That, plus I had a really fat ass. People liked to joke about that—my ass was huge. Finding pants that fit me was always a chore, which is why I guess I thought it'd be great to know how to make my own. I got the zipper right. Put it in, stitched it up, and it worked just fine, too. Did it all by myself—and the zipper's the toughest part.

I did well enough in Home Ec to earn my junior homemaker's degree. That was the highest technical degree you could get in my high school back then. So I guess I wasn't your typical star athlete. See, I was interested in other things. I was *rounded*. I was on the scene, I was involved, I was into what's happening. I was everywhere. I was a member of the Future Business Leaders of America. And I was on the school Nutrition Council. We made posters for the school cafeteria that said Milk Is Good, pictures of dancing apples and bananas that had cartoon smiley faces on them, and charts that broke down the Four Food Groups. I was vice president of my senior class and, like I said, captain of the football team. I made the Honor Society. And I was in Who's Who among American High School Students for 1975. They've got this synopsis about me in the '75 book that lists all my accomplishments. It's a pretty long list.

With a profile like mine, college recruiters were falling all over themselves to snatch me up and have me play ball for them. First they started sending me all kinds of letters and campus brochures. I got so much paper in the mail that Grandma Lou had to set up a special folding table in the living room just to hold it all. Then they started calling me at home. Don't ask me how they got my phone number. All I knew is that, pretty soon, I was on the phone almost every night saying things like: "Yes, sir, that sure sounds fine. Yes, sir, I do appreciate the fine tradition of your school. Yes, sir, football's my life, you know it."

After a few weeks of that, the college reps started coming to my neighborhood so they could hunt me down in person. That's when things began to get really weird. Talk about stress.

I had college reps trailing me all over my hometown like spies. Or maybe kidnappers is a better word. They'd literally steal me away on a Friday afternoon, take me on trips. Buy me clothes, buy me dinner.

Come Tuesday morning, they'd drop me back at school with a smile and a wink that said, *You* know *you want to play for* us*!*

Now keep in mind: I grew up poor. I'd never been wooed like that in all my life. USC. Texas Southern. U Texas. Arkansas Tech. Arkansas State. Florida. Georgia Tech. Georgia. Auburn. U Miami. You name it. They were coming out of the woodwork. Florida won the award for Most Persistent. They hauled my ass out to their campus five times. When the deadline came around to sign my Letter of Intent, they even sent their rep around and he took me to some hotel out of state for the weekend, just to keep me away from the Georgia Tech recruiter. They also paid off my brother Larry, who helped them organize the whole thing.

With all that going on, I found it more and more difficult to focus on what I really liked to do: play football. Russell Ellington finally took me aside and we had another of our famous man-to-man chats. "Simmons," he said, "that's it. No more visiting. You keep carrying on like this, I'm gonna cut you from the team. Now shape up and *focus*!"

Focus. There was that word again.

❖

IT WAS HARD not to pay attention to my visitors, though. They could be awfully persuasive. The recruiter from one school was this large, *large* man named Coach Rune. He was a black, bald-headed man with very white teeth and a body that looked like he'd spent all morning stuffing pillows into his shirt and pants. He talked real rough. Used "fuck" a lot. One time he paid me a visit and we talked. I got the message right away: Coach Rune definitely wanted to be my friend. He patted me on the shoulder and clapped me on the back quite a bit, too. He tried to get all chummy.

On his way out the door, he dropped an envelope on the living room floor. I said, "You dropped something."

He looked at me and said, "No, I didn't."

"Your envelope," I said.

"I didn't see nothing."

"Nothing" turned out to be a thousand dollars in ten hundred-dollar bills. I could take a cue. I picked up the envelope and put it in my pocket.

In all, Coach Rune dropped a few thousand dollars on my living room floor that season. I was making out good, but it wasn't just me. My brother Larry swindled them out of everything he could. He made it his job to answer the phone every time it rang; he wouldn't let anyone else touch the receiver unless he'd screened the call first. He even did this to Grandma Lou. I watched him do this several times. The phone would ring, Larry would pick up the receiver and say, "Hello? This is the Simmons residence." Then he'd listen for a bit. I could tell if it was a recruiter right away because Larry would turn to me, nod, and wink—just like he was telling me, *Wait'll you see what I pull off this time.*

"Oh, hey, Coach Rune," Larry would begin. "Yeah, yeah. How you doing? Right, right. Yeah, Roy's really thinking hard about playing for you guys . . . right. Well, I hope he chooses you, too. But you know what? I gotta tell you. Things've been a little rough around here. Yeah, you know. My Grandma Lou's got the mortgage to pay and the light bill and the food bills—Roy eats a lot, you know. Huh? What's that? What am I *saying*? Oh, you know. Nothing really. I just know how much Roy loves his family. He'd do anything for us. I'd hate to see him take a job down at the supermarket or something to help out with the bills. He's got a great career ahead of him as a football player, don't you think? Shame to waste that talent at the checkout counter just because we're a little short on cash . . ."

It worked every time. Money started trickling into the house and, as it passed through Larry's hands, a little bit of it sheared itself off, which I suppose was only natural. Call it a finder's fee. Call it an agent's commission. Whatever you want to call it, I didn't care and I still don't. Larry earned his money fair and square. He played those recruiters like they were trying to play me.

Then came the gifts. Texas Southern took me to a tailor who fitted me for custom shirts and pants. All the work was done right there on the premises. USC got me clothes, too. Arkansas Tech got me clothes.

Coach Rune eventually upped the ante. They tried to get me some pussy.

On one of my visits to the campus, a linebacker on the team took me to a party and introduced me to this girl. Hooooo, she was fine! Tight body. Long fucking legs. Gorgeous hair. Beautiful eyes. Tits and ass going Pow Pow *POW!* First moment we were introduced, she sidles up to me and puts her arm through mine. "So!" she says. "Hear you're gonna play for *our* team."

Like I said, man, I can take a cue. This girl was all primed up to jump into bed with me. But I wasn't. I was there to play ball and I kept it on that level.

Then there was the man from Georgia Tech, a big-boned man named Coach Franklin Brooks. Funny. I remember him like he was standing right here beside me. He was white, 5'10", and built broad like he'd played ball. In fact, that's the first impression I got when I met that man. *This man's spent some serious time on the gridiron.*

Franklin Brooks grew on me pretty quick. Unlike all the other recruiters, he never came to my house. He respected my territory. He wasn't like Coach Rune, a man who took great delight in thoroughly abusing the NCAA guidelines, which state that gifts and perquisites and grandiose promises must be kept to strict minimums.

Franklin Brooks would say things like, "You're a good player. You've got skills. We can train you. Make you better. It's a lot of work. But if you want it, we'd like to work with you." Franklin Brooks and Georgia Tech never offered me anything. No envelopes dropped on the living room floor, that's for sure. But there was something about the tone of Coach Brooks's voice. That matter-of-fact way of talking began to agree with me.

It got to the point where Coach Rune called my house maybe once every two days. He'd talk to my mother when she was around, or my grandmother, and he'd talk to Larry, who promised to set up appointments with me in exchange for a nominal fee. On the other hand, Franklin Brooks called my house twice in all the weeks I was being courted by schools. And both times he asked to be excused for disturbing me at home.

I didn't want to be bought, but Coach Rune made it tough. In addition to the money Coach Rune kept dropping on me, he promised to buy my mother a new house and give me a brand-new car. I don't care what your value system is. When you're poor and somebody offers to take care of your mama, that shit can look pretty attractive.

Everything came to a head about a week before the deadline to sign my letter of intent. I got home from school at around 2:30 in the afternoon to find Coach Brooks at the house talking with my grandmother. We sat down in the living room and had a glass of sweet tea. Then Coach Rune showed up all of a sudden, which sort of made the situation a little tense.

It was as if these two men had worn masks in front of me up until that point; they'd kept their faces pleasant and civilized. Now, face to face with each other, the masks dropped off their faces. They stared at each other with what looked to me like something close to hatred and started arguing right there in front of me and my family. They argued about their schools, they argued about the athletes in their football programs, they argued about both of them being at the house at that particular time.

"What are *you* doing here?" Coach Rune demanded. Franklin Brooks's was like, "What am *I* doing here? What are *you* doing here?!"

If I thought the NCAA recruiting rules were bullshit before, they were completely out the window by now. Coach Rune started again ticking off all the things he was gonna do for me. "A car, Roy! Money for you! Money for your brothers! A new house for your momma! And girls!" Coach Brooks was like, "I do not *believe* what I'm *hearing*! Who the *hell* do you think you are?" And that's when Coach Rune reached over and shoved Coach Brooks, really hard. Coach Brooks turned cold. He said only one word: "Outside." And just like that, the two men got up and left the room. I remember looking at Grandma Lou and Larry before we got up and followed them without a word.

The coaches walked across the street to the grounds of the kindergarten about 100 feet away from my front door. Then these two very sizeable men started swinging away at each other. It was fucking insane.

It was over in about three or four minutes. Coach Rune brought Franklin Brooks down; he was younger and bigger—Coach Brooks never really had a chance. He got in a few good punches, don't get me wrong, but Rune had his way with him. Then, just as fast as it started, the two men stopped fighting and walked back across the street toward us. Coach Rune was panting and sweating and walking real fast. The first words out of his mouth were, "Roy, I've *got* to fucking *have* you! You *must* play for us! You were *meant* to play for us, Roy, you understand what I'm saying? I've got to have you!" This thought crossed my mind like a lightning bolt. *They're offering money, they're offering a car and a house! Take it, man! Go on and take it!* My family and I needed the money. But the more that thought flickered in my brain—*go on and take it, go on and take it*—the more I realized it made me uncomfortable. In fact, Coach *Rune* made me uncomfortable.

Now it was Coach Brooks's turn. He was walking a little stiff, like maybe he'd hurt himself. He just looked at me, looked at my Grand-mother, looked at Larry. Looked back at me. Then he let his eyes drop to his shoes. I think he was ashamed. "Sorry you had to see that," he said. And then he tuned and walked away, too. Franklin Brooks lost that battle. But he won the war. I picked Georgia Tech.

❖

FRANKLIN BROOKS DIED of asbestos poisoning about a year and a half after that fight in the schoolyard. Somewhere during the course of his life, he'd worked in a factory somewhere, and I guess the cancer got into his lungs. I never really noticed how hard it was for him to breathe, but looking back I guess he was struggling. When he lost the fight to Coach Rune, I assumed it was 'cause Rune was bigger and stronger and younger—Rune was in his early 40s, Brooks was in his middle 50s. Now I guess I see things differently. I guess Coach Brooks had other things to deal with back then, but of course he never let on.

I couldn't make the viewing but I was able to be at the burial service. By that point, I was playing for Georgia Tech and proud of everything I was doing for the team.

Coach Brooks and I had kept in contact. We talked often. He always listened to what I had to say, always thought things over before he opened his mouth to give me advice. When he died, I felt an incredible sadness rise up inside of me. Sadness like I remember feeling when Willy White died.

At the graveyard, I ran into a man who looked just like Coach Brooks. I was so sure this man had to be a relative that I went over and introduced myself. It turns out that man was Franklin Brooks's brother. We struck up a little conversation and shared a few memories of Coach Brooks. "What did you think of my brother?" his brother asked me. And I told him what I knew. I spoke from my heart. "He was a good man," I said, though that didn't even begin to cover it for me. "Your brother was a very good man."

❖

I SIGNED MY letter of intent to play for Georgia Tech a week after the fight on the kindergarten grounds. I held a little press conference in the tiny office of my high school principal. The place was jam-packed with reporters from the local media. Cameras clicked. Flashbulbs popped. Everyone was shouting questions at me. The place was so crowded that I couldn't get to the principal's desk. I signed my letter by asking my mother to turn around so I could write against her back. Which she did.

The place was pure commotion but I remember looking up and catching my grandmother's eye. She smiled at me. Lord, she was so proud. I could see it written all over her face. *My hard work paid off with this one.* Truly, that was one of the most beautiful moments in my life. I was on my way up and I was gonna take everyone with me. I was going to *college*! First person in my family to ever do that. I'd get a good job. I'd get us out of the ghetto. I'd marry Sheila. We'd have kids. I'd buy a big house where we all could live. Grandma Lou would never have to work again. Mama neither. It was all gonna be so beautiful. It was all gonna be perfect. For a while it was, too.

5

I ARRIVED AT Georgia Tech in the summer of '75 and lived in Smith dorm, right across from the famous Varsity Restaurant on Interstate 75. That's an electric highway, man, ol' 75—six lanes of constant, high-speed traffic; it's go-go-go 24/7 from the Great Lakes all the way down to Miami, through Detroit, Toledo, Cincinnati, Knoxville, Chattanooga, Atlanta, Naples, and Tampa. I used sit on the front stoop of Smith dorm and watch the swarm of headlights streaming by like fireflies in the dead of night. Used to dream about where they were headed, same as I dreamed for myself. Back then, wondering where I was headed turned out to be a full time job.

Georgia Tech hooked me up with a job working for Delta Airlines. I was responsible for grabbing the bags coming in off one domestic flight and transferring them to another. I operated a big machine that unloaded these big cargo containers full of luggage off of L-1011s. It was a dangerous job. Those containers could slip up and come down at any moment. If they hit you, they'd kill you, no doubt about it. But I liked it.

The problem was, I was lonely. There wasn't a damn soul on campus in the middle of summer. My family was all back home. Even Sheila was completely preoccupied getting ready to leave for Savannah State, where she was going to major in journalism. I wandered the empty halls of Smith and wondered, *Where the hell is everybody?*

For long weeks at a time, my life boiled down to working at the airport, coming home, and going to the gym every now and then. I shouldn't have worried, though. When school started up, they moved me to another dorm and things really began to cook.

❖

I GOT A new roommate, guy by the name of Al Richardson. He was a freshman linebacker from Miami. To give you an idea of what a bad match this turned out to be, I'll say this: I've always preferred to fall asleep in total quiet. Al liked to blast the radio. As it turns out, I chose to lose sleep so the motherfucker could enjoy his radio.

Now that school was in session, the campus didn't seem so lonely anymore. I began to miss my family a little less 'cause I had a new family, the Georgia Tech football team. We used to eat together in our own team dining room. God, I miss that dining room! You could eat all you wanted! The food never stopped!

Coming out of high school, my nickname was Horse. I guess it was 'cause I was big and fast. But my new family gave me a new nickname. A madman linebacker named John Blue started calling me the Sugar Bear. He was a very witty guy, John Blue. We used to smoke pot together sometimes in his dorm room. He'd walk around the room naked right in front of everyone while his girlfriend from another college played with his little winger right there in front of everybody. John Blue was vain as hell, but he nailed me to a wall with that nickname. Sugar Bear. That was me in a nutshell. I was big and I was soft. Sweet as candy, ferocious as a grizzly. John Blue nailed me right on the head with that nickname, and it stuck.

Academically, I wasn't setting the world on fire. I got the first F of my life in sociology. I nearly died. I guess I thought I could get by without going to class. All the guys on the football team got an automatic A in physical education and we never even had to attend. I guess sociology's a little bit different.

Actually, looking back, I don't remember a damn thing from any class I took in college. And I wonder about that sometimes. Is that just an athlete thing? Or is that what college is all about? You know, for everybody. The things I remember from back then have a lot more to do with life lessons than they have to do with classroom lessons. For instance, let me tell you about my first sexual experience in college.

Early on, some guys from my team and I were sitting around on the front porch of our dorm, hanging out. We used to sit around like a bunch of old ladies, drinking beer and calling each other names for fun. From the stoop, you could look out across the highway to the buildings lined up on the other side. And on top of this one building, I could barely make out the heads of people moving around on some kind of rooftop patio. This was in early fall, and I guessed those guys were up there trying to get a tan. I learned that the building was called the Flex Club.

Now, I used to go to Arby's, which was right on the corner of the same street as the Flex. I liked that damn sweet sauce Arby's put on their roast beef sandwiches. Plus they had a two-for-one deal there. Arby's ran bargains all the time in the campus newspaper, which was perfect for a 270-pound lineman in training. It takes a lot to feed that kind of machine.

I found myself getting more and more curious about what was going on up on that rooftop patio. I used to sit in the booth at Arby's for longer and longer periods of time, watching the cars coming in and out of the Flex Club. One day my curiosity got the better of me and led me down to the end of the street. It was a short journey. But it changed my life forever.

Here's what I saw the first time I opened the door to the Flex Club: row after row of books and magazines. Some of them were erotic literature, but others were sort of like catalogs that told you what was going on in and around the Atlanta gay scene. There were erotic toys lined up on shelves near the front of the house: dildoes, double dildoes, leathers, lubes, masks—a very large selection. Club music was blasting out of speakers positioned high up on the walls, and I noticed lockers lined up on the opposite side of the room. I shut the door and left.

That quick peek inside told me what I needed to know. The place was a sex club. How did I know? There were men hanging around all over the place in towels. And you better believe they all looked gay.

I went back, of course.

It was a warm fall day when I joined the Flex Club, my first membership at my first bathhouse. I can't say it was a proud occasion for me. Actually, I was kinda petrified that I'd run into someone I knew—like a teammate, for instance, or maybe a professor or something. But I have to admit I was also excited. Excited and very, very curious.

At the club, you had a choice: you could rent a locker or a room. I got a room. I went in and changed into a towel like everyone else was wearing. Then I left to go exploring. The way I remember it, I was more curious than nervous.

Right away I found out there was a pool with a Jacuzzi on the lowest floors, but that wasn't what I was looking for. I hunted around the Flex until I found the stairway leading up to that spot I'd seen on the roof from across the highway. I'd been right. There were men sunbathing all over the place on lounge chairs. Some were still dressed in towels. Some were nude. Some were squirting tanning oil on their hands and lathering each other up. One guy off in the corner was openly playing with himself while he watched other guys getting it on. It was Gay Heaven.

On that rooftop, I could move to the edge and look out over the low wall, look right on over at the Georgia Tech campus where I lived. Shit, I could see my teammates sitting on the front porch of our football dorm. The highway hummed between us, constantly moving, go-go-go. There was something else between us, too, now. Something even bigger than Route 75.

From that distance, my teammates would never be able to recognize me. So I waved at them. I didn't see anyone wave back. That was when I realized that I'd truly crossed the line, and I felt this peculiar excitement zip through me like electricity!

The first guy I met at the Flex was also dressed in a towel, a black guy in excellent shape. His body was all cut up and massive. He appeared to be a couple years older than me and he spoke very well. We talked for a little while and then went to his room. He handed me a little plastic capsule and said, "Here."

I asked, "What is it?"

He said, "Look. You go like this." And he broke the capsule open with his strong hands and shoved it under my nose so I could inhale the fumes. My introduction to poppers. Before I knew it, I was high as a motherfucking kite. We did 69. Complete fucking passion. His dick was good, and I know my dick was good for him 'cause we kept up our sucking for a long, long time. The poppers really did their job, man. We even came at the same fucking time. What a rush. Felt like the back of my head was about to explode.

Before the guy left, he put on his Navy uniform. Razor-sharp creases. The whole outfit was fitted to his body. Perfect. For a second I found myself thinking, *uniform?* Like that thought was tugging at something else in my brain, a memory. Then, just like that, it was gone. The guy turned around, waved at me and said, "See ya around." Real normal, like he was leaving for work in the morning. I never saw him again.

But after that I went back to the Flex Club at least once a week. Sometimes two times, sometimes three. Hell, it was only a fifteen-minute walk from my dorm. And no, I never saw any of my teammates there.

Not everything was as simple as all this might sound. I wasn't just into dick back then. I liked pussy, too, but that didn't confuse me. With me it was like, *whatever's happening today.* In fact, while I was running around getting myself acquainted at the Flex Club, I was also fucking this girl from Spellman College, which was this upper-crust, girls' school a couple of miles away on a separate campus.

Her name was Wendy and I met her at a party. I guess we fucked maybe once a week for a few months straight during my freshman year. It got so that I looked forward to her pussy. In college it was always good to have a little pussy on tap, and this girl was definitely available on a regular basis. Wendy was *my* pussy. But then she stopped returning my calls all of a sudden with no explanation. So I went to see her. She closed the door to her dorm room and said, "I have something to tell you."

I said, "Okay."

Then she opened her legs and shined a light down there. She said, "This is why I haven't called you."

The girl had herpes. And that was that. I never saw her again. For the next few weeks I kept a real close watch on my dick to see if anything weird was going on down there. But I guess Wendy must've gotten her shit from someone else. Thank God she didn't give it to me.

❖

As it turns out, I didn't have to leave campus to find sex with men. One day I went to the men's room in the building where the Dean's office was and found this big, round hole in the wall big enough to stick your fist through. I got the point. So I sat my ass down on the seat and waited. Some white guy used to come in and stick his humongous dick through the hole. I'd suck it while I jacked myself off. Then I'd go to class. I never could figure out who he was but I used to have fantasies. Somebody from my team? One of my professors? The Dean himself? Who the hell knew? That was part of the excitement. Not knowing.

Sometimes I'd wait in that toilet stall a long time to suck somebody's dick. Some days I switched it up and got my dick sucked instead. Either way, it turned out to be a pretty disappointing experience. There just wasn't a whole lot of traffic for that kind of activity moving back and forth in that men's room.

❖

I found other outlets, though. There was this tall, thin, nerdy Jewish guy living over at the Alpha Epsilon Phi house. He had an awfully big dick. I used to go over to visit Alpha Epsilon Phi with Eddie Lee Ivery, our star running back. The Phis loved having us over, since football players are sort of like celebrities at a school like Georgia Tech.

Now I had a hunch this Jewish guy was freaky. I could tell just by taking one good look at him. So I took him aside one time and said, "Look, man. We can do this if you're real cool about it. Don't mention this to Eddie Lee." He completely understood.

We went to his room and he sucked my dick. I sucked his. We kept this up for a good long while, too. Sometimes I met the guy twice a week so we could go at it. One time I even let him fuck me.

❖

Meanwhile, Sheila and I were still together even though we carried on this long distance relationship. She went to Savannah State and majored in journalism. She got really involved at her school, becoming an announcer for the campus radio station. We got to see each other every time we came home on breaks and it was good. Meaning there was always something alive there. That spark or attraction or whatever you wanna call it never went away.

We didn't have any illusions about being away from each other most of the time—at least *I* didn't. If she was seeing someone out at Savannah, I never knew about it, and there wasn't much I'd be able to say about it anyway. I was seeing people at Georgia Tech. A lot of people, as it turns out.

Like I said, I still thought of Sheila as the woman I'd eventually marry. Hell, I wasn't going to let my sexuality stop me from having a wedding and a family and a storybook life and all that shit. Yes, that was always the dream with me. It's how I was raised. Grandma Lou used to tell us all the time how every family needs a good man to be a husband and a father. "A good man keeps everybody in line," she'd say. "A good man turns bad things into good." I bought it, too, even though it took me years to finally wonder, *Wait a minute, what the hell's she talking about?* After all, none of the men in my family'd ever behaved like that.

Still, I revered Sheila. I worshipped her. I've got a romantic streak in me that's a thousand yards wide and it affected the way I was with her. I put her up on a pedestal. We hadn't even had sex yet. I wouldn't let myself with her. There was a part of me that wanted her pure and virginal for our wedding day, believe it or not. But all that changed when Sheila seduced me my sophomore year.

We had a homecoming game in the fall, and my mother and Sheila came up to visit. I got each of them a room at the Tech Motel. My mother's room was at the opposite end of the hallway. I didn't want it to happen the way it did. Sheila and I were hanging out after the game in her room. The lights were down real low and there was music playing softly in the background. We started kissing. Before long one thing led to another and we didn't have any clothes on.

I was kinda trying to hold myself back, but Sheila was really into it. There just ain't no stopping a woman who wants to give herself to you, that's the truth. I'd never seen that side of her before and—you know what I'm saying? I was shocked.

All of a sudden she opened right up and I felt myself slide in. Smooth and clean like it was meant to be. And I took my time with her. 'Cause, like it or not, it was a very special moment for me. For her. For us. It was very, very special.

❖

Now you can say what you want about college life; it's got its ups and downs, sure. Those parties used to rock! The Afro-American Association used to throw these all-out blasts at the Black House on 10th Street. That motherfucker used to go full tilt! Cars lined up all down the street. Music playing. People hooking up left and right all dressed up in their fine party clothes. Looking sharp, looking cute. I'd cruise the joint with my teammates and pretend I was looking for pussy, too. I wasn't though. Usually, I was looking for dick.

There was this constant worry in the back of my head about being found out for that, for liking men. But really, one of the things I found out was that if you play things cool and don't rub people's faces in your shit, they'll let you get away with just about anything. Because I was a football player, folks just naturally assumed I was straight—straight and crazy-ass horny. They were right about one part, at least.

I'd venture to say that the stigma of homosexuality among young black men is three or four times greater than it is for young white men.

I got involved in a lot of extracurricular activities in college same as I had in high school. My half-brother Stevie was Basileus of Omega Psi Phi over at Morris Brown, a college maybe three or four miles away from Georgia Tech. Let me tell you: Omega Psi Phi was *the* fraternity to join if you went to school at a black college. They called themselves the Que Dogs.

One time I visited Stevie and I got the chance to see all these little pledges running around obeying every fucking word he said. "Yes, sir, Big Brother! Right away, Big Brother! Anything you say, Big Brother! Anything you say!" That shit nearly got me hard. I was so impressed with the structure, you know? The hierarchy. To me, the frat was a whole lot like the football team, just another family of fellas hanging out and being brothers.

Right away I knew I wanted to be in Omega Psi Phi, too, but they didn't have any black fraternities at Georgia Tech. So I started pledging Alpha Epsilon Pi, which was a primarily Jewish fraternity. But then the Georgia Tech Afro-American Association figured it was high time that Georgia Tech had its own all-black fraternity. So they opened up the first-ever Omega Psi Phi chapter at the school and I rushed it.

The pledge to be a Que Dog lasted eleven weeks even though it was supposed to last six. Shit, man, it was like going through hell on earth. The Big Brothers made us run around the football field over and over and over again. 'Course I was sort of used to that, but it left most of the other guys huffing. But then they made us do all sorts of mental gymnastics, too. Had to learn poems and fraternity chapter history and shit. Had to know the full family backgrounds of each of the Big Brothers. There were twenty-two of us pledges, and each of us was given a new name for the rush period. Mine was Que Lock. Don't ask me why. The whole damn thing was insane before the Brothers figured they could kick things up a notch and get *really* creative.

One time they made seven of us climb inside a Volkswagon Beetle and drive like that all over campus—looping and skidding at breakneck speed—until we finally got to the Dean of Pledges' house where our orders were to pile out on the front lawn, turn around, drop our drawers, and moon him. The Brothers shaved our heads bald and made us wear pledge uniforms at all times: boots, blue jeans, and a white T-shirt. Not so bad until you considered the huge gold-and-purple lamp carved from wood that you wore on a thong around your neck. That motherfucker was heavy, too. Maybe 25 pounds. I was tempted to rip that thing off and throw it out the window on several occasions. But you didn't dare let one of the Big Brothers see you do that. No, no, no, you didn't even *think* things like that. If you made even the slightest mistake with the Brothers—lost focus for just a second—the penalties were swift and hard. One Brother, the biggest one of all, used to step right up to pledges who'd broken the rules and announce in his big, bass voice, "You, sir, have sinned against the Omega Psi Phi way!" Then he'd haul back and smack the pledge across the face so hard he could cause a nosebleed. Sure as hell, he set your ears to ringing for the rest of the night. I know this for a fact because I was considered an uppity pledge. I was slapped very hard on several occasions.

One time I got hit for talking to a female, which was against the rules for rushing pledges. And that Big Ass Black Ass Big Brother Motherfucker says to me, "I saw your ass, there, Simmons. You know what you did was wrong. Stand up and take it like a man." Shit, he cocked back and hoooooo! hit me so hard that the blood flew everywhere. It got so I used to tremble whenever I heard the sound of that man's voice. Oh, how I hated that motherfucker.

Those bastards made us sleep together, eat together, piss together, walk to class together—all so we'd kinda get the idea that we were brothers, you know? When one man went down, the whole line went with him. I knew that already from the football field. I just wanted to be a Que Dog. To me, joining that frat *and* being a part of the Georgia Tech football team were the two highest honors in the universe. That was my life every day for eleven weeks. I lost forty pounds.

❖

FINALLY CAME THE day for our branding, which took place on a Sunday morning. I was in bed asleep when they showed up at my room and hauled my ass out into the sunlight. They led me off to the Dean of Pledges' house like I was about to be tried for a crime. That was the feel of it, anyway.

When we got there, they told me to wash my arm, which I did. Then they set about beating on my shoulder with their bare knuckles till the motherfucker was numb. After that they applied some Betadine, then a layer of Vaseline, which I suppose was to keep my skin from ripping itself up under the hot iron. Then came the brand. Made a goddamn sizzling sound when it hit me. Like I was a T-bone steak.

Damn Vaseline didn't do me no good, neither. My skin came right off on the hot iron. I had a butter knife in my mouth so I could bite down on it, to keep from screaming. That didn't do me no good, neither.

❖

WE STARTED WITH twenty-two pledges, ended up with six. You better believe I was one of the guys who made it. I never entertained the thought of quitting. 'Cause it's true what they say: Only the strong survive.

Meanwhile, back on the gridiron I was making myself useful. For the record, I started all four years at Georgia Tech. The school recruited me as a guard, so that's what I started out doing.

My head coach was a guy named Pepper Rodgers and I admired him. He was very extroverted. He had curly hair and was just a spiffy guy. I remember I took one look at that guy and said to myself, "Whoooo boy. He's gonna be a wild motherfucker." And he was.

See, head coaches are supposed to be conservative. But not Pepper Rodgers. No, sir. He'd holler and scream at us from the sidelines. He'd rant and rave and throw shit at us whenever the spirit moved him. But it was never anything personal, you understand, it was all just part of the job. That man could whip up his own personal shit storm in the middle of a game, but once the whistle blew and the game was over he went right on back to being a human being again. Once you got to know Pepper and his wife, it was truly amazing. They were just a regular, old-fashioned down-to-earth couple.

❖

MAN, I HAD some times playing ball for Georgia Tech. We played for keeps and we were good. I especially loved it when we played our rivals at Georgia. In the back of my head, I was always a little conscious of the fact that, were it not for the efforts of Mr. Franklin Brooks, I could have played for that team. Hell, I could have played for any of the teams we played. That gave me a whole lot of extra inspiration.

One time when we played Georgia I knocked this guy on his ass so hard that the whole right side of my body went numb. I didn't tell nobody about it, didn't signal the coach for a time-out or nothing. I just waited for the sensation to return. And waited. I began to be very afraid.

It seemed like forever but it was actually more like a minute or so. Then I started to feel myself tingling and was like, *Hoooooo! That was close.*

❖

I WAS MAKING a name for myself on the field. One time I clotheslined this guy from Duke, and the *Atlanta Constitution* made a big color spread out of it for their sports section. I was getting lots and lots of good press.

Pepper Rodgers thought enough of my talent that he started to experiment with me. Pretty soon he figured out that he could get more mileage outta me if he moved me around the squads a bit, used me to fill in the holes in his lines. I played noseguard my sophomore year. Back to offensive tackle as a junior. I played guard, and guard only, for my senior year, and that's when I started thinking to myself: *Hey, man, if you can play like this, there just might be a place for you in the NFL.* Before that, I'd never entertained the thought. Never dared to. I was still in the mentality of *I'm just a poor black kid from Savannah, ain't no room in pro football for a kid like me.* Far as I was concerned, I was gonna get my industrial management degree and settle down somewhere with a factory job and, you know, work forty years, retire, and die.

❖

THE FLEX BECAME my getaway spot from the world. It was a perfect retreat 'cause, for one thing, it never closed. For another, I finally got over my paranoia of meeting someone I knew or even recognized there; after a couple of months went by, it just hadn't happened so I started to feel safe. Looking back, it makes sense to me that a lot of the clientele would have come from the college, but that's not the way it was. They were mostly executives. Traveling men. Which was perfect for me. Just passing through meant no real attachments. I hit the Flex about once a week.

I was living a closeted life in my own little closeted world. Nobody knew. I doubt anybody even suspected. Oh, I had friends, sure. Some of them were pretty close, even. But nobody ever got close enough to figure out what was going on. First of all, I was always a little shy. Didn't talk much and kept mostly to myself. Plus everyone I knew—the guys on the team and even my fraternity brothers—they just sort of got used to my behaviors. I guess they figured I was eccentric.

Like the way I'd sort of disappear for a day or so and pop back into your life again like it was perfectly normal. I could tell people who weren't on the football team that I had team business to attend to. I could tell guys on the team that I had some fraternity thing to do. I could tell my fraternity brothers that I had a project due for some class, or I was meeting some friends. Since I hung out with so many different groups of people, I was sort of a part of everyone's life. But at the same time I wasn't really there. It was never unusual for me to be hanging out with folks and then sort of say, "Oh hey. Sorry. I got to go somewhere. See you later. Alright?"

I was just passing through, you see what I mean? No real attachments.

❖

ONE TIME IN my junior year I went to the Varsity Restaurant to get something to eat. I made eye contact with this tall, white guy and one thing led to another. I wound up at his apartment. There was music playing on the stereo and the TV was on without any sound. He'd offered me a gin and juice. All of a sudden my vision became blurred and I felt queasy. Lord have mercy! In the back of my head—and I'm talking way, way in the back of my head—I thought to myself, *Bastard put something in my drink.*

I don't know what happened after that. I sort of remember being on my stomach. I felt some pressure. Don't know what he did to me. I don't know if that was his dick or his arm up there. Woke up with a sore ass the next morning and the guy made me breakfast. Then he gave me a ride back to campus. We made small talk about school and college life and so forth. We did not talk about what had happened. Later on, after I'd had some time to think about it, I was just glad he didn't kill me or lock me in the basement. And then I wondered why, having been raped as a child, I'd let someone do that to me all over again.

❖

I'D SAY ABOUT half the football team smoked pot and I was in the half that—how do they say it these days?—inhaled. As my college years progressed, I began to accelerate my pot use. Pretty soon I was smoking every day or every other day. It wasn't hard to do. When I lived in the dorms we just stuffed a towel under the door. It kept the smell from drifting into the hallway—we didn't want to tip off the dorm's Resident Assistant. Or sometimes we'd put a fan on and blow the smoke out an open window.

Later on I got an off-campus apartment for my sophomore and junior years. I would have kept it, too, but the phone bill was in my name and my two frat brother roommates never paid their share. So the phone got shut off. I moved back on campus senior year so I could receive incoming calls.

❖

WE DRANK A lot, too. Most of the guys preferred 8.00 Beer, which I didn't really care for, I'm not much a beer man. I could only drink it cold. One time we went to a rush party and they had a keg that was so iced down that the beer came out almost frozen. I kept drinking and drinking and drinking and drinking. It was odd: the ice-cold beer made this warm feeling in my belly. I was so fucked up I could hardly stand, barely walk, my speech was all slurry. It was one of the only times in my entire life that I've allowed myself to get that crazy, that completely out of control. And I learned from that mistake, too. Later on, the idea of being that inebriated scared the hell out of me. *Got to be more careful 'cause I never want to lose control. Lose control and maybe I'll act in a certain way, say a certain thing, do a certain deed that'll let people know. They'll find out. Learn my secret.*

During the Peach Bowl, we stayed at the Marriott Hotel for a week and I was introduced to Jack Daniels by Lawrence Lowe, a linebacker who was like my little brother. The night before the Peach Bowl, I met and partied with the Purdue players. Turns out Purdue had a mother-fucking huge Omega Psi Phi chapter. So I got a chance to meet a lot of my fraternity brothers who I'd be clashing up against the next day, head to head.

Purdue whipped our asses. I can't even remember the fucking score, but it was pitiful, man. Just pitiful.

❖

IN 1979, SOME teammates and I were sitting around my room listening to the NFL draft over the radio. I'd been looking forward to it for a long time. Everyone expected me to go in the very first round. It was in all the Georgia papers. *The Peach State will surely offer up a grand harvest of recruits for this year's NFL draft. From Georgia Tech, running back Eddie Lee Ivery, tackle Kent Hill, and jack-of-all-trades Roy Simmons are expected to be taken in the first round . . .*

Eddie Lee Ivery and Kent Hill went in the first round all right. The draft that year chose 330 players and Eddie was number 15, the Packers snatched him up; Kent was number 26, he was chosen by the Rams. You shoulda heard the whooping and hollering in my little room when that happened. Everyone was screaming their heads off, it was outta control.

"All right, Roy," Eddie said. He had a smile on his face and a beer in his hand and he was proceeding to get very, very drunk. He thumped me on the back. "All right now, Sugar Bear. Here comes your turn!"

The first round finished up at player number 28. Eddie thumped me on the back again and said, "You're first choice in the second round, I bet." The second round finished up at player number 56. I hadn't been chosen. Eddie shrugged and said, "Get ready. Here it comes." The third round went by—nothing. And the fourth round—nothing. In the fifth round my teammate Don Bessilieu, a defensive back, got picked up by the Miami Dolphins, he was player number 134. By this point Eddie wasn't saying a thing anymore. Nobody was. They were flicking glances back and forth as if to say *what the hell is going on?!?* But nobody wanted to speak. I guess they didn't trust that what they said could help the situation any.

Kent phoned me as the fifth round ended and said, "Roy, man! What the fuck is going on? I don't deserve to go. You do." I said, "I don't know, man." And I didn't. I had no idea what was going on. Somebody passed me a joint and I smoked it.

The sixth round came and went. They didn't call my name. And just like that, the first day of the draft was over. Nobody knew what to say to me. I really didn't know what to say either. As it was, I think I just muttered, "Know what? Fuck that. Fuck *everybody*. Nobody better call me after that shit, 'cause I'm not going no-fucking-where."

I was hurt. I was goddamn inconsolable. Everyone knew I played the game well. They knew I'd been shafted. And to this day, I have no idea why things worked out the way they did. The only clue I ever got was this: later on I heard that the NFL had problems with the fact that I'd started in four different positions during my time at Georgia Tech. Shows what you get for being versatile.

That was a horrible night for me. All my friends were celebrating, whooping it up, and getting ready to fly out the very next day to cities around the United States to meet their new teammates. Me? I smoked another joint and had some more beer and tried to act like I didn't fucking care.

The next day I got up and went to the bathroom to take a shower. I wasn't in there long when a few of the guys burst in hollering, "Roy! Sugar Bear! You got a phone call!"

To which I said, "So?" My mood was fucking grim.

"It's the New York Giants! They wanna speak to you!"

To which I said, "Fuck 'em." And I meant it. I took my time in the shower.

When I finally got out and toweled off and walked down the hall and picked up the phone, I said, "Hello?"

"Roy Simmons?"

"Yes."

"This is the New York Giants. You've just been drafted in the eighth round."

The eighth round? I had no idea what to say to that. *The New York Giants?* Shit, I was a Dallas Cowboys fan. I idolized Dallas's fullback, Robert Newhouse. I had a poster of the Dallas Cheerleaders on my bedroom wall. Dallas was America's Winning Team back then. Everybody else was just a team.

"Mr. Simmons?"

"Yeah."

"Still with me?"

"Yeah."

"Can you come out to New York today?"

"No. But I'll be there tomorrow."

I was still mad when I hung up the phone. But then I started thinking, *Fuck the Cowboys. My ass is going to the NFL!*

❖

MY CONTRACT WAS negotiated for me by an attorney and my starting salary was set at $40,000 with a $10,000 signing bonus. In the late '70s, $50,000 was a great big pile of money. I was thrilled! In fact, I was so excited that I kinda forgot all about the fact that I never actually graduated from Georgia Tech. That's the sad truth of it and I got no one to blame but myself. I'd done so well in high school I could have graduated a year early but my performance in college was pitiful. I let football and the fraternity and sex become my curriculum. I got lazy. If I went to a class and didn't like it? Hell, I'd just drop it. And most of the time I was too fucked up to attend the classes I *did* like. Cut it any way you want it. I still need thirty more credits to get my industrial management degree. And I have no one to blame but myself.

I went north to Orange, New Jersey, and stayed with Aunt Betty for a few days. I was still angry and maybe even a little embarrassed about the whole draft thing. But a lot of that went away when I found out Betty's house was only twenty minutes from Giants' Stadium.

So there I was, just a few days after getting that phone call, staring out at all the empty rows of seats, looking down at the empty playing field, thinking about how my life was about to change. I loved that stadium, man. Really loved it. And I have to say, the team locker room was very plush. Thick carpets. Beautiful new lockers with individual keys. Coke machines and wide-screen TVs in the sitting area. Beautiful bathrooms with excellent mirrors you could spend all day shaving in. I thought, *I could get used to this.* Little by little, that's just what I did.

Aunt Betty's house was also really close to something else I was about to get used to. It didn't take me long to venture into Manhattan.

6

S OMETIMES I'D DRIVE through the streets of New York City just
to look at all the people. Blacks, whites, Asians, Hispanics, Jews,
Europeans, and everything in between. Amazing! So much variety.
In Savannah, we thought we had variety if two friends liked to read
different newspapers!

I was learning the vibe, you know? Picking it up the ways of the
streets little by little, the way you pick up the words to a cool new song
you hear over the radio a few times. It seeps into you gradually. I learned
as I went. And I learned a lot.

Greenwich Village was electric! And Harlem was divine. The West
Side, the East Side, Riverside, Morningside—ain't no damn place in
the whole wide world as beautiful and magnificent as New York City.
You can still walk the streets and hear folks chattering away in every
language spoken on earth. You can eat the foods of every culture, and
that shit's cooked fresh by the actual native peoples, too. And talk
about entertainment! I went to clubs where they had people fucking,
live and on stage. I went to the famous Badlands bar and hung out
with all the movers and shakers, the dealers, the thugs, the party boys,
and the glitter girls. I went to a black club called Peter Rabbit's where
jazz musicians used to hang out nodding in the back corners, stoned
outta their minds but ready to thrill you with their instruments at any
moment. Then there were places where they had all kinds of female
impersonators walking around. Most of them were for hire and I
thought, *Hooo, man! I like this shit!*

For the first time in my life, I had money—lots and lots of money. I also had some brand-new, killer connections through the NFL. I had prestige. I was a professional football player for a team whose home town was New York City. That's wild! That's amazing! But the best part of it all? Apart from maybe San Francisco, there's no place better in the whole damn world to find gay sex than in New York City.

❖

STILL, I HAD to maintain my focus. Coach Lewis and Coach Ellington from high school would have been proud of me. I realized that professional football is big business and I was determined to make my mark early on. The Giants' training camp was at Pace University in Pleasantville, New York. My roommate's name was Ken Johnson and he was a running back from Florida. Later on, he got cut from the program, but I never figured out why. Seemed to me like Kenny had all the right moves, but that's not always why they hire a player. Sometimes there's personal reasons. Sometimes there's shit happening under the surface that you don't know about that they're taking into consideration. But I missed Kenny when they cut him. He was one of my first friends coming into the world of professional football. We bonded, talked about our families and our lives and college life and what we hoped to accomplish playing pro ball. We started to dream together, but it ended for him real quick.

The coaches worked us hard all summer long. We pulled two-a-day sessions in the stifling heat. And I began to meet the guys I'd be playing with, assuming I made the team, which I knew I would. Getting drafted don't mean you get a free ride. Hell, nobody gets a free ride in training camp, you gotta earn your place. But I was confident. I looked around and took a good hard look at the talent pool. I was just a kid from Savannah, Georgia, but still I found myself thinking, *This is it? These guys are pros? Hell, I can do this!* I knew in my heart I was one of the best. I had absolutely no doubt in my mind at all.

❖

WHEN I KNEW I was on the team for sure, I called up Sheila. She was overjoyed.

"You made it?"

"I made it."

"You really, really *made* it?!?"

"I really, really *made* it, baby!"

Then I called Aunt Betty. Same reaction. Everyone was so proud of me. Making the team was one of the happiest days of my life. They held a press conference which was very prestigious, a great tradition. Again with the flashbulbs going off all over the place and the reporters pushing their microphones and tape recorders up into my face. But there wasn't anything mean-spirited about it. Everyone was so excited. The fans were hopeful. Maybe this would be the team, you know? Maybe this would be the year.

A little later on, my cousin Alisha asked me to visit her elementary school so she could show me off to her friends. Man, those kids loved it! I signed posters and told stories and showed them how to handle a football. It was a good feeling, you know? Cousin Alisha told me, "I'm so excited to have a professional football player in my family."

I didn't know how to tell her how excited I was to *be* the professional football player in the family. I didn't know how to tell her how I wanted the best for us all, how I thought that I could move us all up. How elated I was that finally—finally!—I was in a position to make sure that the Simmons family never wanted for anything ever again.

I told her, "Whatever it takes, girl. Money. Prestige. Shaving ads. More money. You know I'm gonna do it all and do it right. For us, Alisha. I'm doing it all for us."

❖

YOU'VE PROBABLY HEARD of some of the guys I played ball with on the Giants. There was a man by the name of Lawrence Taylor, for instance. This man was a thoroughbred. He may well have been one of the most talented ball players I ever got the chance to work with or watch. And everything you've heard about him, no matter how outrageous—I guarantee it's true. That's the beauty of being a thoroughbred. They're not like the rest of the population. They're brilliant. They're insane. They're completely unpredictable. And they're so valuable to NFL culture that everybody—coaches, owners, the fans, the police—everybody on the goddamn planet lets them practically get away with murder.

One time I took LT out to Foley's bar and he had so much to drink that he just all of a sudden bit through the glass in his hand and started chewing it up like cornbread. Another time during the season he came out to Aunt Betty's house on a quiet Sunday and just let himself in. Aunt Betty was like, "Who the hell is that—is that Lawrence Taylor?" But before she could get a handle on the situation, he'd walked straight up the steps to my third-story bedroom and busted down the fucking door. I was in bed with this girl named Angela and she screamed like we were under attack. Screamed hard enough like to bust my eardrums.

LT was drunk, of course. He fell to his knees and burst out laughing. Then he screamed, "Roy Simmons is up here fucking!" Loud enough so that I'm sure they heard him all the way off in Newark. I got him to go back downstairs with me and we hung out in the living room and had a drink while Angela tried to pull herself together. Which took a little bit of time cause that girl was out of her mind with fear.

❖

THEN THERE WAS Beasley Reece, who gave me no end of inspiration during my rookie year. Beasley came from Waco, Texas—and there's something about Texans, man. They're not like people from other parts of the country. Everything they do, they do it bigger. One time I was in the locker room with Beasley and he says to me, "Roy Simmons. You know what?"

"What," I asked.

"You are one very bad motherfucker. Did you know that?"

"No."

And he smiles and nods and says, "Yes, sir. Yes, you are. That's what I see when I look at you, Roy. One very bad motherfucker. In fact, I don't even think you *realize* how motherfucking bad you are. You don't realize that, do you? *Do* you?" That Beasley made it sound awfully good.

"Well, listen up, man," Beasley said. "'Cause I'm telling you the truth. You're bad. You're *bad*! You're *motherfucking* bad! I just want you to know that."

"Okay."

"You know that now, right?"

"I know that now, yeah."

"That's right. Now you do." And just like that, he walked out. I still don't know what exactly he was talking about, but he used to talk to me like that all the time. In the NFL, you got some guys who used all of their energy to lift other people up. And then you had guys who used everything they had to crush other people down. Beasley's still kind of an inspiration to me even now. In 1976 he was a ninthround NFL draft pick outta North Texas State. The Dallas Cowboys snatched him up as pick number 264. That's even lower than my ranking in the draft. But Beasley never let that stop him. He left the Cowboys—a dream team—after only one year and wound up with the Giants in '77. He worked real hard and pretty soon made Defensive Captain—he was one of the fastest runners in the league back then. And his career just kept on going, he really put his nose to the grind stone. He had a great run with the Tampa Bay Buccaneers after moving to their team in '83. And this man who'd started out so low on the NFL draft totem pole eventually got inducted to the NFL Hall of Fame in 1997. Today, he's a highly regarded sportscaster and a role model for athletes and sports fans, young and old alike. Now that's what I call a career.

❖

ALVIN GARRETT NEVER crushed me down. In fact, Alvin became one of my closest friends. He was a pure southern gentleman with a fine southern accent. And Lord! He just loved to go out and party! He'd drink till he got drunk. One time he brought a girl over to my aunt Betty's house. I told Alvin to go right on ahead and do whatever he had to do. Which he did. A day or two later he got the goddamn crabs. Poor dumb sonovabitch. Later on, I'd follow Alvin down south.

My gay side took a beating in the locker room as far as my pride was concerned. There I was surrounded by all these fine-looking men. Couldn't have a single one of them. Didn't even want to think about it, lest I give myself away somehow.

I was real attracted to Billy Taylor and I liked Earnest Gray's body. I used to watch him walk by in his towel and think *Huh, Gray's Anatomy.* But Odis McKinney for sure had the baddest physique on the whole motherfucking team. That man was chiseled from marble. He was hammered out and cut up in all the right places! Then there was Johnny Perkins. Otis Wonsley.

I kinda dug Gary Jeter a little bit, too—he was a great defense player. Jeter was fun, he and I argued back and forth like bitches in the locker room. Jeter used to make fun of me all the time, called me "fat-ass" and "cocksucker" and "faggot" and "fairy." We hammered at each other like that constantly. Looking back, I think he might have even known I was gay. At very least, I'm sure he suspected. We never talked about it outright, but there was something about the way we interacted with each other, some kinda hidden subtext to our conversations that was solely based on perpetuating an unmentionable secret. We could be discussing the weather or Bo Matthews's newest expensive purchase or a new play we'd just learned or an upcoming game. Didn't matter what we were discussing *on the surface.* Underneath it all, our conversation always felt to me like this: *I know you're a homo, Roy. You can't fool me./That's okay, Gary, I'm not trying to fool anybody. You cool with it?/Yeah, sure, I'm cool. Don't make no difference to me. But don't think for a second that I'm not gonna give you shit about it./That's fine with me, Gary. I wouldn't expect anything less from a half-brained, witless screw like yourself./Cocksucker./ Asshole./Fat-ass./California surf boy.* And on and on like this.

With all this sexual tension floating around in the air, it made things tough for me. Not exactly uncomfortable, but definitely challenging. Like I said, I could look, but I could not touch. I had to get by on peeks. It was all about total conditioning of the self that allowed me to survive in that environment. And as far as I could see, I was all alone in my struggle. I was the only one fighting that particular battle.

Bo Matthews was the first guy on the team to buy himself a Rolls-Royce. The team *owners* didn't even have Rolls-Royces. But that's the way Bo Matthews was. He had the cash and he liked to flaunt it. He used to dress himself in very fine clothes, like a gridiron aristocrat.

One of my teammates, who used to sit near me in the locker room, was the one who eventually turned me on to cocaine. One time I saw him snort the shit an hour before game time. Once, he was on the phone in my hotel room and he tossed me a packet of coke and kept right on talking. Mind you, I never really liked coke. It got me all depressed. But I had to do *some*. It was sort of expected. I ended up snorting a little bit and throwing the rest behind the bed whenever he looked away.

I never smoked crack with anyone on the Giants while I was with the Giants. But I know for a fact that some of my teammates got together and smoked crack at their homes. I particularly remember how I once heard about an upcoming house party that sounded like it'd be a real crazy time. I got really excited about it but a few of the guys suddenly got all squirrelly about me attending. This was very strange behavior since we'd pretty much been inseparable up until that point. They kept trying to talk me out of attending, and I wasn't having it. The stranger they acted, the more I wanted to see what it was they were trying to hide from me.

As it turns out, they didn't want me to see guys from the team free-basing. When I got there, a few of my teammates were standing in the kitchen. They spent the whole night there, huddled around a beaker that was boiling away over the gas range. At the time I knew nothing about the process of making crack. You heat cocaine with ammonia or sodium bicarbonate and water to remove the hydrochloride. The result is an relatively inexpensive, smokable form of the drug that delivers a very intense high only ten seconds after you inhale. My friends knew that I'd never tried crack and I guess they were trying to keep me ignorant of it, trying to keep me from experimenting. Looking back, I thank them for that, I really do. I only wish that I'd taken their hint and steered clear of the stuff later on.

❖

IN TRAINING CAMP my rookie year there was a player named John Mendenhall who took it upon himself to try to hurt me. We regularly beat the shit out of each other in training camp, but this guy had some sort of special agenda with me, don't know what it was. I thought it over some and made up my mind that he didn't have any right to hurt me. So I decided to try and break his fucking leg on the field before training camp was over.

I think he sensed what was going on. I went after him a few times and he backed off real quick. He said, "Yo, man. Whoa, whoa, *whoa!* I got a fucking family, yo. I got children." I was like, *Whatever, bitch. Stay the fuck away from me.*

Later on, I hit the locker room and there he was, perched up on his stool like some sort of weird-ass gargoyle. And he says to me, "Roy Simmons! You know what? You look like a guy who could use this. Go on. It's yours." I guess he figured my aggression toward him sprang from that fact that I hadn't gotten laid in a while 'cause he gave me a pass to a club called Plato's Retreat, an adult fuck club. His idea of a peace offering, I guess. I pocketed the damn thing and sort of grunted at him. Let that be his thank-you.

❖

PLATO'S RETREAT WAS in Manhattan, not far from the West Side Highway. I walked right on in and hit the bar and ordered my usual, a Long Island Iced Tea with top-shelf liquor. Best medicine in the world to work out some of the jitters. Back then I was running around 275 or 280 pounds, so it took a *lot* of medicine, five Long Islands, to get my buzz on. I had a pretty high tolerance.

I gotta give this to Mendenhall, though, Plato's Retreat was wild. Up until that point, I'd never seen anything like it. There was a sofa area with candles up front that sort of lulled you into thinking that maybe the place was normal. Then you'd move through these curtains and get deeper into the place. You started to find these little booth areas where you could slide on in without even introducing yourself and watch folks carrying on. Some were naked, some wore clothes.

I watched guys getting their dicks sucked all over the place. Then this one girl takes a guy's dick out of her mouth, hikes up her miniskirt and sits down right on top of him, starts humping away. She didn't seem to care that anyone was watching. In fact, I think she liked it.

Deeper in, you found even more interesting stuff. Girls walking around in G-strings and nothing else. You had to pay for them, of course, and they were probably there for the folks who wanted to do ménage-à-trois and so forth. Basically, whatever you wanted to do could get done, so long as you were willing to pay for it. Which was sort of the same way I was beginning to look at the world now that I'd joined the NFL.

In spite of all that, I have to say I was a little disappointed in the place. I didn't indulge in anything except the liquor. At that time I was most certainly into other things, which they didn't feature on the menu. I'd go to the Village, for instance. The gay guys hung out on Christopher Street, that much was obvious. As far as bars went, there was a place called Keller's and another called Two Potato. I never liked Keller's. The place was a fucking meat market. You'd go inside and it was wall-to-wall sausage, guys slammed up against one another. Not my kind of environment at all. I never left Keller's with anyone except myself.

Two Potato was another story. People ask me if I was ever worried that someone would recognize me. I mean, here I was, a relatively well-known guy, a professional football player, publicly visiting an openly gay venue in the middle of New York City. Didn't that scare me? No. Not really. The truth is most people can't smell shit for what it is even if you rub their goddamn faces in it. Back then I was also in the habit of hiring hustlers and taking them out to hotel rooms. Not exactly what you'd call discreet behavior, but none of that matters if nobody's watching for it in the first place.

❖

THE FIRST BATHHOUSE I went to in New York was called the Everard on West 28th Steet. We called it the Rod. There were other places in town, like the Barracks over on 42nd Street, but the Rod was the cleanest and that made all the difference in the world to me. This one older gay man worked the window as you came in, and he was very cordial. He was also a huge Giants fan. He couldn't believe his eyes when he saw my ID.

"Simmons?!"

"Yeah."

"*Roy* Simmons?!?"

"Uh huh."

"*The* motherfucking Roy Simmons!?!?"

He was so excited, looked like he was about to mess his drawers, man. Which would've made two of us. I was so damn frightened that someone had spotted me that I think I just stood there that first time with my mouth hanging open onto my damn chest. As it turned out, I shouldn't have worried. This guy knew how to play it cool. I never once had to tell him to keep his mouth shut; he already understood that. And thank God he did.

This man could have really fucked me up. He could have got my black face splashed all over all the local tabloids if he'd wanted to. But he didn't. And I appreciated that. I appreciated *him*. I got in the habit of bringing this dude team stickers and memorabilia and paraphernalia and shit. One time I brought him an actual football. He went crazy over it.

The Rod got to be comfortable. Sort of like the New York version of the Flex Club. It got to be like home. So I started hitting it maybe once a week or so, just like I'd done down at Georgia Tech. There were five floors at the Everard and each one of them catered to a different type of sexual activity. One floor had a bunch of rooms designed to act out your fantasies. There were mirrors hung all over the place and bondage equipment available to play with. One floor had an orgy area with movie screens for porn films. There was a weight room area. A sauna area. A massage area. A dance area. Combine all this with a wicked sound system running throughout the whole place and guess what you've got? A gay man's paradise. The Rod made the Flex Club look like a kindergarten version of what a sex club should be.

❖

I'D FLY HOME to Savannah during breaks and the off season. I had a routine where I'd pick up a rental car, then go to see Gerald, even before I saw my family, before I saw Sheila. We'd hit the fine nightclubs on River Street rather than hang out at all the little black clubs in the city. A lot of times we stuck to the tourist zones 'cause it was easiest that way. No one there knew us and we were guaranteed not to know them.

Eventually I'd make time to see Sheila, of course. Despite everything that was going on in my life back then, despite all the men I was into,

I just couldn't shake that girl from my mind. I was always thinking about her. Looking back now, I'm not sure if it was love or idealization or my romantic streak or what. Part of me knew that I was doing her wrong. It was one thing to be seeing other people, but it was another thing entirely to be doing the shit that I was doing.

That was the Great Conflict in me. Maybe that's the Great Conflict in every man living a closeted life. On the one hand, I had a female who was willing to give herself to me completely. And I loved her right back. But no, not completely. 'Cause with me, there would always be this *other side* that I could never let her see. In truth, it had nothing to do with her, that's the way I saw it. I was like, *Shit. If they can separate church and state in this country, then one man sure as hell can separate his love life.*

Besides that, I just couldn't get enough sex. I'd go out at night and be with a man, come right back home and still have plenty left to throw Sheila a piece, too. Maybe that was the problem with our relationship: the guarantee. I always knew I could have sex with Sheila. With men it was more of a challenge. With men, I had to put my game face on and get down to some serious hunting.

She never knew all the shit I was wrestling with. Hell, no one did. *Was I born like this? Was it cause of Travis? Is this really me? Or am I just sort of acting something out?* I never could get any clarity. And my Great Conflict kept working overtime to keep building my Great Big Lie, brick by brick, day by day. Sheila was the biggest victim of all. There's so many Sheilas out there. So many women, so many wives living with men they don't truly know.

Maybe I should've trusted her more. Maybe I should've gotten help. Maybe I should've just come clean and let the chips fall where they may. I'm sure I should've done a lot of things, looking back. But I didn't. I kept right on doing what I was doing, thinking that everything would work out right in the end. How wrong I was.

❖

ONE WEEKNIGHT DURING my rookie season I went to the Rod, same as usual. I walked in and handed off some Giants paraphernalia to the guy at the window.

"Hey, Roy! Cool T-shirt!"

"Figured you were a Large."

"You mean I can have it?"

"'Course, man. Enjoy."

"It's perfect. It's great! Thanks, Roy."

"No problem."

I went upstairs to the same room I always rented, changed my clothes, and wrapped myself in a towel. When I stepped into the club, I had it in mind to go around searching the place, like I always did. Don't ask me what I was looking for, anything that turned me on, probably. But I had the searching part down pat by that point so that's what I did.

That's the night I ran into Joe. He wasn't wearing anything but a towel. I'd never seen him before in my life. But when he smiled at me, I knew him. It was like—somehow—I already knew him.

He said: "What's up?"

And I said, "Oh, you know. Not much. How 'bout you?"

Honestly, that was all it took. Joe became the male love of my life.

❖

HE WAS A year younger than me. Gentle. Caring. Loving. He had a wide smile that showed off bright, white teeth in the middle of his brown face and sort of lit me all up inside like I'd been drinking good brandy. He was handsome. Nice hair. A rich baritone voice. Cool.

Obviously, he worked out a lot. He had lots of muscles and looked very strong. Nice, hairy pecs. He reminded me of me.

I think Joe had rented a room at the Everard, too, but we wound up back at my space. We started kissing and feeling each other out. Somehow it all seemed, I don't know, better than with other guys. Easier. More natural. Loving. He fucked me, I didn't fuck him. That's how it happened the first time.

❖

I LIKED JOE, pure and simple. I liked his mannerisms; I liked the way he spoke. I felt a connection with him that was instantaneous and real and vital, like taking in air when you breathe—you don't have to think about it, it just happens. And somewhere in the back of my mind I knew that this was unusual, finding someone who made me feel this way in a *place* like that.

I'd never considered having a relationship with a man that went anywhere above the line of casual sex. But that's just what happened the moment I met Joe. He was that special. We exchanged numbers.

A week later we met at the Everard again and I found out more about him. Joe worked for a bank in New York City. He lived in East Orange, just one town away from where I was staying, which seemed like fate to me.

Finally I said, "Hey, man. This feels pretty good, doesn't it?"

"Yeah, it sure does."

"Then why don't we do better than this. Let's get the hell out of here, huh?"

We left the Rod and went back to his bachelor pad. And there? Let me tell you. The sex was good. It was *real* good.

Turns out Joe loved football, too. Turns out he was a Giants fanatic.

I said, "You know what? I play for the Giants."

He looked at me with a sly grin. "Yes," he said. "I know."

7

I LOVED BEING a New York Giant. I was number 69. Fitting number for me, right? I tell you, there's no kinda feeling in the world like running through that locker room tunnel and popping up inside a big ol' bowl full of 75,000 fans with everybody screaming their heads off. Talk about your heart beating fast! You can smell the sweat dripping off the guy next to you. Smell the layer of moisture lying like a blanket over the turf. On some days, you can even smell the crowd—the open containers of beer, the hot dogs, the thick, oily scent of grease paint on the fans who've done up their faces in red, white, and blue. Then they start to chant, 75,000 voices all raised up in the same magnificent prayer, feet stomping, hands clapping: "Let's go, Gi—ants!" *Boom! Boom! Boom boom—boom!* "Let's go, Gi—ants!" *Boom! Boom! Boom boom—boom!* I'm telling you, that's the best high I ever had, and I've been high a lot.

I can still hear the roar of that crowd in my head. I miss it. Just the thought of that crowd makes me want to go back in time, go back to that very same stadium, strap on my helmet and pads, pull my jersey on, blast out on that field and knock the shit outta somebody. Just like I used to. Just like the old days.

Like the time we kicked ass on the Dallas Cowboys. Serves them right for not drafting me. What a feeling! Victory. Pure adrenaline. We fought hard on that one, too. Randy White, the Cowboys' nasty defensive tackle—that sonovabitch exploded off the ball one time and hit me so hard he came down straight across my helmet and cut my nose in the middle. That hurt so bad I wanted to kill him. And I would have, too. But we ran some traps on his ass. Worked him into our plans, so to speak. We got our licks in good. Ol' Mister Randy White didn't walk away from that game smiling, that's for sure.

Looking back, what the hell was I thinking? How on earth could I have thrown all that away for some bottles of liquor, a few one-night stands, and some goddamn brown dust that you have to buy in secret on street corners?

❖

YES, I WAS seriously into dick back then. But I also had an eye for the ladies. If that doesn't make much sense to folks, then try looking at it this way: I was on top of the world, and when you're on top of the world, you can have anything you want. All you have to do is ask for it and someone'll give it to you. Most times you don't even have to pay for it. That's part of what being on top of the world means.

I've always loved the company of women. I've always enjoyed sex with women. So when I had an urge to meet someone or be with them, I followed it. That's another part of the life of a pro football player: lots of women on tap. During my rookie year I met a girl named Roslyn at a team bar called the Front Row. Sent her a drink through Dennis the bartender and then went over and introduced myself.

"Hi. My name is Roy. I play for the Giants."

She knew that already. 'Course she did. The Front Row was a groupie bar. Everyone there knew all the players' names and stats by heart. The men dropped by just to say they were a part of the action, and the women were there to get laid. Or better.

I asked Roz if she wanted to step outside and smoke a joint in my brand-new '79 Lincoln Town Car, which I'd parked right beside the fence in the Front Row parking lot. She said she'd be delighted.

❖

NOW ROZ WAS an interesting woman. In some ways she kinda reminded me of Big Cat because they were built the same. Roz was maybe 5'9" and stout. She worked as a social worker and came from a black bourgeois community over in Rutherford, New Jersey. Very well-bred and well-mannered, with a college education and the whole works.

She came off as kinda shy, but I found out later on that she was four years older than me, which means she was actually taking advantage of a younger man. And boy did she take advantage! Again and again! Time was, I found out Roz had this real wild-ass *wild* streak running through her like a river.

She gave me her number that first night we smoked reefer in the car and I eventually called her. We had sex for the first time maybe a week or two later and Lord, that woman knew how to move! To this day I don't know a single woman who can move like Roz moves. That was another reason to be with women; as much as I liked dick, there's nothing in this world like a woman who's great in bed. No matter how much I felt for Joe, he could never give me that same kind of pleasure.

After that first night, Roz and I got it on all the time. Sometimes she'd sneak into Aunt Betty's house at three in the morning and we'd start in on each other anywhere we could. One time my little cousin Alisha caught us. Roz and I were tearing into each other like a couple of wild animals right there on the kitchen floor when little Alisha walked right on in looking for a glass of water. She got the strangest expression on her face all of a sudden, like, *What's going on?* Being a child, she had no idea.

❖

I LIKED ROZ so much. We'd go out and walk around the Village, have dinner at the Pink Teacup. I'd get her tickets to the games and she'd come around and hang out with some of her friends. Or sometimes we'd just spend time by ourselves. She was easy to be with like that. No need to talk, no need to push, or convince one another of anything.

Like I said, I liked Roz, but I don't think I loved her. I say this because I got bored with her from time to time. That was okay, though. She wasn't the only woman I was seeing. Like they say: variety is the spice of life.

❖

Nigeria was a beautiful light-skinned girl with a gorgeous body! And take my word for it—she could suck and fuck you outta this goddamn world! She was 20 years old and she had *skills*. When she got you into a bedroom, you were all hers and it was best to surrender. Nigeria lived with her mother down the street from me in Orange. In no time, I got her pregnant. That was unfortunate, because she really wanted to have the baby. But her mother stepped in and made her get an abortion.

Then there was Kathy, a white girl who was tomboyish but feminine. She was tough—oh *Lord*, ol' Kathy was tough! You never, ever went and made the mistake of fucking with Kathy. That girl would rip your heart out if she could! Talk about passion!

For a while I was with Angela, too. She was part Puerto Rican and lived in the projects out in Passaic. Unlike the other women I was seeing, she was soft-spoken and wise. A little bit big, but a whole lot of cute. Sometimes for fun I'd have them all over to Aunt Betty's house at the same time. Angela, Roslyn, and Kathy would be downstairs in the living room talking with Aunt Betty, or my mother who was visiting, while upstairs I was screwing Nigeria. Looking back, today I realize I was a dog. No two ways about it. But like I said, for the first time in my life I was on top of the world. I was testing the limits because I'd had so little for so long. Of all the ladies, Roz would always wait the longest. And after being with Roz who was simply the last link in the chain of Nigeria-and-Kathy-and-maybe-Angela before that, I'd pull out my little black book and drive into Manhattan. Park my car at the Port Authority and catch a cab to a club or maybe one of the bath houses. Have myself a man to cap off the night. Or maybe two. You never knew. Sometimes I got lucky.

❖

In addition to all the women, Joe started to become a part of my life more. I found myself really wanting to see him, which took me by surprise. I'd never considered being in a relationship with a guy, but more and more that's what I felt myself wanting. In a way, he was my easiest lover to be around cause everyone assumed he was just a good friend. He came to all the games and even hung out in the locker room from time to time. He met all the guys on the team and they liked him. He even came with me to training camp my second year—Alvin, Garrett, Larry Heater, and Bo Matthews all knew him, though who's to say if they ever suspected he was more than just a buddy to me? Joe met my family, too, and they all loved him, almost as if he was a part of the family.

My cousin Betty liked Joe so much she wanted to go to bed with him, and I had to put on an act to convince her. "No, no, girl. Listen to what I have to tell you. That man? He is no good for you. I seen the way he gets with women and you'd do well to keep your distance." The whole thing broke poor Betty's heart. She liked Joe that much.

❖

IT'S EASY FOR a gay person to hide out in the open when everyone else in the world is convinced you're straight. I don't know how to explain it. I guess it's the *What You See is What You Want to See* syndrome. I never went outta my way to act gay *or* straight. I was just being Roy Simmons all the time. That was a full-time job all by itself!

But one night me and Aunt Betty were out shopping and this woman walked right up to me and said, "Roy Simmons! Ooooh, child! You play for the New York *Giants*!" What could I say? "Child, you gonna have to excuuuuuse *me*! But can I touch your butt? I just *got* to touch your butt 'cause your butt is *lookin'* so *fine*!" So what did I do? I laughed and let her touch my butt. It was no big deal for me, but it meant the world to her. *Lord*, if that woman only knew! But she didn't. And she never would. Not even if I'd told her the direct truth. Like I said, people see what they want to see.

In the spring of 1980, I met someone who would change the course of my life, although I didn't know it at the time. I guess you never do. Maybe that's the way it's supposed to work. I came in for lunch at the Front Row with my friend Wilbur, who worked for a carpet company. It was the off season and everyone in the place was moving around real slow, on their own time. We ordered up a load of the Front Row's famous chicken fingers with barbecue sauce—they used to call 'em Moon's Chicken Lips—and I struck up a conversation with this thirteen-year old kid I'd seen around the place a few times. He had a job there working as a busboy. He kept showing up at the Front Row with his head bent down over a hand-held Atari football game.

I asked him what kinda game he was playing. That damn thing in his hands kept making all these high-pitched electronic noises. *Bleep bleep bleep! Screeee screeee! Bee-boop! Bo-beep!* I said, "Hey, man. What *is* that?" *Breee breeee breee!* The kid said, "Football." And he didn't even look up from his game. Which made me think, *Whoa, this kid's got focus.* But later on, I found out he was actually painfully shy.

I said, "Football? Really. You know, I play football for the Giants." *Bee-doop! Bo-deep! Screeee screeeee!*

"I know," he said, still not looking up. "You're Roy Simmons, you play Offensive Guard. You're a really good player and I want your autograph." That was how my first conversation began with one of my dearest friends. In fact, this thirteen-year-old kid would one day grow up to be the man who would save my life.

His name was Jimmy Hester and his father was a major motherfucking Giants fan. The Hesters were close friends with a guy named Tom Mullen who was part owner of the Front Row at the time. Jimmy was a freshman at Paramus Catholic High School and he was always on the move. Always moving and always stoned. Jimmy and marijuana were inseparable.

He was a real good kid, obviously very bright. Turns out he was the youngest damn regular in the place, sure, but he was one of us, see? He was part of the gang.

From early on you could tell that Jimmy knew how to work a crowd. I think he took that busboy job just so he could walk around and meet all the players and get their autographs. He was a huge Giants fan.

It got so he was known as the miniature mayor at the Front Row. The women and girls in the place would all flock to him and hit him up for the special knowledge he carried about each player. He knew their stats, but he also knew all about their personal lives. The kid sure knew the value of information. It didn't take long for him to befriend everyone in the damn place. The kid was just that way, a natural-born diplomat. My teammates and I used to buy him Alabama Slammers and he'd drink 'em from a brown coffee mug while he worked.

❖

IN JUNE OF 1980 I went home to be with Sheila. And when we were together that time, something seemed different. Not different "bad," but different "good." The sex was like it was new. Amazing. That woman and I fit together like we were two long-lost pieces of a jigsaw puzzle. It wasn't like we came together, even. More like we sort of fell into each other.

That was the first time I think I really understood how much she cared about me. Not that she'd ever been shy about showing me before. But the way we made love that time in June, I'd have to have been an idiot not to know that I was her one and only. For a second, that made me a little nervous. The closeted part of my brain was saying, *She can think whatever she wants, but who's more important, her or Joe?* Meanwhile, the other part of my brain—the side that still thought I could have a fairy-tale romance and marriage with a good southern woman—said, *You're in love, you're in love, you're in love, you're in love!*

When Sheila and I parted that June, she seemed especially satisfied with herself. Later that summer I was alone in my room at training camp when the phone in the hallway rang and I picked it up. It was Sheila on the other line.

"Roy," she said. "I have something to tell you."

"Hey, what is it?"

There was a little pause. And then she said: "I'm pregnant."

There was another little pause. This time it was mine. "Really? You're—what? You're—pregnant? You're—really?"

"Yes, I am!"

At this point, I'm not really sure what I said. I think maybe I just started repeating, "Oh wow," over and over and over again. *Oh wow oh wow oh wow oh wow oh wow.* I was over the moon, man, I was thrilled! There'd be adjustments to make, of course. My life was screaming along at a thousand miles per hour right then. But I figured, *Okay. So I'll adjust. Don't know how I'll do it just yet, but I will.*

I told Sheila I loved her. And I think we made plans for her to come up and visit as soon as we could work it out. Then I went out to the field and told a few people I was gonna be a daddy.

In my mind? Damn! This child was gonna be the first of many, many more to come. The first of ten, maybe, who the hell knew? I'd wanted that storybook family my whole life and now it looked like I was gonna get it. Or so I thought.

❖

I BROKE MY thumb that year in training camp and the team had this little cast made up that I would wear off and on so I could still play. The pain I was in? Hooo! Like to make me wanna cut my arm off every minute of every hour of every day that whole damn season. The throb in my arm didn't hurt my drinking at the Front Row, though. If anything, it helped me out in that department more than ever. All that throbbing in my hand made me wanna down top-shelf Long Island Ice Teas all the more, which I did. With great frequency. I was also smoking pot at the time. With great frequency.

I remember really clearly the first time Jimmy came up to me at the bar and said, "Hey, man. You got any pot?" The child was fourteen years old at the time. I said, "What the hell you know about smoking pot? You're too young to be smoking pot." I said this even though I knew Jimmy walked around stoned 24/7. But trying to argue with Jimmy is like trying to piss against the ocean. Sooner or later, everything that comes out of you gets thrown right back in your face.

Jimmy just looked at me sensible-like and said, "Roy, look at it this way. If I don't get pot from you, I'm gonna get it from someone else. You wouldn't want me going to someone else, would you? Of course not. I just want to smoke a joint and get stoned. It's not the end of the world. Now, will you help me or not?"

What could I do? I laughed. I was not keen on giving this child reefer. But the way he asked for it? Shit. He was cool and collected, like he was negotiating a major business deal where he'd already worked out all the angles. I tell you, man. From early on, Jimmy was one sharp character.

I gave him the bag of pot I had on me at the time and said, "Don't you ever tell anyone I'm giving you this."

❖

SHEILA DID COME up from Georgia. I was still living at Aunt Betty's house, since that provided a connection to my family and Georgia and my childhood and the South. Sheila moved in with me at Aunt Betty's and we set up having a life together, but it didn't cramp my sexual promiscuity.

I still saw Roz all the time. She knew I had a girlfriend and she knew my girlfriend was pregnant. It didn't matter to her. Hell, I even met Roz at the Front Row on the day Sheila flew up from Savannah. I had drinks with Roz right before I left to pick up Sheila at the airport. But since Roz didn't care about Sheila and Sheila didn't know about Roz, it was kinda perfect. It actually worked out. 'Course, nobody but nobody knew about Joe, so that was perfect, too.

But something started to happen. All of a sudden there was this unexpected side effect of Sheila living with me. See, by that point my love for Joe was growing every day. Joe knew about Sheila, too, and no, he wasn't totally overjoyed with the idea of me getting married and my wife having a baby. But it wasn't like he couldn't deal with it. Hell, he *wanted* to deal with it, he displayed this incredible willingness to make sure everything went smoothly. And that just made me love him all the more.

All the while though, this little voice kept screaming at me in the back of my head: *"WHAT THE FUCK ARE YOU DOING?!?"* I didn't know the answer to that question. Even after all these years, I still don't. I was trying to have it all, I guess. Sheila was one smart cookie, though. She began to figure something was up. She didn't know what, but she didn't have to. In a million years I bet she would never have been able to guess the particulars—hell, who could have? But once she started having her suspicions, the whole damn thing began to unravel.

❖

IT STARTED OFF with my aunt Betty catching a look between Sheila and our friend Thomas in a rearview mirror. Thomas used to hang out at the house a lot and he was driving my family to Philadelphia to see the Giants play the Eagles. The way I've heard it told, Betty was in the front seat, Sheila and my mother were riding in back. And Betty swears she caught Thomas smiling at Sheila and making flirty faces with her by looking at her through the rearview mirror. Normally that might not have seemed like all that big a thing, but Betty's a sharp cookie, too. She'd apparently caught all sorts of little looks like that flying back and forth between Sheila and Thomas at the house while I was away at practice.

Plus, whenever I was away, Sheila was always telling Thomas how good he looked, snuggling up to him, touching his arm, and giggling, but she never did that to me. Betty noticed that, too, and I guess she made up her mind to lay down the law. I guess she figured she was just looking out for me.

One day Sheila called me up all upset and said she needed to talk to me right away, could I please rush right home. So I did, and when I got there, she was a wreck. She was crying profusely. When I asked her what was wrong, she told me how Aunt Betty'd accused her of making eyes at Thomas. I didn't ask her if it was true 'cause frankly I didn't want to know. Besides, I didn't want to blow my cover. All I knew was that a line had been drawn in that house. Aunt Betty stood on one side and Sheila on the other. A decision had to be made.

I loved my aunt Betty and of course I loved Sheila. So you can imagine the turmoil going on inside me when the two of them went at it. I asked Aunt Betty what happened and she told me what she saw. Then I asked Sheila for her side of things and she said, "Roy, none of that ever happened. Do you hear me? None of it. Please. You have to believe me. You have to trust me."

I did. I trusted her. I *believed* her. But that meant it was time for Sheila and me to leave Aunt Betty's house and get out on our own. That was the only way I could see to make the situation work. Within a week we moved into the Sheraton Hasbrouck Heights, which gave discounts to people associated with the New York Giants.

❖

MOVING TO THE Sheraton didn't make things better. In fact, it made things much, much worse. 'Cause with Sheila and me living alone in a hotel room, it became totally impossible to disappear like I used to for long periods of time. At Aunt Betty's there were people around for

Sheila to talk to and occupy her time. In the hotel room, there was only a whole lot of nothing.

Some nights I'd go back to her, some nights I'd go to Joe's apartment, and she never questioned where I was. It was the same set of tricks I'd pulled back in college. Being a member of so many groups, I'd just play one off against the other. It was easy. I could tell the folks at the Front Row I was going to see Sheila when in fact I was out with Joe. I could tell Sheila I had a late team meeting when in fact I was at the Front Row. I could tell my teammates that I couldn't hang out for another drink cause I had to go somewhere and no one would question it cause everybody had their own shit going on back then—mistresses, girlfriends on the side, wives who were into kink, you name it. The only rule we followed as teammates was: don't spill the beans. Even so, I never felt comfortable enough to disclose my gay side.

I don't believe it was the sex that eventually became a problem for Sheila, since I never had a problem pleasing her, even after I'd just been with Joe. But I think she was getting lonely. She'd moved up from Savannah to be with me full time, to have a baby and a family, only to find me gone most of the time. We were practically strangers.

Sometimes I'd bring Sheila down to the Front Row, where we'd meet Joe and his girlfriend. Yes, Joe had a girlfriend—I couldn't stand that bitch. She was built real thick and had a good job and was kinda pretty. She was also intelligent, but I hated seeing him with her. She was just a piece of fish to him, which is a gay term for the woman you keep around so nobody gets suspicious while you fuck other men. Sometimes, instead of Sheila, I'd bring Roz. So it was like this: Sheila knew Joe but she didn't know about *me* and Joe. Roz knew Joe but she didn't know about *me* and Joe. Roz knew about Sheila but Sheila didn't know Roz. I knew about everybody and Joe knew about everybody. Joe's girlfriend knew everybody, too, except she was missing the part about me and Joe. She was most definitely missing that part. Is it any wonder that the whole house of cards would eventually come tumbling down sooner or later?

❖

IT WASN'T MEANT to last. The pressure started building up and some-thing had to break. That something was me, I guess. I felt like I had shit piling up on top of me like a mountain. Living in a hotel, looking for a permanent place to stay on the side. Impending fatherhood and marriage and all the responsibility that would bring. My drugs and my drinking, which were both cruising along at high levels. My relation-ships with Sheila, Roz, Joe, and—honestly?—anybody else who came along at the right time . . . or the wrong time, depending on how you want to look at it. Oh, yeah. And then there was my livelihood. I was a professional football player working the offensive line for the New York Giants. And we were having an okay season.

All of a sudden, my attitude toward Sheila started to change. Yes, I loved her, I know I did. But I just couldn't be bothered. Whenever I was with her, I started to just zone out, you know? Like the way you do just before you're about to get hit real hard by a tackle who weighs sixty pounds more than you do. You sort of leave your body and wait for the crash.

I started staying out for longer and longer periods of time. I spent a lot of time at the Front Row bar. I spent a lot of time with Roz and Joe, sometimes together, sometimes one on one. And whenever I got home there was this temperamental pregnant woman who cried at the drop of a hat. Pregnant woman are like that, you know. They get very emotional. Anything can set them off. You have to go far around the bend to pamper them. And I didn't. In fact, I wouldn't.

I was faithful to no one, dishonest to everyone. I needed support almost as much as Sheila did, but I wasn't ready to seek that for myself. At least Sheila had the good sense to turn to the man who should have been there for her.

❖

LOOKING BACK, I think I caused that situation in order to self-destruct. Call it my own demons. Sheila had been with me since the third grade, and here I found myself trying to protect my relationship with Joe from her. That made no sense. But neither did the way I took her lover for granted. Nor did the way I chose to dedicate myself to the side of me that she knew nothing about, my gay side.

My worst nightmare from that time was this: having Joe walk up to me one day and say, "Roy, I'm falling in love with you. But we can never be together. Look at what's going on! You're getting married! You're having a baby! You're going to be a daddy! All I'm going to be is hurt. I can't do this anymore. I'm glad we had what we had. But it's over."

Joe or Sheila. Sheila or Joe. Joe or Sheila. Sheila or Joe.

In the middle of all the confusion, I started repeating a phrase to myself, over and over and over again. It was a wise old phrase that everybody's heard: If you love something, set it free. *Set it free*, I thought. *Hell, yes! Set it free.*

It wasn't Joe I was willing to part with. It was Sheila.

8

SHEILA TRIED EVERYTHING. She asked me to speak with my cousin Mona, who was wise in the ways of the heart. She asked me to speak with a counselor. She asked me to speak with a priest. Nothing worked. "Roy, I'll leave you," she said. "I swear I will." But by that point I was too far gone. Plus, right around that time I had acquired a new preoccupation, a gay club in Newark called Murphy's which had been introduced to me by my other cousin Linda, the second-oldest of Aunt Betty's five daughters.

Linda knew I was gay even before I came north to play for the Giants. She was a dancer, and dancers—they just know. I helped support Linda financially when she went to study at the Alvin Ailey dance studio and we had no illusions about each other. Linda knew I was gay and I knew her for what she was—a fag hag. Some women just don't feel comfortable hanging out anywhere but in gay bars.

Then one day I was out on the field at Giants Stadium running my practice drills. One of the trainers came out and said, "Roy Simmons? Simmons! Phone!" I went inside and took the call. It was Mona, and she said, "I'm taking Sheila to the bus station, Roy. She's leaving you." Mona sounded pretty upset.

Despite my causing everything that led up to this, it was still hard for me to process. I repeated, "What?" again and again in disbelief. "What do you want me to do, Roy? What do you want me to *do?*" Mona was beside herself. It didn't help that I started yelling at her. Stupidly, I took the low road. I said, "What business is it of *yours*, huh? Why are you taking her away from me, this ain't your business!" The idea of

Sheila leaving me when she was five months pregnant was suddenly so horrible, I figured: kill the messenger. Looking back, I had one hell of a nerve.

"She's going to Rhode Island, Roy, she wants to be with her aunt. What should I do? What do you want me to *do*?" How could I answer that question? I didn't *know* what I wanted her to do. I should've taken control. Doesn't matter what I decided to do in the long run, what mattered most in that moment was that I handle the situation personally, take control of my own damn life. Even if later on Sheila and I decided it was best for her to leave, that made no difference. What mattered was how I *handled* this crisis.

I should've done the right thing and said, "I'll be right there." Had I really wanted to stop her, all I had to do was go to my coach and say, "Coach. I gotta go, got a family crisis. I'm sorry, I gotta leave. I gotta leave *now*." But I didn't. I hung up the phone. I don't remember exactly what I said before I put the phone back in the cradle, but that doesn't really matter, I guess. The *words* don't matter. What matters is the words I *didn't* say, and I didn't say *I'll be right there*.

I jogged back out on the field and tried to pretend that nothing had happened, which didn't work. I fucked up every play we ran that afternoon. I was a wreck. Completely unfocused. When I got back to the hotel room she was gone.

❖

THE FOLLOWING YEAR, Betty and I rented this beautiful three-story house together that sat on a cliff at 601 Fifth Street in a town called Carlstadt, about fourteen miles from New York City. Carlstadt was a nice place, with Italian neighborhoods where everyone knew each other. You could walk down the streets and see the same smiling faces every day. You got in the habit of waving to people, genuine goodwill passing between folks you barely even knew.

Just me and Betty and her five-year old son Terrence. Sort of like the family I almost had with Sheila, only this one wasn't mine. It had no commitments. No real attachments. This one just had the smiles and the goodwill. Truly a storybook family.

Losing Sheila didn't hurt as much as I thought it would. In fact, losing Sheila didn't really hurt at all. Instead, it left this dull sort of numbness in me, like the pain I'd felt that time playing Georgia when I knocked that guy on his ass so hard that I lost the sensation in my body. And just like I did back then, I didn't tell anybody about what was going on with me. Didn't signal for a time-out or anything. I just waited for the sensation to return. Besides, I still had Joe, whom I counted on more than ever.

Then, during my second year on the Giants, I had my first and only sexual experience with a teammate. This guy was on the offensive line, and one night during the off season he and I went to a club out in Alphabet City where we drank way too much Tanqueray. On top of that, we took some quaaludes. At first we thought everything was fine. Hell, we were having a great night, nothing in the world was stopping us, we had *energy!* So we headed back to the car and I drove us through the tunnel. We came out on the Jersey side and hit the turnpike. The quaaludes hit us all at once. All of a sudden the world started to warp and bend and stretch itself out like taffy pulled real slow from both ends.

What I remember most is my teammate mumbling at me from the passenger seat, like he was talking through a thick cotton robe he'd wrapped around his head. "Roy?" And I answered, "What?"

"Roy?!" he asked again. And I'm like, "What, man, what!? Speak to me, dammit!" He said, "Man, I don't feel so good." I guess the chemicals had really set in. So I said, "Oh my God. Oh my God! Okay. Just hang on. Let's just make it home." And I concentrated on that road straight ahead of me like it was a coiling, poisonous snake about to strike us at any moment.

Somehow we made it back to my house in Carlstadt. I dragged my teammate outta the passenger side of the car and into the garage, which I'd turned into a den just to give myself an extra room where I could relax and have some time alone. I laid my friend out on the couch and went upstairs to throw water on my face. When I got back down, he was stretched out and mumbling.

I sat down next to him and started. Running my fingers over his forehead, just to comfort him. His skin was hot, but at the same time he was kinda cold and clammy. When I ran my fingers through his hair, he seemed to like that, too. He shifted a little on his side and mumbled some more. To make a long story short, he asked me to suck his dick. So I did.

Now you gotta remember, this guy and I were pretty close! No, I'm not gonna tell you his name. All you need to know is that we hung out all the time. He might have known I was gay, I don't know. If he did, he never talked about it, just like we never talked about what happened on the couch that night. It just sort of went in the closet and got locked in there with all the rest of my secrets. When you're living in the closet, some of your finest moments get buried like that. They get locked away in darkness, tucked away so deep that you almost begin to believe they never really happened.

❖

MY SITUATION WITH Joe was getting out of control. I went back to the Everard and I swear I spotted Joe. That freaked me out, 'cause all of a sudden the thought of seeing him at the Rod had an effect on me. A real big effect. My hands were shaking. My heart started thumping. My forehead broke out in a cold sweat. I was thinking, *What the fuck is he doing here? What's he need other men for? Ain't I enough for him? Who the fuck's he think he is?* I was jealous. Once again, I was living with a double standard, where it was okay for me to mess around but not my partner.

I went through every floor of the Rod searching for him. Didn't find him. Must've been someone who looked like him. By that point, I was acting kinda insane. I went back to my little room and changed my clothes, then went back to my house in Carlstadt and called his ass. I wanted to make sure he hadn't been there. I wanted to make sure he was alone.

I got no answer at his place, which is when I figured it had all gone to hell. 'Cause Joe and I were a lot alike in so many ways, like I said. But in many ways we were different. In *key* ways, we were different. Whereas I now felt ready to commit to him in ways I'd only ever dreamed of, he was still this insanely private individual who couldn't stand it when I'd try to hold his hand in public or grab his ass.

"What the hell is wrong with you?" he'd hiss at me. "Jesus, man. Somebody's gonna see."

In the back of my head, though, a thought was beginning to brew. *And just what's so wrong with that?*

❖

MY SECOND YEAR playing for the Giants we were 4 and 12, not a particularly stellar season. That was the winter of 1981, when Jimmy Hester started hanging around my house. He lived with his folks in Little Ferry, about twenty minutes away from me. He had a moped and he used to drop by my place for parties, but he never got out on the living room floor and danced. He'd just lie there on the floor by the speaker and drum his fingers to the beat instead.

I hadn't been in touch with Sheila even though it was the last months of her pregnancy, and Jimmy especially found this odd. He kept asking me questions about it, questions that were particularly nosy for a fourteen-year-old kid to ask of an adult.

"Roy," he said. "I don't get it. Where's Sheila?"

"Jimmy, don't worry about it. She's with family."

"But she's pregnant, right?"

"Yeah, man."

"So . . . shouldn't she be with you?"

The way he was talking almost made we wish he was still the same scrawny kid I'd seen playing that damned Atari football game. I would've preferred the *bee deep boop* and *breeee breeee breee* of that damned thing to Jimmy's third degree. I felt lousy about how things with Sheila ended up. I hated myself for letting it all happen the way it did. Still, I couldn't muster the courage to reach out to her.

Instead, I said, "Look, Jimmy. This ain't for you to figure out so just leave it alone." Jimmy shut up, but I could tell he wasn't satisfied with my answer. In some ways, neither was I.

It didn't help matters when I got a phone call later that spring from one of Sheila's friends. She said, "Roy, I'm at the hospital with Sheila. She's about to have the baby." There it was again, that numbness. Sheila was already in labor and couldn't come to the phone. I think I told the caller to tell Sheila that I loved her and I wanted to come see her soon. 'Course that's just a guess, really. That part of my life is all pretty hazy to me now. Why shouldn't it be? Back then I spent my time doing three things and three things only: drinking, drugging, and fucking.

She gave birth to a girl; I learned that later on. She was born on March 23, 1981, a sweet little girl named Kara, my own flesh and blood. My darling baby daughter. When I heard it was a girl, I went out to a tobacco store and bought a whole bunch of those prepackaged cigars—you know the ones, they're done up all in pink and say "IT'S A GIRL!" on the wrapper. I passed one out to every guy on the team. That's a perfect example of where my head was back in the day. I had the nerve to celebrate my daughter's birth while doing absolutely nothing whatsoever for the baby herself or the mother—my beloved Sheila.

In June of '81 my life took another major turn when I invited my mother and three younger brothers up from Georgia to live with me. They'd been living on welfare in the drug-infested west side of Savannah, dodging eviction notices and scrounging up change to eat with. Ricky was thirteen; he was the oldest. Then came LaTwan, eleven, and Gary, ten. Rather than send them money, I wanted them out of that entire scene, out of the environment. I wanted my family with me so I could personally make sure they were being taken care of.

I'd gone through college pretty much all alone, no family around me to speak of except those times I'd visit on the breaks and so forth. Then, of course, playing pro ball and living out my ways in New York City was another thing altogether. I still felt isolated, especially with Sheila gone and Aunt Betty sort of distant after we left her house.

But now? Now I was playing father figure to brothers who were young enough to be my own kids. I'd come home from practice at the stadium and fix lunch for everybody, then head back to the field. Sometimes I took everybody shopping. It was a happy life. A good life. I have great memories of that time. Makes me wonder why I couldn't have tapped more of that goodness welling up inside me more often. That goodness had been there my whole life, but the drugs and the sex and so forth had pretty much stuffed it down, leaving no room for anything else to emerge.

I guess word got around that I was generous, though. Pretty soon Alvin Garrett and my other teammate Larry Heater and his wife and their baby moved in, too. Why not? The house was big enough, and this way, everybody could save money. My cousin Betty was still there with her two kids—she had two kids by this point 'cause she'd slept with my teammate Nate Johnson, a receiver, whom I'd told her not to fuck with. So at one point we had twelve people running around that house in Carlstadt. Twelve people! One big happy family!

Later on, though, Roz pointed out something to me that I found rather interesting. She gave me this real thoughtful look and said, "Roy? You know what? I think you're scared to live all alone by yourself." Looking back, I think it was actually deeper than that. I now think I needed to live in chaos in order for my life to make any kind of sense to me. Maybe that sounds ridiculous, but as long as I was swallowed up by chaos, I know I never really had to confront my own personal demons. The house, the kids, the people, the parties—it was all distractions I set up for myself to keep my mind off my own pain.

❖

I WAITED THREE days after Kara was born to drive up to Rhode Island. Sheila was cold to me, but then, why shouldn't she have been? Still, I could tell that part of her was happy to see me. Which was good, 'cause I was real happy to see her, too. Happier still to see this little ball of cuteness she had clutched up in her arms. My daughter, Kara.

I call her this "little" ball of cuteness, but that's not quite right. That girl was big and she was heavy! She kicked and squirmed. Sheila was an excellent mom to her, any fool could see that. So I sat there running my fingers through the kinky little curls in her hair. Touching her tiny little lips with my fingers. Swirling my thick old thumbs into those tiny little hands of hers. I fell in love, if the truth be told. I fell in love with my own baby girl. I cried, that feeling was so big.

I took Sheila out shopping and bought her some things for the baby—a stroller, some clothes. I gave her some money, too—maybe about $500 or $600. Sheila accepted it all with that same frosty look on her face. She said thank you like she was talking to a house burglar.

She had every reason in the world to hate my guts. Hell, no one could have hated me more than I hated myself. But we went together that night like husband and wife and I knew right then that she still loved me. It was obvious in the way we still fit together. Pieces of that old jigsaw puzzle.

That was my second chance. My last chance. And I blew it. I could have made amends right then and there. Could have played the part of Romeo coming home to save his Juliet in her darkest hour. I could have taken them back to Carlstadt. I had an extra room in the house set up for Kara if only I'd invite them to stay with me, if only I'd chosen to deal with my problems head on and confront them.

But I didn't. I left Providence alone and that was the end of my dreams for a family. Five months later, Sheila decided she wanted to move back to Georgia. She hopped a flight that took her from Providence to Savannah by way of Newark. I met her at Newark Airport and kept her company during the layover. We didn't say much. And I held Kara for a while. Good Lord, she was getting big so quick!

❖

THE GIANTS AND the Jets were doing a charity benefit at a place called the King's Court, which was sort of a famous New Jersey health club back in the day. Jimmy was there, of course, since by that point he was everywhere that the Giants went. One night he had a chance encounter that launched his motherfucking career as a serious player in the entertainment industry.

You gotta remember, this was the age of disco. You couldn't hit a club or a major function back then without hearing excellent tunes from Quincy Jones, the Bee Gees, Donna Summer, or Earth, Wind, & Fire. Kool & the Gang was still big. So was this dude named Dan Hartman. But one of the songs I remember most was called *I Like What You're Doing to Me* by a group called Young & Company.

Jimmy'd just bought the 12-inch single 'cause he heard the famous DJ Frankie Crocker playing it all the time on WBLS radio. Back then, if a record was good enough for Frankie, it was good enough for anyone in the whole wide world. Frankie Crocker was the king, man. Ain't no way to describe who he was to New York music 'less you were there.

Ain't never been anyone like Frankie Crocker. He was that kind of beautiful.

Jimmy met an unbelievably gorgeous girl at the benefit party and he struck up a conversation. "So, what do you do?" Jimmy asked. And she said, "I'm a singer." To which Jimmy shrugged and said, "Oh, well. I probably don't know what you sing, but tell me anyway." And she said, "Oh, we've got this little song called *I Like What You're Doing to Me.*" Wouldn't you know it? That gorgeous girl was Jackie Thomas of Young & Company. That Jimmy's got a lucky streak like a Georgia hound dog—damn thing just never quits.

Jimmy started jumping up and down. He was so excited he couldn't contain himself. "I can't believe this! I can't *believe* this! I'm a big fan of yours!" And he started taking Jackie Thomas around to meet all my teammates, giving her the royal treatment.

Well, things worked out so well that Jackie Thomas invited Jimmy and a few guests to see Young & Company perform at the Copacabana. So he went and brought along my teammates Leon Perry and Nate Johnson, who were a big hit, of course. I tell you, the kid was a natural-born networking genius. Here he was, an underage kid living it up in the one of the swankiest joints in town *and* he was responsible for bringing the life of the party.

A little later on, I walked into the Front Row and mentioned to Jimmy that Frankie Crocker—*THE* Frankie Crocker—was throwing the Giants an end-of-the-season party at a club called the Underground. And you should have seen that boy's reaction to *that.* Jimmy *loved* Frankie Crocker. He started jumping up and down again he got so excited, saying, "I gotta go! I gotta go! Roy! You gotta get me in! Please, please! I wanna bring Young & Company."

I had my doubts about the whole thing at first. Jimmy was still underage and I didn't want any trouble, not even for his sake. But finally my love for him overruled my hesitation—Jimmy had never let me down yet—and I cracked open my date book, which was full of tiny blue passes for the end-of-the-season party. I gave Jimmy ten passes, good for a total of twenty people. From the look on his face you would have thought I was giving him the keys to heaven's gate.

He spared no expense. He rented a white jump-seat limo out in

Jersey which he used to pick up Young & Company and bring them into Manhattan. He brought Jackie Thomas to the Underground and escorted her through the front door like she was a princess. He made the rounds and introduced her to every player on the Giants' team. Then he took her to meet Mr. Frankie Crocker himself.

❖

NOW IF YOU'RE too young to remember, Frankie was the King of Cool. He could take your breath away. Frankie didn't go with the flow, Frankie *was* the flow. He was purely original. He had a super-cool deep voice that felt like it was coming from somewhere down beneath the earth. And when he started off a sentence with one of his catch-all phrases—"Ya know what ahm sayin', cats? Ha ha ha, yeah. Back in da day . . ."—man, the resonance and soulfulness and raw sexual power of his voice made Barry White sound like a squealing teenage girl. Frankie could shut down a whole room just by opening his mouth. His voice had a power.

I could tell Jimmy was awestruck. But not so awestruck that he didn't remember to make the most important move of the evening, the move that I'm convinced launched his entire career. Jimmy walked right on up to Frankie Crocker and presented his stunning new friend, Ms. Jackie Thomas. "Frankie Crocker," said Jimmy, "I'd like you to meet Young & Company."

"Oh oh *oh*!" said Frankie Crocker. "Look who's in the house!" And he got on the mike and told everybody what good fortune they had to be in the presence of such a fine and talented musician. You should have seen the look on Jimmy's face as Frankie announced Young & Company to everyone in the Underground. Jimmy was beaming. The kid from New Jersey had finally arrived. He'd taken his shot and won big. He was on his way up. But I would pass him soon on my way down.

❖

WHEN YOU'RE "UP" there's a whole fantasy lifestyle at your fingertips. It's the American Dream—luxury at your beck and call. There's perks and frills and lovely things everywhere you look. People recognize you when you're "up" and they fall at your feet to serve you. Flight attendants give you their phone numbers and free booze. Hotel clerks trip all over themselves to fetch redcaps to haul your luggage, provide you with clean towels for your feet, fresh soap for your face and hands—and room service! Lots and lots of room service! Waiters pay extra-special attention to you in restaurants—service is always impeccable. And the people eating at other tables will shift their chairs around so they can get a better look at you. They'll watch how you eat—you can see them do this out of the corner of your eye. I guess this sort of thing happens when you're even a little bit famous in America. And it's exactly this feeling, this superstar energy, this pampered extravagance that goes on every day and everywhere and leads many a good and righteous-minded person into thinking he can get away with anything. Living the "up" life dares you to push the envelope as far as it will go—wide open if need be. Once you open that door, you can never really go back to living the way you were before. In short, I found living "up" to be more addictive than crack, heroin, or any other drug I know.

People tended to recognize me most when I traveled with the team. It was easy to spot me. On my own, however, was another story entirely. I'd leave my teammates on the road and go my own way. That's when my other life kicked in. In San Francisco, I'd hop BART and ride into Berkeley, over to a bathhouse, and troll around for men. I'd do it the night before a game. Long as I got back to the hotel in time for the team meeting at 9 p.m., which I always did. Long as I fulfilled my obligations to the New York Giants, whatever I did in my free time was my own business. In fact, that's the way the whole team saw their own lives—football was just a job, like working in the post office or a loan office.

In San Francisco, Dallas, and other cities, I'd hit places that belonged to the Club Bath Chains. These are private gay venues designed to satisfy the needs of the business traveler. I'd gotten me a membership as soon as I found out about them. The membership you bought in one state was good for CBCs across the country. The Ultimate National Closet Fraternity.

The men I got with at these places were probably married, probably just as closeted as I was, sneaking off whenever they were traveling on the company dollar. I can't tell you how many men I met in this situation. And the beauty of it all was complete anonymity. For once, I didn't have to lie to anyone. If someone asked me during the course of polite conversation what I did for a living, I'd just say, "play ball." Polite conversation never got you very far in a bathhouse anyway. Guys were there for sex, pure and simple.

Nobody from the Giants ever found out. If they even suspected, I never knew about it. Why would they? As far as they saw, I still fucked women. In fact, Alvin, Larry Heater, and I once had a contest to see who could fuck the most women in a week—you know: male ego bullshit. I won with seven. You'd think professional athletes would have more pressing matters to command their attention, but there was a lot of this kid nonsense going on.

In fact, I suspected that two of my teammates were fooling around with each other. I won't mention these men by name, but all you had to do was watch them with the eyes of someone like me who also played around with men. They were way too buddy-buddy with one another for it to be a purely heterosexual friendship. They waited for each other to come out of the shower in the locker room, went everywhere together after practice and games—hell, they did everything but hold hands. They'd gone to college together, been drafted together, they even shared an apartment together. These two men were inseparable.

'Course, it's sometimes tough to tell with football players, I admit. Professional athletes take what I guess you'd call an above-average interest in another person's physique. It comes with the territory. It's one of the demands of the profession, our bodies are our trade. So it's only natural that you start looking at the bodies of your peers with a professional interest. But you never let it get beyond that, on the surface at least. Not unless you want to blow your cover.

Besides, wild sexual behavior was generally excused in the world of pro football anyway, because everyone knew that we were largely out of our minds. You had to be mostly crazy in order to play in the NFL. It came with the territory. Just think of the kind of person it takes to make a living in that sport. Basically, your job is to trot onto a stadium field, crouch down, and when a signal is given, run full tilt into a long line of men, each of whom is roughly as big and powerful as a young rhinoceros, each of whom wants to do you serious physical harm. You had to be clinically insane to tangle with the likes of Lawrence Taylor, for instance. "Mean" Joe Green was in the twilight of his career when I played with the Giants, but you could still lose a tooth or break a limb if he caught you blind-side. If Randy White started hunting your ass, you'd best run and run fast. The NFL was the only home these violent bad guys had. Without football, where else in society could these men work—and be paid as much money for their time?

Shit, when we threw a party, you knew you weren't going nowhere for the rest of the evening. I once hosted a toga party and my guests were the Jets, the Nets, the Cosmos, and the New Jersey Generals. That's a whole lot of testosterone under one roof, so I had to be prepared. I made sure all the bedrooms had locks on the doors so people could go on in, close up, and get to their sucking and fucking. Must've been 150 people in and out of the house at one point or another with me shuttling back and forth to Harlem with my cousin-in-law Levi while the whole thing was going on so that we could keep the place stocked with enough drugs to go around. Cocaine, reefer, uppers, downers—you name it, it was on the coffee table, laid out like a buffet.

My younger brothers were there sometimes, too. There'd be girls on the floor, guys on the floor, drugs lying around all over the damn place, cigarette and pot smoke floating up along the rafters like an indoor rain cloud. And here in the middle of it all are these three preteenage boys wandering around with eyes as big as hubcaps. Gary used to like to hide in the bathroom 'cause he knew he'd see naked women that way. Sometimes they played the whole game to their advantage, too. Players would give these kids fifty bucks to shuffle off somewhere and sit by themselves so they could free up a bed, a patch of floor, or an extra stretch of kitchen countertop. I'm telling you, it was wild! Eventually the cops came around 'cause they'd gotten complaints about the noise and I had to promise them again and again that I'd work to keep the party quiet. Fat chance!

❖

ALL THE WHILE I was still fucking around with men like there was no tomorrow. One time I met a guy named Ari in an elevator of my aunt's building in New York City. I'd stopped by to deliver my aunt's rent to her landlord, and there was Ari standing in the elevator when the doors opened, just like he'd been waiting for me. Such a distinguished-looking gentleman! Gray hair. White beard. A white linen suit with flare-bottomed pants, and sandals instead of good shoes. He looked like some kinda beatnik poet or something. A southern aristocrat who'd taken a walk on the wild side or something. But he was gay. I could tell that just from the way he looked at me. Again, like so many times before; it was all about the eye contact. Eye contact started many a gay affair for me.

We looked at each other for just a moment when those elevator doors opened, and he gave me this little smile like he was saying, *Why yes, come on in. We might as well get to know each other since we're gonna end up fucking.* I said, "Hi. I'm Roy." And he said, "I'm Ari. How are you?" in this deep, baritone voice. After that, the conversation was easy.

I learned that Ari was married with two children, which didn't mean much, of course; lots of gay men are married with children. He suggested we meet sometime for lunch and I agreed—of course I agreed! We already had that vibe going between us, so why shut it down?

❖

WE STARTED MEETING at the Everard and sometimes I went to his place on the Upper West Side when his wife was away in Israel. His apartment was a showplace. It was like a magical indoor jungle with a big fountain sitting right there in the middle of his home gurgling water in a steady rhythm. You could tell he'd spent a great deal of time on the lighting design, since all the lights were recessed and positioned at strategic angles to show the place off, the artwork, the architecture, the gorgeous antique furniture, and the many levels that ran throughout the apartment. You had to be careful walking around Ari's place. There were so many sunken areas and drops and stairs that you'd trip if you didn't mind your steps.

The first time I went to his place was for what he called "a party." I ain't never been to a party like that before or since! When I got there, at maybe eight o'clock, I was the first one to arrive. We shared a bottle of Cristal and some cocaine. For a while it was just the two of us. We started kissing and I gave him a hand job. Then—all of a sudden, guys started showing up. The doorbell kept ringing on and off, on and off, like a phone chime, and all kinds of men started streaming into that apartment!

Before I knew it, there was some serious shit going on in that East Side apartment. There was fucking, there was sucking, there was biting, there was chewing. Lemme tell you this: if the police had come to break up *that* motherfucking party, ain't no doubt about it, man, we *all* would've gone to jail for total indecency.

❖

NINETEEN EIGHTY-TWO WAS the year that Jimmy's parents split up and I became sort of his big brother. I'd pick him up from school sometimes, or he'd ride his moped over to the house and hang around with me and my friends. It was a tough time for Jimmy. He was going through some serious emotional shit. It was a tough time for me, too. I was going through my own swamp of serious emotional shit, but mine was about to have incredible repercussions for my livelihood.

See, the weight of everything I'd been going through all this time began to pile up. I felt cut off. Adrift. Disenchanted. Flat. Numb. Confused. Depressed. And maybe a dozen other things, all of which felt terrible.

One time I was driving Jimmy back to his house after we'd spent the day hanging out together, and I figured he's been a good friend. A real true friend to me. He's a young man, that's true, but he's got capability beyond his years. He can handle this, I know it. Shit—he might handle it better than I can.

Like I said, Jimmy'd never let me down. So I pulled the car over to the side of the road and we sat there for a moment in front of the tiny Police Department in the little town of Moonachie, New Jersey. For a long moment, I didn't say anything and Jimmy just looked at me, confused. I'd made an important decision the previous week and I had to share the difficult news with someone.

"Roy," he said. "What is it?"

Okay, here we go. "Jimmy," I said. "Any day now you're gonna be reading something in the papers about me. I just wanna tell you now. Don't question it, I'm okay. You get what I'm saying?"

He was like, "No. I don't get what you're saying. I have no idea what the fuck you're talking about. What's going on?"

That's when I told him I felt I needed to take a year off from football.

9

J IMMY SAT THERE and listened to me talk for a while, listened to me try to explain what was going on in my head, the confusion, the hurt, the stuff beneath the hurt that felt like—well, I guess I'm gonna use that word again: numb. Numbness. He sat there and listened with his eyes full of shock and confusion like I'd suddenly started speaking gibberish to him, which I suppose in a way I had. Then, after a few minutes, I stopped my mouth from running and just sat there staring back at him. And Jimmy said: "Roy, *are you out of your mind?!?* Man, listen to me: football players don't *do* this!" *Oh yes they do,* I thought. *Bisexual football players with deep, dark secrets do.*

We talked for a little while longer and watched some of the cars cruise by us on the small-town road. After a while a quiet settled between us. I guess that was the point when we both realized we'd said enough and that nothing we had said *was* enough. There was nothing else to do but sit like that, in silence. Finally, Jimmy said something I've never ever forgotten:

"Jesus, Roy. You know what? It's obvious that I'm gonna have to really make it someday just so you'll have someone to take care of you." I'm telling you. It was like he could see into the motherfucking future.

❖

JIMMY THOUGHT I was making a major goddamn wrong decision, and so, by the way, did the coaches and management of the New York Giants. Coach Perkins called me into his office and sat me down and started to lay into me real hard. He said: "Dammit, Simmons! People just don't *do* this! Where the hell do you get off pulling a stunt like this? You've got a great thing going here. Are you out of your mind? Are you insane?"

Hell, I thought. Maybe. I guess I don't know anymore. I guess maybe that's a distinct possibility.

To make matters worse, some serious words had been going around the team management and the sports community in general that the Giants were looking to build their entire offensive strategy around me and Billy Taylor, our star running back. That's a huge motherfucking responsibility. There'd be extra time on the playing field, extra time spent working with the coaches, press conferences, speaking engagements, shaving ads, spotlights. Too much for me, man. Too fucking much.

See, when the president of a corporation or an officer in an army assumes a position of that magnitude—well, we all know what happens next. They're no longer allowed to do certain things that they may have liked to do. Suddenly they just can't act the same way they used to. From out of nowhere you've got all these people relying on you, and there's no room for error. It's like riding a motorcycle at top speed in the rain: one slip and you're done—and maybe you even end up taking a few people with you. That's a heavy cross to bear. That's heavy weight to pull and I didn't feel ready for it. I didn't feel strong enough.

I was already pulling so much weight along behind me as it was. There was Nigeria and Kathy and Angela and Roz. There was Sheila and Kara, and every member of my family—my cousins, my aunts, my brothers, sisters, aunts, uncles. There were all the men I'd met in bathhouses—far too many to count, in fact—and there was Joe, too. Heaviest of all, though, was that other weight, the one I carried square up on my shoulders, the awful fucking weight of cocaine. Jesus. How's a man supposed to haul his ass out on a football field dragging all that shit behind him and still hope to play like a champ?

❖

I TOLD THE Giants I was mentally fatigued, and as you might imagine they completely flipped. There were all sorts of meetings with the coaches and managers, meetings where everyone looked at me like I was some kind of space alien they had to try to communicate with. I apologized to them over and over again but held firm with my decision. No, I wasn't trying to cause problems. I just needed some time off. I felt a little confused about where my life was going. I felt—like I said—mentally fatigued. After a dozen or so attempts to set me back on the straight and narrow, the coaches sent me to a Dr. Joel Goldberg for an "evaluation."

Dr. Goldberg was the Giants' career consultant, which I think was some sort of euphemism for the fact that he was a head shrinker specializing in acute gridiron disorders. He didn't practice clinical psychology so much as administer vocational aptitude tests, and he tried to help us find work out of season. I remember standing in this man's office and answering a whole bunch of questions. He said, "So. Coach Perkins says that you say you're tired."

"That's right."

"Mentally tired or physically tired?"

"I just need to take a time out, that's all."

"And you think this is normal?"

"Did I say that?"

"No. No, you didn't. I'm just trying to gauge how you feel about all this."

I shrugged. "When you're playing the game and you need to think something over you call a time out. So that's what I want to do. I'm calling time out."

Dr. Goldberg just looked at me. He tapped his pen against his desk for a few moments. Then he said: "So. Tell me. Do you *like* playing for the Giants?"

"Yes."

"Are you sure?"

I nodded. But here again I was holding back a bit. If I'd been honest at that moment, I would have told Dr. Goldberg how angry I was that Perkins had called me into his office earlier in the season and told me to stop hanging out with my friends. "Roy," he said. "You and I both know there's a couple of guys on this team who like to cut loose in a big way off the field. I'm telling you: stay away from them. They're a bad influence on you. They'll only lead you into trouble." Man, that upset me! Those guys were my friends! I was so close to them that I left Perkins's office and turned right around and told them everything he'd said.

But how could I begin to articulate the deep-down anger I felt about the weird charade I saw constantly being played out all around me. In the NFL, you can be a wife-beater, you can do drugs, get piss-ass drunk and wreck your car, sleep with as many groupies as you want behind your wife's back, and destroy private property whenever you went on a rampage. No matter what sin you committed, the team would accept you back into the fold. If anything, the team would hold you in higher esteem! You earned your bones if you were arrested for assault. You put a notch in your belt each time you smoked opium after stomping the Philadelphia Eagles for the bunch of incompetents they were. Sometimes I wondered where the boundaries lay, if any truly existed at all. A man who played professional football could get away with pretty much anything, but never—under any circumstances whatsoever—could you announce that you were gay. That was the one unpardonable sin, the big taboo, the league secret. All those other antics were nothing but entertainment compared to that.

No, I never mentioned any of this to Dr. Goldberg. Again, that would have required complete honesty, which was something I shied away from back then because honesty would also have meant telling Dr. Goldberg about the drugs and the woman I screwed and the men I had and the baby I didn't have and Travis the Neighbor and Gerald and Wayne and Stick and maybe even a little about Willy White, assuming that really *did* happen, which I'm still not sure of even to this day. Complete honesty was too big a door to walk through at that time in my life. So I just nodded when Dr. Goldberg asked if I liked playing for the Giants and nodded again and said, "Yes, I do. Why wouldn't I?"

❖

IN AN EFFORT to keep the press from roasting my black ass on the front page of every goddamn tabloid in the country, I called a press conference and broke the news of my crazy scheme to the world. "I'm taking a year off from football," I said. "But I'll be back." Everyone thought I had lost my mind.

Without my paycheck from the Giants, I was gonna have to handle expenses a little differently, so I moved out of the house in Carlstadt and set up house in the basement of my aunt Rosetta's apartment out in Amityville, Long Island. It was a major downshift in lifestyle, but it was affordable. I wasn't paying a whole lot of rent. Dr. Goldberg got me a nice job working out at Kennedy Airport, and once again I was a baggage handler, just like I'd been in college. Who says you don't learn anything in school? Sometimes I also worked as a Clipper Club attendant supervisor for Pan Am.

Everything was suddenly so different. 'Course it was, I wasn't "up" anymore. But still, I felt it was gonna be all right. I commuted from Amityville to Jamaica, Queens, using the Long Island Railroad and the New York City Q10 bus. Sometimes I brought my lunch along, sometimes I read the paper. I was a regular Joe for the first time since I could remember, and that felt good. I felt like a regular person.

❖

DOWN IN SAVANNAH, Sheila and Kara were living on welfare. I wasn't really talking to Sheila but I'd send her money every now and then, whenever I could, which wasn't really much. Hell, with the money I *wasn't* making at the airport I couldn't afford to lease a car, let alone funnel money down south.

At that point, my conversations with Sheila (whenever she actually returned my phone calls) would go something like this: I'd say, "Hi, Sheila. It's Roy. How are you?" And she'd snap, "Just send the goddamn money!" I didn't like her anger, didn't understand it at all back then, if the truth be told. Now I do. I had an obligation to Kara, which I'd never lived up to. So I told her that I wanted to come down and see Kara, but she was real clear on this point; she said that no, I didn't need to see Kara, what I *needed* to do was send money and send it fast.

Hell, I needed money, too. Sometimes Roz would wire me money and that helped out so much. That woman would give me the shirt off her back, to say nothing of her good advice and honest opinions. But she was sending me so much money that Jimmy began to joke around and call her "Western Roslyn" instead of "Western Union." A lot of the time, without knowing it, she was really sending me money for drugs.

❖

DR. GOLDBERG CALLED me up all the time during that year and kept asking me the same questions. *How was I doing? What was I doing? How was the job? How was my life? Was I happy? Was I sad? What were my thoughts about returning to the field next season? Was there anything he could do?* He was always very kind like that.

I didn't have much to tell him, really. I found myself repeating the same old things to him during our conversations. Yes, I liked the environment I was in. Yes, I liked my shift at the airport, 3 P.M. to 11 at night suited me just fine. Yes, I liked the low-pressure atmosphere plus the fact that I was in charge of hiring and firing. That was something I'd never had to do before and I took to it pretty well. Yes, I liked the fact that I had to wear a shirt and tie to work. I wasn't lying about that, either. I *did* enjoy wearing a shirt and tie! And yes—oh yes! I just loved the people I worked with.

They was regular, decent, beautiful folks. No one knew that I played football, or at least no one volunteered that information to me. A few people told me, "Hey, man! You look like you play ball." And if it came up like that, if someone asked me directly, I'd never lie to them. I'd say, "Well, I did." Some of them were like, "Dang! Why the heck didn't you tell me?!?" To which I'd say, "I don't know. I guess I just didn't think it was important."

Eventually a lot of people figured out who I was, and they made me feel special. 'Cause here I was, some sort of professional football player on the lam, hanging out with them.

What I didn't tell Dr. Goldberg was that I was still drinking and drugging and sexing it up whenever and wherever I could. No change, really, from when I was playing for the Giants. It's just that I wasn't running into a stadium every once in a while in my uniform while 75,000 screaming fans went nuts and cheered me on. I didn't tell Dr. Goldberg anything about my private life, and maybe I should've. Looking back, I suppose that's what I took time off from football to deal with in the first place. But then, like I said, at that time in my life I was not into the concept of complete honesty.

For a guy who had no car, very little money, and the obligations of a full-time job in the service industry, I was partying my ass off. Never mind that Sheila and Kara were living on welfare at the time; I was all about me. By that point Jimmy was becoming a big shot on the club circuit and he could get my name on the guest lists of some A-list places. Plus, being an attendant at the Clipper Club meant that I had access to all the liquor in the cabinets. I'd fill my attaché case with little airline-sized bottles of hooch and take it home with me. In fact, little smuggling stunts like that gave me the means to start my days off right.

Breakfast always started out with gin and juice or maybe a nice screwdriver. By the time I left the house, I was at least into my second or third. Then, as the day went on, I'd switch off to whatever took my fancy. Whiskey. Bourbon. More vodka. More gin. If I had to estimate, I'd say I was doing maybe ten drinks a day. I was smoking pot practically every day at that point, too. Plus a little coke at night on the side.

Honestly, though, I never let myself get too out of control. After all, I didn't have a car and I knew that wherever I wanted to go I'd have to walk my own ass out there. That meant I had to keep myself in pretty good shape.

❖

Roz would drive out to Amityville and pick me up sometimes. We never stopped having sex, that was just something that Roz and I did, didn't matter how long it'd been since we'd seen one another or whatever else was going on in our lives. Sex with me and Roz was a constant activity, like eating or breathing.

But then there was this new guy I met by the name of Tyrone. He was an ex-marine who worked security at the ABC television network; we met in the New York City subway and I liked him right away 'cause he was well-traveled. He'd been around the world during his service, so he had plenty of stories.

After we started hanging out together, I brought him up to the

Clipper Club a few times, got him a few cocktails. Then I started taking him to the clubs down in the Village that I liked to go, and he started taking me to his favorite places. We got pretty close, close enough that I got to know and like his entire family out in Brooklyn.

He was into young guys, I was into older men. Tyrone used to hang out with the big, *big* boys, you know? The muscleheads who could fuck you and then fuck you up if they so chose. In that company, ol' T was like the little brother who liked to just hang around and suck dick, but I was never into that crowd. I found them a little intimidating.

❖

I WAS ONLY making ten or eleven dollars an hour. And sometimes, what with the cost of drugs and short-stay hotel rates and child support (when I paid it) and food, I just didn't have enough to go around. Because of the situation, I almost said to hell with it all and went back to play for the Giants, just for the money's sake. But whenever things got really tight, it was Dr. Goldberg to the rescue. I called that man so many times that I can still recite his phone number to this day. And he never refused me a loan. He'd send me small amounts—$50 here, $75 there. A hundred, maybe two hundred when things got really, *really* tight. All in all, I'd say he loaned me close to two grand, which was a lot of money back then.

I don't think he was aware of my addiction. Or maybe I should say it like this. If he was aware of my addiction, I don't think he was aware of the *depth* of my addiction. Otherwise, I can't imagine he would've sent me all that money, that just wouldn't make sense. And you know what? He never asked me where that money was going. Every time he called, we'd talk a bit and he'd just offer me some sensible advice. "Take care of yourself, Roy," he'd say. "Call if you need anything at all. And always remember to do the right thing."

I trusted Dr. Goldberg. I trusted him so much that one day I visited his office and we sat down and talked and I told him about how I grew up, and about Grandma Lou and Rudolph and my mother, and even about the rape. I told him about Travis. Later on he asked me if I was gay and I told him that yes, I was. "Hmmmm," he said, and he played with his pen for a bit and wrote something down on his notepad. "You know?" he said. "I had this gut feeling that you were." I think that man had a soft spot in his heart for me. Maybe that's why he never asked for the money he gave me to be repaid.

At Christmastime my coworkers showed me how much they appreciated me by piling gifts on my desk—dozens and dozens and dozens of liquor bottles tied with red and green bows. The only thing going through my head was *Goddamn! Let's have us a drink!*

❖

DURING THE TIME I worked at the airport, Jimmy Hester was finishing up his senior year in high school. At the age of seventeen he'd already begun to create a working public relations company for his own little self. In May of 1983 he was in the middle of final exams, but that didn't stop him from picking up the phone and tracking down the marquee player of the USFL, Herschel Walker of the New Jersey Generals.

Jimmy had made it a point to know all the numbers of all the pay phones in all the locker rooms at Giants Stadium. And he was now determined more than ever to cut his way into the music business, which in his mind meant upping the ante on his relationship with Frankie Crocker. So Jimmy waited until the Generals played at Giants Stadium. And somehow he got hold of Herschel Walker in the goddamn Generals locker room.

He did it by calling the pay phone and simply asking, "Is Herschel there?" To which someone said, "Who's this?" And Jimmy said, "It's Jimmy," just like he and Herschel had known each other their entire lives, like they were the oldest buddies on earth. He did it so convincingly that whoever had picked up the phone brought Herschel to the line. He picked up the receiver and said, "Hello?" And just like that, Jimmy was off and running.

"Herschel, how are you? My name is Jimmy Hester. I threw parties for the Giants with Lawrence Taylor and Frankie Crocker. You know Frankie Crocker? The DJ? One oh seven point five FM?"

Herschel was like, "Oh yeah, man, I listen to Frankie. Great."

And Jimmy said, "Perfect. Listen. Do you mind if Frankie and I throw you a little end-of-the-season party for you and your teammates? They tend to be pretty cool. We use places like the Underground and nice clubs and such. Can I make that happen for you guys, too?"

What the hell else was Herschel going to say? "No, no. Don't mind at all. In fact, that'd be real nice."

"Great!" said Jimmy, and then he closed the deal. "Gimme a better number to reach you at. I'll coordinate with Frankie and call you back with some dates."

Now I think you know what happened next. Jimmy called Frankie and basically said, "Frankie, how would you like to host an end-of-the-season party for Herschel Walker and the New Jersey Generals? I just talked to Herschel and he thinks it's a great idea, he'd love to have you do it. Can we make this happen?"

Jimmy threw the Generals a very successful little party in Manhattan at the same time I called the Giants and let them know that I was ready to come back to work. We worked it out over the phone and I showed up to the May mini-training camp a week early with the rest of the rookies.

Now, this time around I was determined to make my mark with the Giants. I moved back in with Aunt Betty so I could have easy access to the stadium. And when I first set foot in that training camp I was of the mind that I was there to inherit the job they'd been talking about for me when I left. I wanted to be head of the offensive line, goddammit. I finally felt I was ready.

In my absence, however, the Giants had drafted a few more linemen and the coaching staff had experienced some pretty heavy changes. For instance, Tom Bresnahan was the new offensive line coach and that was one thing I didn't particularly mind. But head coach Perkins was gone. He'd left the Giants at the end of the '82 season to take up his dream job at the University of Alabama coaching the Crimson Tide. And to fill the absence, George Young, the Giants' general manager, promoted Bill Parcells off the defensive line.

Parcells and I hadn't interacted too much the first two years I'd been in New York. Offensive linemen don't spend too much time hanging around with the defense guys, they're like on a whole different planet.

Therefore I barely knew the man. But I guess he knew me. Seems to me like he had all sorts of opinions about me right from the get-go, and none of them were good. I suppose taking off a year hadn't helped me look good either.

I knew something was up when they changed my position during the second week of training camp. Now they wanted me to play right tackle, which was held down by the starting guy on the line, a man by the name of Gordon King. At first the move didn't bother me too much. My attitude was like, *Oh well, I'll just kick Gordon King's ass and win this job.* But Parcells's mind was made up. He was convinced that I was a bad seed. And before I got to cracking my own shell, sprouting shoots, and putting down roots again, he was gonna dig me up and throw me aside, make room for another plant which he could groom more easily to his own tastes.

❖

EVERY NFL TEAM has a guy on the staff called the Turk. This is the man whose job it is to roust you out of bed in the early morning hours and dash your dreams to tiny little bits. You can think of the Turk as the football equivalent of Donald Trump in the TV show *The Apprentice*. 'Cause the Turk's job is basically to pop into your life, look you square in the eye, and tell you, "You're fired."

In the third week of training camp, I heard that dreaded knock on my door. I opened it up and there was the Turk, that slimy bastard. He said, "Coach wants to see you. Bring your playbook." And just like that he walked off down the hall.

I stood thereon the threshold watching this little shit walk away and feeling my stomach drop into my heels. Meanwhile, my roommate, a wide receiver named Floyd Eddings, came up behind me saying, "Who was that?" He caught a glimpse of the Turk walking away down the corridor and started moaning, "Oh no! Oh no! Oh no, Sugar Bear, no . . ."

Oh yes. Oh I'm afraid fucking so. All that time at Kennedy Airport trying to sort things out—for what? For this? All those people who believed in me . . . my family, my friends . . . what are they gonna think?

The night before, I'd rolled this nice fat joint and left it in my top clothes drawer. Right then, I felt this incredible urge to smoke that damn thing up and *then* go into his office. Maybe pin Parcells against the wall and start yelling in his face that he'd made a mistake. That I was better than he knew. That he wasn't giving me a fair shake. Anything. Anything at all to take the edge off.

'Course I didn't do that. I just glanced over at the top drawer and thought to myself, *I'll get you when I come back, baby. Just you wait right there.* And I began the long walk over to Parcells's office.

❖

MY MIND WAS whirling so fast all through the meeting that I barely heard what Parcells was saying to me. "Simmons," he said, "we are not a charity organization, we're the New York Giants, our business is football . . ." Meanwhile, all I heard myself saying in my head was, *I know I'm better than any of those motherfuckers on that line. I know I can play this game tight. I know this is about something else, it ain't about football.*

"This is not a place where you can take off whenever you want and come back whenever you want and leave us hanging while you go off and indulge yourself in God knows what. This is a football team. A *professional* football team. And professional football teams require discipline, hard work, and commitment . . ."

When he fired me, I just got up and walked out the door. I despised that man for years, too. I didn't care how much of what he said was my fault. I hadn't deserved to be fired.

A lot of players came to my room and told me they were sorry. I still had a lot of close friends on the team. They were like my family. We hugged each other and said our good-byes. I felt low. I felt really, really fucking low.

The first person I called was Jimmy. When I told him what happened, he was positively stunned. "Oh shit, Roy." That's all he kept saying. "Oh shit, oh shit, oh shit, oh shit." I wasn't being a whole lot more articulate. I think I kept saying, "Yeah. I know. Uh huh. Yeah. I know."

"What are you gonna do?" he said. It took me a second to figure out a response. "Right now," I said, "I'm gonna head over to Central Park and sit down and collect my thoughts." Which seemed like the best idea I'd come up with in a long, long time. But first I made sure to grab the joint I'd left in my top clothes drawer.

I smoked that first joint in the training camp parking lot, loaded up all my bags into my rental car, and drove over to Central Park. I wandered around for a while until I found a nice, secluded place away from everybody. There was a great big rock poking up from the ground and I climbed on top and just sat there for a while, thinking. Then I smoked another joint. It all started to sink in. *No more Giants. No more football. No more Roy Simmons, Fantastic Fucking Athlete. No more of the life I'd known for years. Now what?* I called Jimmy again from a payphone.

He said, "Roy, look. Everything's gonna be fine. Let's do this. I'll take you out to Studio 54 tonight. We'll drink champagne. We'll do some blow. We'll dance, we'll let off some steam. This isn't the end, I'm telling you, this isn't the end. We'll figure something out."

"Okay, Jimmy. All right." It sounded better than any idea I could come up with myself. I drove my car back to Aunt Rosetta's place. Later on, I picked Jimmy up at his home in Little Ferry, New Jersey, and we headed into Manhattan, where we quickly got down to some really serious partying. Mark Fleischman, the owner of Studio 54, gave us the VIP treatment, which meant that we didn't pay the cover, didn't pay for drinks, and were allowed access to the private back rooms, which were essentially drug dens for the rich and famous. Jimmy's friend Helen was with us—a girl we always called Meadowlands Molly, who was sort of a Giants team groupie. I even took a spin on the dance floor with Joan Rivers, whom Mark Fleischman introduced me to. It was a good time. It was a very, very good time.

The next day, the phone rang. Aunt Betty was on the line. "Roy," she said. "The Washington Redskins just called. They want you to call them back right away." Man, life's something, right? Just when you think the whole world's flushing you down the toilet bowl, something else comes along and makes everything all right again.

I don't know how they do it these days, but back then, when a player got cut from an NFL team at training camp, their name went out over a wire service for the next 72 hours so that everybody else in the league knew what was going on. Basically it was like saying, *Hey everybody! Here's who's looking for work.* My name went on that list the moment the Giants cut me from training camp and my skills caught the Redskins' attention. I guess what I had to offer filled a hole in their roster at the time. Just luck, really, that's all it was.

❖

In 1983, the Redskins were the defending Super Bowl champions, so you *know* I took this call real seriously. I called them back and spoke to Joe Bugel, the offensive line coach, who said to me, "Simmons, I want you to get down here and join our training camp. I think we might have a place for you. Can you get out here today?"

"To Washington?"

"No. Training camp's in Carlisle, Pennsylvania." I'd never heard of the place before. I thought about it for a second. Mostly, what I thought about was Jimmy. Then I said, "No. I can't. Not today. But I'll get there tomorrow, how's that?" That sounded just fine to him. So I flew out to Carlisle and joined the Redskins training camp. I noticed how Joe Bugel kept a close watch on me over the course of a few workouts. Finally, after a few days, he came up to me and took me aside so we could talk privately.

"Simmons," he said. "You can play here. I want you to join the team as a backup guard." And just like that, I was playing professional football again. This time I was hired at a salary of $100,000. I'd need every penny of it, too.

10

ONE THING YOU gotta know about the Washington Redskins: we used to beat the shit outta each other in training camp. I never practiced as hard as that with the New York Giants! These guys were some serious motherfucking football players. Like I said, they'd won the Super Bowl the year before, and you didn't have to look twice to see they wanted to win it again this year, too. They wanted that win real bad.

This is probably a good place to tell you about "the rules" for hitting people. When you're a lineman, that's pretty much what your job is—hitting people. It may sound like fun, but trust me, after you do it for a little while it can really start to screw with your head. You get a lot of linemen in the NFL who are screamers. That's their way of dealing with the tension. They scream in the huddles, they scream in the lineup. They scream just before they enter or leave the field. They scream before they hit you.

My personal preference is to stay silent. I'm not saying I never screamed; hell, once or twice it seemed like the right thing to do, and I'll say this for it: it *does* relieve a certain amount of tension. But mostly I liked to keep all that energy to myself. I found that screaming dissipated my mojo. Didn't want to just toss it off on the field like it was useless, nothing. I preferred to keep my mojo bottled up tight, saving it for the right moment when I could use it to my best advantage. One key run. One key push. The guts it took to push back against three defense tackles at once on a tidal wave sack.

Part of the challenge of joining the Redskins was learning to understand all these new screams. When you're a member of a professional football team, you get to know your teammates about as well as if you'd married them, as far as playing the game goes. You could tell when somebody was having an off day or when somebody was feeling exceptionally sharp. You quickly learned how to read everyone's body language, both on and off the field. You learned everyone's habits, too. It's part of being one of the gladiators in the clutch, part of being in the brotherhood. It's useful knowledge. Very useful.

For instance, those screams are like a whole separate language in the NFL. They're like tells in poker. You can learn a lot about a person from the way they use their voice in a game. I worked with quarterbacks who I could tell were feeling confident at any given moment because of the precise timber of their voice when they called out a play. One lineman on the Giants used to *huuuuuuf!* a certain way precisely one second before he exploded out of his three-point stance. Another guy, an offensive guard, used to scream sometimes, sure. But he only screamed to intimidate people, which actually meant that he wasn't feeling so confident about his ability to punch through the defense. When people ask me these days if I speak French or Spanish or Italian I tell them, *No. I don't. I'm sorry. I never learned those languages.* But I speak Football. I speak many dialects within that language, too. Offensive T-formation. 10—10 Drop Back 5. Chug 20 Hut. Quick 34—35 Trap. In these tongues, I'm 100 percent fluent.

The Redskins were a great bunch of guys and we got on real well. But the thing I couldn't get over was their damned locker room. Man, what a shithouse! Place looked like the men's room at a municipal swimming pool. Bare concrete walls, cracked sinks, industrial-grade mirrors, banged-up rusty lockers. I was like, *Y'all just won the damned Super Bowl! What is the problem here? It don't take all that much money to renovate a locker room and make it nice and plush. Put some spare change into a new coat of paint, for crying out loud!*

What can I say? I guess they had different priorities.

❖

QUARTERBACK JOE THEISMANN and I got on real well. That guy was spunky! Talked and talked and talked and *talked*. He could back up everything he said, and that was what made Joe different from any other quarterback I played with. Theismann was a very smart man and he knew the game of football. If he said, "I'm gonna drop back, fake left, break right, backpedal three steps, and drop a pass right down the line so we gain six yards," that's *exactly* what he'd do. You could count on that shit like you count on a wristwatch. Joe was an artist. The man was fucking *precise*.

Not a lot of people know this, but Theismann was an allover athlete, too. In 1971, he got drafted into the NFL by the Miami Dolphins, *and* by the Minnesota Twins for Major League Baseball. He turned them both down! Crazy-ass man wanted to play for the Toronto Argonauts in the Canadian Football League. Now that's a man who knows his own mind. I envy that kind of clarity and willpower. Sometimes I think, *if only I'd been that level-headed*. No doubt about it. I could have spared myself and a whole lot of people I care about some tremendous pain and suffering.

When he finally came back to the NFL in '74, he started out as the Redskins' punt returner. Then he worked his way up. Became starting quarterback in 1978. Set several Redskins franchise records. Most career passing attempts. Most career passing completions. Most career passing yards. He made Pro Bowl MVP, Offensive Player of the Year, plus NFL MVP in '83, and lemme tell you, he deserved it all.

I wasn't there when Theismann's career ended. That was in 1985 after I'd moved on to a different team. I remember how it happened, though. *Second quarter against the New York Giants. Theismann hands off to offensive lineman John Riggins. Riggins flea-flickers the ball back to Theismann. Theismann drops back to make a throw, but all of a sudden three of the Giants linemen show up and fall on him. They just destroy him.* You could hear Theismann's leg snap even on the TV. It was a gruesome injury. Broke his right thigh like a twig. 'Course it came as no surprise to me that one of those three Giants lineman was my old friend, Lawrence Taylor. That crazy sonovabitch. I always had this feeling that he'd hurt somebody someday.

❖

SPEAKING OF JOHN Riggins, he had to be one of the greatest players I ever got to see in action. He was getting up in years back when I played with the Redskins; he was thirty-four years old, which was practically an old man for a professional football player back then. But you'd never have known his age from the way that man moved. Lord, he could kick ass! He was un-fucking-stoppable, he'd run all over motherfuckers and then come back and stomp 'em some more. The guy was an animal—power, speed, grace, and cold-blooded intelligence.

In Super Bowl XVII, when the Redskins beat the Dolphins 27–17, Riggins broke all the rushing records. Up until then, no other running back had rushed more than 400 yards in four straight playoff games; Riggins tallied 610. No other running back had ever gained more than 158 yards in a Super Bowl; Riggins gained 166. He even made the longest touchdown run from scrimmage in Super Bowl history. I'm telling you, the man was an animal. He was a force of nature on the gridiron.

Riggins did so well in Super Bowl XVII that he considered walking away from the game. But then he told the press, "Aw, you guys know me. I change my mind every five minutes." I thank God he *didn't* walk away. I thank God I got a chance to play with him.

❖

THEN THERE WAS the beautiful Dexter Manley. No doubt in my mind why he was such a Redskins fan favorite. Such a sparkling personality, Mr. Manley. And what a great player! I think he still holds the Redskins' franchise records for career and single-season sacks. Dexter was big and Dexter was fast. When he went after a quarterback, that quarterback was very, very afraid.

I still remember how Dexter went after the Dallas Cowboys QB, Danny, back in the 1982 NFC Championship game. Dexter hit that man so hard he knocked him clean outta the game! And then later on, the Skins had Dallas trapped inside their own ten-yard line. It was Dexter—beautiful Dexter!—reached on up and tipped a pass thrown by Gary Hogeboom, the backup QB. Not much contact on the ball, just the tip of Dexter's fingers, but it was enough to foul the pass. The ball dropped into the waiting arms of our man Darryl Grant, who ran the ball in for the killer TD and sent the Redskins on their way to Super Bowl XVII.

Dexter had his problems, of course. Very bad drug addictions. But Coach Joe Gibbs was such a patient man, an excellent teacher. He could've canned Dexter's ass a thousand times for all sorts of misbehaviors, but that wasn't his style. He'd sit Dexter down and talk to him like they were father and son. Not just because Dexter was such a talented athlete and valuable to the team, but because that's just the kind of man Joe Gibbs is. He never cursed and he never talked over you. He took everything we did in stride. He'd just look us in the eye—and say, "Come on now, get your dang thing done." I still remember the way he talked, with a wonderful Carolina accent. All of us respected him. I think Dexter thought Joe Gibbs was the Second Coming.

One time Dexter showed up in the locker room wearing a handsome monogrammed shirt. I wasn't thinking that day. I went up right up to him, reached out, and felt the fabric. I touched him in what I guess he considered an inappropriate way. I said, "Damn, man! This shit is really nice." Meaning the shirt. Dexter pulled away from me and said, "Look, man. Don't you ever fucking touch me. Got it?" Oh, I got it, all right. I was like, "Fuck you, you big black bastard." But from then on, I never had a thing to say to him.

❖

MAYBE THE WEIRDEST thing about playing for the Washington Redskins was the time we played against my old team, the New York Giants. That whole week, the Redskins' coaches sat me down alone in a room and picked my brain like nobody's business. "All right, Roy. Come on, now, think. Can you remember the offensive plays?"

Hell, yes. I remembered them all like the back of my hand. Flow 38. Quick 34–35 trap. The 338–339 Screen. Ride 12–13 straight up. Lemme tell you, those coaches were suddenly very interested in everything I had to say. I talked for hours and hours while they all took pages and pages of notes. Felt like I was holding my very own private press conference.

During the game against the Giants, I couldn't stand to look over at Bill Parcells. I still resented him for cutting me from the team. We kicked the Giants' asses, and that felt good. But the nicest part about that whole experience was getting together on the field after the game with my old teammates Billy Taylor, Danny Pittman, Mike Dennis, Jeter, Gray, Simms. We were just like family again. It didn't matter which team we played for. I tell you, we were just like family.

❖

Now, DURING ALL this time, I'd taken up residence in Reston, Virginia. After I got cut from the Giants, my mother'd gone back to Savannah along with Ricky, Gary, and LaTwan, but my brothers tended to visit a lot. I got used to living in the D.C. area pretty quick. What a city! Sometimes I'd head to Georgetown and hit Champions restaurant—they gave us a nice team discount. Or, if I really wanted to treat someone to a nice time, I'd take them to Morton's steakhouse.

'Course, to satisfy my other needs, I'd sometimes head for the gay clubs in the downtown area, places like the Brass Rail, for instance. I'd park my car just a few blocks down and tiptoe right on in. It was risky, man. Hoooooo, that was risky! But you know what they say about old habits dying hard. Didn't matter how risky the whole thing was to me, it was a risk I was willing to take. Shit, man—it was a risk I felt *compelled* to take!

In D.C. my gay life was as active as ever. Tyrone came down to live with me for a little while but that was a totally platonic thing. I'd bought this beautiful new stereo system but I didn't know how to do all the wiring. So Tyrone came down since he was a jack-of-all-trades. He fixed up the stereo and we started blasting out Ashford and Simpson all day, all the time. In fact, every time I hear Ashford and Simpson today, I always think back to those times in Reston with Tyrone and me walking around the house in our drawers and nothing else. Like I said, though, it was totally platonic. I didn't want Tyrone—not emotionally, not sexually. I didn't want anybody, the truth be told. Anybody except Joe, that is.

❖

JOE WAS STILL up north, working and living and doing his thing. I wanted to keep in touch with him so bad that I went out and bought us matching state-of-the-art Sony answering machines. Cost me $250 apiece! These things came with little remote controls that you could hold up against a phone's earpiece when you called your house. You pressed a button and the remote gave a little beep that was the audio equivalent of a four-character digitized code. The beep interacted with your message unit and allowed you to retrieve your voice mail from any location.

One time I was over at Joe's place. I cracked open the control panel on his remote and glanced at the dials that contained his four-digit code while he was on the toilet in the bathroom with the door closed. Now I could set the dials on my own remote to Joe's frequency and call up his machine whenever I knew he was out. I could retrieve his messages then rewind the machine so he'd never suspect I'd been there. It was a horrible breach of trust, I know, a pure act of betrayal. But I couldn't help myself. I was hooked on Joe. I made myself sick over many occasions wondering, *Why doesn't he call me? Who's he going out with while I'm gone? Is he in love with somebody else? Was he ever in love with me? What did I ever do wrong to him that he'd go and treat me like this?* And so on. I was like schoolgirl pining away for her first big crush in junior high. I was a mess.

Of all the messages Joe received routinely on his machine, one guy got me suspicious immediately. He wasn't a coworker, he wasn't a friend—leastways he wasn't a friend that Joe had gone out of his way to introduce me to. In my mind that meant that he was Joe's boyfriend. His fling. His affair. Maybe they were in love or maybe they were just fooling around. Either way, he wasn't me and that made me insane with anger. I was like a man possessed. Joe was mine. No one else deserved him. And he deserved no one else but me, regardless of the fact that I was seeing my own people on the side.

Eventually, I confronted Joe with what I knew. I asked him who this mystery guy was who kept calling and calling. That probably wasn't the brightest thing in the world to do. In order to admit that I knew some guy was calling Joe, I also had to admit that I'd stolen his four-digit code and accessed his voice mail. Joe was not amused.

I said, "Dammit, man, why you lying to me?! This guy calls you every goddamn day and you're saying ain't nothing going on?!"

"How do *you* know he calls every day?"

"Say what?"

"Simple question. How do *you* know this guy calls me every goddamn day? You been at my answering machine, man?"

"What? No. Hell, no. 'Course not."

By this time I'd gotten used to lying to so many people that I was beginning to grow completely unaware of when I was even lying to myself. Joe told me this man I was talking about was just a workout partner from his gym. Nothing more. Certainly no hanky-panky going on. I didn't believe him. Still don't. And after that incident our relationship began to change. Joe was a little cooler to me overall. I saw him looking at me sidelong more often, like I was an animal whose tricks he'd grown used to. We held it together, though. Once or twice a month, Joe would come down over the weekend to stay with me in Reston. He came to visit me at the Redskins training camp in Carlisle while I was there, and we went out to catch a movie. We saw *Purple Rain* together. It was a beautiful film and we both cried and held hands during the tender parts. I have such wonderful memories of Joe like that. When I think of us together during those Redskins days, all I can do is smile.

❖

DRINKING AND DRUGGING at my place became something like a national pasttime. My teammates from the Redskins would drop by and indulge themselves, Tyrone indulged himself, Joe indulged himself when he came down. I picked up the tab for all the liquor and all the drugs 'cause I liked having all my friends around. Lord, it got expensive! I even picked up the tabs for my young lover, Ray, whom I kept on the side.

Right around this time, I made one of the worst mistakes of my life. I started freebasing cocaine. It happened like this: I remember seeing these two young black women on the opposite side of the street where I lived. I used to see them every time I drove home, practically every day. And you know, after a while I started saying to myself, *Maybe I should go over and introduce myself. I'd really like to meet them.* That southern hospitality gets in you and stays there.

So one day I did just that. I pulled the car over and introduced myself to these nice young ladies. Their names were Bonnie and Monnie and they were fine-looking, done up in nice clothes. They were really short—barely came up to my chest—and they had painted nails and drove a nice car. Bonnie was enormously well endowed up top and Monnie wasn't all that far behind, but I wasn't really attracted to them in a sexual way. I told myself I just wanted some company.

I introduced myself to them and offered to make dinner for them. I told them who I was and I figured, *Shit, that's okay. Anyone staying in this complex must be respectable, must have a lot of cash. You gotta be a professional person to afford living in a place like this.* Well. They were professionals, all right. Professional drug dealers. Worst damn mistake I ever coulda made.

I got to know them pretty well. I even had sex with Bonnie once. Pretty soon they were stopping by the apartment maybe once or twice a week. We had dinner on those occasions and drank some. Eventually they asked me if I smoked and I told them I did. Meaning reefer. Which wasn't what they had in mind, I guess. "Reefer, huh?" They both giggled like I'd just said something cute. Then Monnie said, "You mind if I go into your kitchen and do something?" I said, "Sure, go right ahead." I was curious.

Well, of course they got right to it and cooked up some cocaine. I ain't talking 'bout crack, here, I'm talking the real fucking deal, bringing the drug back to its natural form. After a while, I wanted to see what they were up to, so I got up from my chair in the living room and went into the kitchen. There they were, doing their thing over the gas range. Monnie had a pipe in her mouth and she was puffing from it like an old sailor hanging out on a fishing boat dock, watching the sun go down. They both looked up when I entered the kitchen.

"You wanna try it?" Monnie said.

"Sure. Okay." So Monnie got a kitchen chair and climbed up on it so she could reach my face—that's how short she was—and she put the pipe in my mouth and held a lighter to it and told me to pull when she started the flame. Which I did. And you know what? That first time I pulled? It was really nothing. I felt nothing, no effect at all. I was like,

This is good. No, fuck that. This shit feels great! Who the hell said freebasing was bad for you? This shit feels wonderful!

A very, very big mistake.

Out of the clear blue a few days later, I found myself wandering around the city looking for a head shop. I bought myself a bowl, a pipe, a torch, the works. And every day after that, I'd come home from work, cook up, and freebase in my kitchen. I got some excellent cocaine from a dealer in our community who knew it was bad news to sell me anything but the finest shit. Freebasing beat getting stoned any day of the week. Freebasing cocaine was a totally different kind of high. No stress, no anxiety, no hassles. Just light up, inhale, and let everything be A-OK.

❖

ROZ CAME DOWN to see me a few times. We were still in touch, but the cocaine started to change all that. She wasn't into freebasing. Hell, she wouldn't have that shit at all. For Roz, smoking reefer was one thing, smoking cocaine was another thing entirely. She just wouldn't do it, it made her nervous, and that drove a big wedge between us.

One night while she was visiting Reston, we got into a big argument. She said the smoke had changed me. Said I didn't care about her anymore or some such nonsense. Said I was devoting more time to drugs than I was to her, to my family, to my job. I sent her to bed. Even if this was true, I wasn't having any of it.

She stayed a whole week one time and I remember it especially 'cause I had a bitch of a time getting high. I always had to be careful whenever Roz was around. It was like she was holding me to an entirely different standard of behavior.

❖

THE REDSKINS MADE it to Super Bowl XVIII and my world sort of exploded. Here I was playing for the best damn team in the NFL, the reigning champions of the game. We were about to go back into the arena to win that damn title again. It was a dream come true for me. I'd finally made it to the top. You couldn't get any higher in pro football. We were headed down to Tampa, Florida, to do royal fucking battle with the goddamn Los Angeles Raiders. It was gonna be a blood bath, baby!

'Course I invited my old friend Jimmy down. Hell, I invited *everyone* down, and I do mean *everyone*. I paid for the tickets to the game, I paid for the hotels, I paid for the rental cars. It was full-fledged insanity.

Tyrone was in one room with John, whom I knew through Alvin Garett, and my lover Ray. Joe came down, too. Aunt Betty made the trip with two of her friends. Then there was my mother and my four brothers, Larry, Gary, Ricky, and LaTwan. My sister, Catherine, was there, too. Jimmy, Nigeria, and Kathy all had rooms in the same hotel as mine. And there were two other people, I knew, too, a married couple who were die-hard Redskins fans. They came to all the games and I'd met them outside the stadium on numerous occasions; I'd promised to get them Super Bowl tickets if we went.

I booked three rental cars in all—one for Joe, one for my aunt, and one that I shared with (of all people) Dexter Manley. I never got a chance to drive that damned car, though. Dexter hogged it all week.

Everyone was doing drugs that week. Jimmy brought an eight-ball of cocaine down with him, and once he borrowed my rental car so he and Larry and Cat could make a run for alcohol. Somehow they wound up slamming the car into a muddy ditch. They had to have the damned thing towed out. Don't ask me how that happened.

We kept this up all week—the drugs, the booze, the sex, the secrets. Since no one knew I was gay back then, I had to keep up this huge charade while I was shuffling back and forth to Joe's room. I also shuffled back to Nigeria's room. I think I popped in on Ray a few times, too. It was a fast pace and hard to maintain. Hoooo, it was crazy!

The night before the game had to be the worst, though. I didn't screw anybody, but the drinks and the drugs never stopped. My little entourage and I skipped out to all the bars in town and I saw my teammates out all over the place, too. Everybody was drinking hard! I saw a few of the Raiders out, as well, and they weren't taking things any easier. The whole thing was goddamn insane.

To make a long story short, we got our asses waxed the next day.

There's really no better way to put it. I wish I could say there were some outstanding plays that day, but no, there weren't. We played like we were drugged—go figure. Like I said, the Raiders had partied hard, too. But they obviously wanted it more.

❖

GARY POMERANTZ, A sportswriter for our hometown newspaper, the *Washington Post*, called that day the "most one-sided game in 18 years of Super Bowls." I'd like to say he was wrong about that, but I can't. That game was fucking humiliating. We'd won 31 out of 34 games that season; we'd won 11 games straight leading up to the Super Bowl. We were favored to win! We had a record-breaking offensive team! But the Raiders' defense ran all the hell over us. Their cornerbacks, Lester Hayes and Mike Haynes, doused us on just about every play. Our receivers couldn't get no game—Charlie Brown was only able to make three catches, Art Monk made only one. The Raiders' defense even threw a wet blanket over John Riggins, held him back to 64 yards on 26 carries. That's chump change for a guy like John. They sacked Theismann six fucking times.

I guess the worst part came at the end of the first half. The Raiders were leading us 14 to 3. Their punter laid the ball down right on our 12-yard line with 12 seconds to go. Don't even ask me what the fuck we were thinking. But Joe Gibbs opted not to run out the clock, nor did he opt to go for the deep pass to try and move the ball downfield. We went for a short play instead.

Theismann dropped back into our end zone and threw this crazy swing pass to our running back, Joe Washington. Washington never got hold of the ball. Jack Squirek, a Raider nobody'd ever heard of until that moment, jumped up and made his whole career in an instant. He snagged the ball in mid-flight at our 5 and ran the ball in for the touchdown. The half-time gun went off and we were trailing 21–3. Later on, I heard Squirek quoted in the newspapers. "I was surprised when they threw it. I was even more surprised when I caught it."

Later on Gibbs talked to the press, too, and tried to reason out that play. He said that when you got so little time left, there are only two choices. "You either fall on the ball or try to get something. I didn't like falling on the ball. I was hoping we'd get 20 or 30 yards and maybe get a field goal." Well, we didn't.

I was in the game on special teams and I also played guard toward the end. About the best thing I can say we did on special teams was block a punt after the Raiders scored their first touchdown five minutes into the game. But that wasn't even our doing, really. The Raiders' punter made a lame shot that bounced off the elbow of one of their own players while his back was turned.

We tried like hell to score in the third quarter. We knew we had to do something to stay in the game, but nothing worked. Riggins managed to get in a one-yard touchdown run, and that was great, 'cause it gave him six consecutive postseason games with a touchdown, meaning he broke Franco Harris's record from the Pittsburgh Steelers. But the Raiders blocked the extra point, so we were left at 21–9 with less than eleven minutes to go in the third.

The Raiders hammered us almost immediately with another touchdown. This one was made by Marcus Allen, the L.A. running back, who played his ass off that day. Now the score was 28–9. Then Allen made another touchdown with just seconds left to go in the third. He ran the damn ball 74 yards and fucking shamed us. Now we were 35–9 and everyone knew it was over. Marcus Allen drove a knife through our hearts with that play.

In the final minutes of the game, Theismann told us in the huddle, "Let's play hard and go out with class. We've had a hell of a year." He was right, but it felt empty somehow. We'd done so well that season. I guess I'd hoped for more. I guess that year we'd all hoped for so much more.

❖

AFTER THE GAME, I was simply disgusted. I got in the car and Jimmy climbed in with me. I said, "You got any shit?"

"Yeah, right here."

"Well, gimme some, then." So we both snorted up and I started driving down the highway. I took Jimmy back to the hotel and dropped him off. Then it was just me, back out on the road in the rental car, snorting coke and blasting up I-95. I don't know where I was headed. I made sure to keep my speed to an acceptable limit. Last thing on earth I needed right then was to get pulled over by some angry cop. But I was so angry! We'd gotten our asses whooped and I felt like—no, I *knew.*—I'd never get another chance like that.

Twenty, maybe thirty minutes later, I turned around and drove straight back to the hotel. Everyone was real quiet and somber, but I put on my best face and was like, *Well, that's the way it happened. Tough luck. Look forward to the future 'cause the best is yet to come.*

How motherfucking wrong I was.

❖

I GOT MY Super Bowl ring a month after the game, and Lord, was it beautiful! It had eighteen diamonds, and a ruby, too! It said *Washington Redskins, Super Bowl XVIII* on it clear as day plus a picture of the Redskins helmet, and it even had my name on it: *Roy Simmons.* Made me feel so proud! I think it was valued at something like $3,200. We're talking 'bout a serious piece of bling!

Now I'd met this pretty boy named John way back when I'd been with the Giants. He was a mixed black and Puerto Rican guy, a musician, a guitar player from 42nd Street. Not the greatest lover in the world, if the truth be told, but handsome enough to keep around for a once-in-a-while thing. About two weeks after I got my ring, John called up and said he needed to get out of New York, could he come down and stay with me for a while. I said sure, and he came down to stay for a week.

One night while he was there, I left him in the apartment and took an old high school friend of mine named Barbara out for dinner. Barbara'd moved up to D.C. many years before and had made a nice life for herself working in the FBI building. It was nice to see someone from the old neighborhood, I can tell you that! We went over to Morton's Steakhouse and ordered us some beautiful, expensive cuts of meat. Barbara couldn't get over my ring. I took it off my finger and put it on hers and she wore it all through dinner.

When we were finished eating, we made plans to meet up with another friend of ours, Althea, the very next day. But Barbara had another idea that she thought was pretty important. "Roy," she said. "Let me hold your ring, huh? Just overnight, I promise. I just want to have it for a little while, okay? I can give it back to you tomorrow, would that be all right?"

I gotta tell you, my reaction was, "Noooooo way! Uh-uh. Sorry, girl. I worked hard for that bling and it don't make no sense to me letting it outta my sight, not even for you." She was disappointed, but she said she understood.

I got home that night at about one in the morning, went into the apartment, took off all my clothes, and draped them across a chair in the living room. John was knocked out on the couch, so I tiptoed around quietly, trying not to disturb him. Then I went into the bedroom, took off all my jewelry, and put it in my jewelry box on top of the dresser. The box had a little lock on it, but I didn't latch it up. I was tired, I'd had a few drinks. I was even too pooped for hanky-panky, so I closed the door to my room and went to bed.

Dumb fucking move.

The next morning I woke up, took a shower, got dressed, and went to put on my jewelry. But it was gone. All of it. Gone. And so was John. I ran around the apartment saying, "Oh my God, oh my God, oh my God."

I had a gold necklace that I'd had since my days with the Giants. It had my Giants number on it in a big gold pendant: 69. Gone. I had a gold bracelet, my diamond cluster ring, and a diamond horseshoe ring, which my brother Larry had given me 'cause horseshoes are the symbol of my old fraternity, Omega Psi Phi. Gone, too. And my Peach Bowl ring! I'd had that damned thing for years. Gone. And my Super Bowl ring. Uh huh. That was also gone. I hit the motherfucking roof.

To show you how stupid that sonovabitch was, he hadn't taken the damn plane ticket I'd bought for him, which was sitting right out in the open on the dining room table along with about $200 in cash that I'd planned to give him for traveling money. He was stupid, all right, but obviously not as stupid as me.

I called the police. Within 15 minutes, detectives were swarming all over my apartment. They listened to everything I told them and took notes on little notepads. They nodded their heads a lot. Then they started asking me questions. *What does John look like? What does he do for a living? Did he have any friends, relations, or acquaintances in the area that I knew of? Did I know if he had much money on him?*

Then they asked me, *How would you describe your relationship to this man?* And I told them, "He's a friend. He's just a friend." They closed their notebooks and said the chances of recovering my jewelry were slim.

After the cops left, I searched the house again and found a black wallet that John had apparently left behind. I guess he'd been in such a rush to get outta the apartment, he wasn't thinking straight. There wasn't any cash in the wallet, but I found a phone number in the 718 area code—New York City—and I called it. It was John's sister, who lived in Staten Island.

I told this girl what her brother had done and then I put my intentions to her in frank terms. "I'm gonna find him, fuck him up good, and have his motherfucking ass disposed of." She freaked out when I said this. She began to plead with me over and over again, "He didn't *mean* it! He didn't *know* any better! He has *problems! Please* don't hurt him!"

But I told her, "It's too late for that. That's done now. Listen. If you see him, tell him he can keep all the other jewelry. But I want my fucking Super Bowl ring back and I'm coming up to New York to get it." The very next week, I flew up to New York to find that motherfucker and kick his ass good.

I got a rental car at the airport, drove into the city, and parked at the Port Authority. Then I walked from Broadway to Eighth Avenue and started combing up and down Times Square. I passed the porn halls, the seedy bars, the run-down restaurants, the pimps, and the whores. I remembered that John liked to shoot pool, so I combed all the pool halls, too. Talk about a tour of filth. Back then, Times Square was the worst kinda place—chock-full of the worst kinda elements.

I was dressed in my most intimidating outlaw outfit, a black leather suit and thick-heeled boots, perfect for stomping some goddamn friend-betraying, crackhead jewelry thief. Everywhere I went, I got right up in people's faces and said, "Have you seen John? Have you seen this guy?" I had to describe him to folks since I didn't have a picture of him. What a totally pointless exercise.

Of course nobody'd seen him. A young, black man in Times Square? *Yeah, we've got a few of those here.* After a few hours, I gave up. The next day I flew back to D.C.

There were messages from the police waiting for me on the answering machine at my apartment in Reston. *Mr. Simmons, we're just calling to follow up with you in the case of your stolen jewelry. Unfortunately—as we said—we believe that our chances of recovering your merchandise are slim. But we'd like to reinterview you in the hopes of coming up with a new angle. If there's any possibility of tracking this gentleman down, we'd like to do it and do it soon. Is there anything else you might have thought of in the last few days? Anything at all that might have motivated your friend to do this?* I'm thinking, *You mean like the fact that we're lovers and this was the ultimate fuck for him?*

Which is when it hit me: the danger I was in. John had gotten my jewelry, sure, and that was terrible. He was a motherfucking crook who deserved to have his skull fractured. But he'd also made off with something else that was precious to me. Something priceless, in fact: the secret of my homosexuality. If that motherfucker wanted to, he could out my ass, tell the papers, tell the world that I liked sleeping with men. That little shit really got the last laugh after all. If he wanted to, he could destroy me. Yeah, I probably should have thought of that sooner. But I was a slave to my anger. Logic didn't pertain to the situation.

Later on, I called up Barbara and told her my ring had been stolen. She said: "Oh my God! That's horrible!"

"Yes," I said. "It surely is."

She waited a beat before adding, "See? I *told* you you should have let me have the ring that night!"

❖

NOT LONG AFTER that, the Redskins cut me from the '84 training camp. Again, it was unexpected, though I guess it's *always* unexpected.

Nobody ever wants to *believe* they're gonna get cut. I remember Joe Gibbs calling me aside and telling me the team management's decision, but I don't remember exactly what he said to me. Mostly I remember the feelings, not the details. The intent, not the words. I gotta say, though, this time, I wasn't so depressed. Gibbs was kinder about cutting me than Bill Parcells had been. He said they'd hired me on to fill a slot that they were now eliminating. The Super Bowl fiasco had caused the team to reconsider it's entire offensive strategy. I said I understood. But after he was done, I began to feel so goddamn low that I was ready to go someplace else—anyplace else—and ready to do it right away.

As it turned out, getting cut from the Redskins was sort of a blessing in disguise.

11

THE VERY NEXT day I got a call from a representative of the USFL Jacksonville Bulls. This man was very nice, very cordial and respectful, and he offered me a $100,000 salary to join his team. $100,000! Sometimes I almost think there really is some kind of force out there keeping an eye out for me. How else could you possibly explain these tremendous bouts of good fortune?

Now, I have to admit: up until that point, I'd always considered the USFL to be a fake bunch of pretenders in funny-looking uniforms. I figured they weren't real athletes; they were B-list wannabes looking to make a name for themselves in the minor league before making the jump to try and become real professional football players. So the offer from the Bulls took me by complete surprise. I was like, *You gotta be kidding me. These cats aren't the real deal, this is humiliating.* I changed my opinion of the USFL pretty fast, though. Hell, back then $100,000 was enough to change *anybody's* opinion pretty fast. Especially mine.

A group from the Bulls' management flew up to Reston and I met with them at the Sheraton Hotel near my apartment. They told me about how the Bulls were trying to build a real sharp offensive line and I told *them* what I knew to be true about offensive lines by that point in my career. I told them that a line is only as good as the weakest man on it. Individual players can be stars, sure, but it takes a cohesive team to make the game work properly. They listened to everything I had to say, and then they started offering me incentives. Now my $100,000 was up around $140,000.

❖

FOR ALL THE shit I once talked about the USFL, I gotta say: I really grew to love the city of Jacksonville. I loved the area I lived in, a beautiful community called Bay Meadows. I loved the clubs, the night life, the local grocery stores, the neighbors. Pretty soon, I even grew to love the guys I was working with. Hell, these players weren't hacks. They were outstanding athletes and it was my blessing to play with them. Guys like Mike Rozier, for instance, our star running back who'd won the Heisman Trophy in 1983 and led the NCAA Division I rushers with 2,148 yards in 275 attempts. And my old friend from the Giants, J. T. Turner, took a job with the Bulls, too. He was playing guard right along side me. In many ways, it was like old times. 'Course, what we didn't know then is we were both in the twilight of our careers.

I was living large, man. Really large. The money was beautiful. The money was fine. But like I said before, I was gonna need every last cent I earned. I had some serious—and I do mean *serious*—drinking and drugging to do, and none of that comes cheap. But when I say I was living large, I'm talking about all the perks a guy can get when he plays pro football. For instance, Mike Rozier used to ship girls in from Nebraska for us! Not your typical job incentive.

On some occasions I was blowing a grand or more a day on drugs. My house became the focal point for all the partying. My teammates were very into the scene. They'd come over to my place and get totally wrecked. If I thought that guys in the NFL did a lot of drugs, I was shocked to see all the drugs guys did in the USFL.

Drugs were the center of our culture. The prevailing attitude on the team was, "Let's get this practice over with so we can get back to Roy's place and tear that fucker up." And that became the cycle of our days. *Come home from work. Get fucked up. Eat something. Sleep a little. Get up. Go to work. Come home from work. Get fucked up. Repeat.*

My brother Larry was living with me at the time. He'd come down from Savannah and got a good job as a carpenter, but mostly I remember him functioning as the Chief High Coke Cooker for our little parties. With a little practice, he got really good at it, too.

Now, during our festivities I was always the one who held himself

ROY SIMMONS | 157

back a bit. When your house is chock-full of these totally fucked up motherfuckers getting loony, you kinda want to stay on your toes. Since I was generous and single and liked to party, my teammates used my house like it was some sort of private club or opium den. They'd come in, smoke up, drink up, and lose all control of their civilized selves. Once they walked in my door, the guys practically forgot who they were.

I can't tell you how many times one of the wives would call my house looking for her husband. "Roy?" she'd say. "Is so-and-so there?" And most of the time I had to answer, "No, I don't know where he is, sorry." Sometimes what I said was true. But most of the time I was lying through my teeth. Either the husband in question was somewhere in the house and I just didn't want to be bothered to look for him or he was in the house and had left explicit instructions not to be disturbed. *Do Not Disturb* might have meant he just didn't want to talk to his wife. Or it could have meant he was fucking some girl in one of my bedrooms. Pretty much the same thing, when you think about it, I guess.

Every morning, when I woke up, I'd clean up the house and take out the trash. All the liquor bottles went into the garbage. The beer cans, the overflowing ashtrays, the bongs we'd cracked the night before throwing them at each other's heads: all into the garbage. I wanted my house as neat as a pin so that the next night's festivities could start off with a brand-new slate. I loved to have a good time but I refused to live like a slob.

Before practice, I'd drive the garbage bags over to the McDonald's and take them around back to the Dumpster. This way my neighbors would never see evidence of what we'd been up to, though I gotta say, unless they were deaf, dumb, and blind, they must have had some inkling we were throwing raging parties every night. But nobody ever complained. That was just another reason to love the city of Jacksonville!

I'd drive over to the stadium, then, and show up at practice with a sack full of ten to fifteen Egg McMuffins. They didn't last more than a few seconds. My teammates were hungry and Sugar Bear provided. Plus, in case you didn't know, the Egg McMuffin is one of the most reliable hangover remedies on earth. It'll cure what ails you, I guarantee.

❖

SOMETIMES I WONDER what my career would have been like if I hadn't been so into drugs. But then, in some ways, I have to admit that the drugs in some crazy way may have actually helped me play football better. When the Bulls were slated to go up against the Birmingham Stallions, word came down the pipe that the defense guy I'd be covering personally was this unbelievably skilled motherfucker, a real heavy hitter. He'd won all sorts of awards and everyone in the league thought he was hot shit.

For a brief moment or two, all that talk stopped me dead in my tracks and made me think about cutting down on the drugs. I didn't want to humiliate myself in front of this badass, you know? But then something inside me snapped and said, *Hey, Roy! You done all right so far with your regime, huh? You really gonna let some shitface Defense slob from Ala-fucking-bama change your tune?*

The answer to that was no.

I kicked that boy's ass all over the fucking field when we went up against the Stallions. I did it with great pleasure, too. Drugs or no drugs, NFL or no NFL, gay or straight—it didn't make a difference. I was still one of the baddest motherfuckers around.

I don't wanna give you the wrong impression, though. I sure as hell had my clean periods. In fact, I had real long periods back then when I got off the shit and stuck to my business. When I first started playing for the Bulls, I even joined the church.

See, I met this woman named Denise through some of my teammates. She'd been in the navy and we became good friends. She'd had her days of drinking and drugging, but that was all behind her now. She'd found her salvation at the Church of God By Faith, and *Lord*! To hear that woman talk about how much better she felt!

"Roy," she said, "it's like waking up one day and you're born *again*! I mean literally and for *real*! You enter the world all *new* and *fresh*! *Everyone* deserves to have an experience like *this*! Everyone deserves a second *chance*!" It sounded good to me!

So one day I went to church with Denise. And let me tell you, it made such an impact on me! People from all walks of life, all coming together on a Sunday morning. While most of teammates were sprawled out in bed, snoring off the party we'd had the night before and grumbling in their sleep as the booze and the coke and all the shit we'd eaten worked its way outta their systems, here in church was the happiest group of people I'd seen in a long, long time. I'm talking about genuinely happy people. Everyone smiling and walking right on up to greet me as a newcomer, say hello, and thank me for coming. These people had life in them, any fool could see that. We sang the most beautiful gospel hymns, too—songs that made me weep with shame at the life I'd led up to that point.

But I was still desperate. If the truth be told, I still felt lost in the world. Going to church down in Florida proved to me that I needed an anchor. Throughout my life, I hadn't had one, except for one person—Roz. Impulsively, I phoned her up and asked her to marry me. She was at work in Jersey when she took the call and she listened very carefully to what I had to say. Amazingly, when I was through stuttering and stammering my way through the proposal, she said yes! She actually said *yes!* I was overjoyed.

Next came the wedding plans. Roz's mother started shopping for dresses. I told Roz I didn't have money for a ring just yet, and that was true. I guess we both half-believed that my proposal came from a place inside me full of real love, not just my need for a good wife, a caretaker. Two weeks later, though, I couldn't deny that bleak, empty feeling that was rising up inside me again. Same feeling I'd had when Sheila and I were living at the Sheraton Hasbrouck Heights. Like it just wasn't meant to be. Like I was kidding myself. It was like I was asking myself, *Hey, man, given everything you know about yourself to be true, you sure this is what you really want? You sure you wanna be married? You sure Roz doesn't deserve someone better?*

Two weeks later I called her back and told her I had to break the engagement off. It was one of the few honest things I did back in those days. It crushed me to do it, but there was no way I could put Roz through what I'd done to Sheila. "I thought it over," I said. "I just don't think it's the right time." She was heartbroken.

❖

IT WAS MY turn to be devastated when the Jacksonville Bulls folded in '85–'86. I'd only played for the Bulls a year, but already I loved the team. I'd badmouthed the USFL all throughout my NFL days, and here I was happier than I'd ever been in my whole damn life playing for the Bulls.

It was a tragic situation. We'd heard rumblings about the team's collapse early on from the media and team representatives and finally even the coaches. I guess when you boil the situation right down it was a question of inadequate financing. I could also blame the NFL. They're such a monopoly in the business of professional football that they pretty much choked the life right out of the USFL. Not enough fans, not enough funding. By the end of my first season with the Bulls, the rumblings increased to a roar and the roar continued to get louder. Before my second season with Jacksonville, the team collapsed, and all of a sudden there I was without a job in pro football for the first time in seven years.

Little did I know that would be the last time I ever played pro ball. If I had known this, I might have done things a whole lot differently. I was still running a drug habit that cost me about $1,000 a day. That's a beast that requires a lot of feeding. Not to mention, that was money that could have gone to my daughter, investments, a future for my family. Uh-uh. I should've cut back on my excesses the moment I got the bad news. But the damned thing about hindsight is that it's always 20/20, while in the moment you only think you're seeing clearly.

I didn't lose my apartment in Bay Meadows right away. I was able to hang on to it for another few months. Eventually I gave it up and moved into a cheaper housing complex on the south side of town. My brothers Ricky and Larry came with me, of course. I wouldn't have it any other way.

With all the uncertainties I suddenly faced, I found myself turning more and more to the church. Denise and I got closer, and with her help I also came closer to kicking my drugging and drinking. Lord, that woman turned out to be just like a sister to me, kind and caring and compassionate. A true friend, a very spiritual person. I eventually moved in with her in order to save money—Ricky and Larry got their own place—and I remember how she and I spent long hours talking through the night. We talked about addiction and serenity and how the only way a person can ever hope to be free of the raging jones for drugs was to completely and utterly surrender his spirit to the Lord God Jesus Christ. These days, I'm convinced that a person has to live through this for him or herself in order to fully understand the enormous challenge this entails.

Denise, Denise. God bless that woman, she almost worked me loose. But all her hard work was about to come crashing down around her. I was about to ruin another friendship.

❖

MY FRIEND DANNY was heavy, heavy, *heavy* into cocaine, and we ended up staying out all night one time, hopping from one bar to the next, ordering drinks, downing them, ordering more. Danny was a millionaire so he could party in style. I never had to worry about who was picking up the next round. We blew through enough coke to constitute the gross national product of Peru. Eventually I made it back to Denise's apartment. It was one in the morning and I stumbled on in. Don't ask me why I did this. Looking back, it obviously wasn't the smartest thing in the world to do. But I went straight to the door of Denise's room and opened up. She sat up in bed as I turned on the light and she shrieked.

"Oh my God! Oh my God—Roy!"

"What! What is it?"

"Your eyes! Your eyes are . . ."

"What?!?!"

"Glowing!!!"

The rest of the evening didn't go so well. Denise was very, very upset with me and she got even more upset when I asked her to return the $400 microwave I'd given her as a present. I was low on cash and needed every last damn cent I could get my hands on. Now that I'd fallen off the wagon again, I wanted to buy up every last drug I could find in the Jacksonville area and do it. Reefer, coke, crack, booze—didn't matter one bit to me. I wanted to get high and I wanted to get high right goddamn *then*!

Denise refused to gimme back the microwave. She kicked me outta the apartment and I never saw her again.

❖

YOU MIGHT BE wondering where my old beautiful lover Joe was through all this. I was pretty much wondering the same thing. Our relationship had cooled a bit when I moved out to Reston, Virginia. It got positively icy after I pulled that thing with the answering machines. I don't once recall Joe coming to visit me in Florida. I think he was the only one of my friends who didn't. So, for all the love I had for that man—and I had so much—we were pretty much finished as a couple. As friends.

Joe had always told me that he wanted to marry a good woman someday. Have a home. Have kids. Have a life. It always pierced my heart to hear that. Because there was no room for me in that life. Joe was essentially admitting that our love wasn't meant to last, that I was no big thing in the long run. Plus, take a look at all I'd thrown away for him! Sheila! Kara! My whole damn shot at the storybook life I'd wanted all throughout my youth. I was like, *How dare this motherfucker drop me like that? How dare he do anything but stay with me and love me and cherish me for the rest of my goddamn life!*

But that's just what he did, and he did it sly. He didn't drop me all at once in a face-to-face conversation. Didn't even pick up the phone and tell me long distance. No, Joe just preferred to let the whole relationship die quietly, strangled by a 1700-mile-long cord that ran from Newark down to Jacksonville, Florida.

❖

I DID GET closure later on. Although my relationship with Joe cooled substantially after the answering machine incident, I never stopped loving him. I even felt the need to apologize. So a few years later, I was back up north and I finally picked up the phone to call him. Doing that meant I had to suck in my gut. Swallow my pride. But I did call him. He said he was glad to hear from me and we set up a dinner date at our old favorite place, The Pink Teacup down in Greenwich Village.

I was so glad to see him when he walked through that door. Glad to see him and terrified at the same time. I jumped up from my seat and gave him a fierce hug that lasted a long, long time.

We sat down and ordered and spent the next few hours doing a good job talking about nothing of any real consequence. Anytime I asked about how Joe was doing, he just sort of laughed and said that everything was fine, fine, fine. I'd press him a little, try to get something out of him. Some little detail, some hint of what he was doing, who he was seeing. When he answered me, it was like he was trying to explain something complicated to a child who could never understand. "I'm good, Roy," he'd say. "I'm really, good. So. How are you? Hear from Roz lately?"

Later on Joe dropped me off at Penn Station in his brand-new black Lincoln Navigator. We had about twenty minutes before my train got in, so we sat in the car and talked a little more. More polite talk, that's all it was. Every word was another disappointment. Finally the clock rolled around and Joe said, "Well, I guess it's time." He sounded relieved. "This was fun, Roy. It was really great seeing you."

I couldn't let it end like that and started talking like a mad man. I said stupid things like, "Hey, man! Me, too!" My voice sounded way too happy in my own ears. Way too cool. "I really enjoyed dinner! Whoa, such a nice time! Really nice seeing you, too! Hey! We should do it again some time. Some time really soon, you know? Think we could do that? You wanna do that? I love your truck, man, really love your truck, and you know what? You look good! Man, you look really good. You still working out or what?"

Joe smiled politely and said that yeah, we should do it again sometime. Sometime real soon. Then he looked at his watch and said, "Hey, you'd better get going or you're gonna be late."

Okay. I get it, man. 'Bye.

I gave him a hug and climbed out of the truck. Joe waved through the window and drove away, he left me standing on that dark corner right there in the heart of New York City. And just like that, I knew he was gone for good.

❖

I ENDED UP staying in Jacksonville. Got a job working for AT&T in the Equal Access department, nine to five making $11 an hour. How the mighty have fallen. I was in big trouble. The bills were running way too high and the drugs were costing way too much. The more I did drugs the more I wanted *more* drugs. Larry and I would drive down to Miami every other weekend and pick up kilos of the shit. At this point Larry was supplementing his income as a carpenter by working as a dealer. He'd learned a lot by apprenticing himself as the Chief High Coke Cooker to the Jacksonville Bulls. Thank God he did, too, 'cause I sure as hell was too poor to keep up my lifestyle. Larry used to toss me a bone every now and then, slide me a little packet of shit 'cause he knew I was in need.

Sometimes I'd look at Larry and wonder, you know? This was the same kid who'd once fleeced Florida Southern University for everything he could pull from them. He was a natural-born hustler, like Jimmy Hester. He had talent and he had the moves. He was making money. He was going places. Me? I was going nowhere fast.

I lived like this for nine months before I ran out of everything: money, options, gumption, and patience. It was time for me to get the hell outta Jacksonville.

With no money, I moved back home to Savannah but I didn't want anyone to know I was in town—not friends, not family, and certainly not the media. I avoided everyone. I'd left Savannah with the world laying itself open at my feet. How could I tell people I was back again with no job, no prospects, no direction, and a raging drug habit? And what if they somehow found out I was gay on top of all that? Maybe coming home was the worst move for me to make, but I felt I needed an anchor back then; I figured I'd find it there. I was wrong.

❖

MEANWHILE, JIMMY HESTER was taking over New York City. He had stepped up his party-brokering enterprises big time. He threw an NFC Championship soirée at the Visage in Manhattan the night the Giants beat the Redskins 17–0 and earned the right to take a shot at the title in the upcoming Super Bowl XXI.

You shoulda seen the guest list for that bash! Chris Rock. Mike Tyson. Salt-N-Pepa. Jimmy's contact list was beginning to look like a Who's Who in American Entertainment. I always knew the kid had it in him, but he was really stretching himself now, really going for the gold. I guess almost everybody on the Giants showed up, too. Lots of guys I knew were there. LT. Carl Banks. Leonard Marshall. Mark Collins. Terry Kinard, Sean Landeta, Mark Bavaro, Phil McConkey, and Byron Hunt. I didn't go. The thought of attending made me feel too weird. But Jimmy did such a good job pulling that damn party together that Lionel Manuel, William Roberts, and Andy Headen approached him with the idea of putting together a Super Bowl video.

Football team videos were all the rage back in the mid to late '80s. The Chicago Bears had come out with their smash hit, *The Super Bowl Shuffle*, just the year before. I guess everybody in America really appreciated seeing William "The Refrigerator" Perry shaking his ass and getting his groove on. The Bears had touched a nerve and now the Giants wanted to follow suit.

Jimmy called me up and told me everything that was going on in his life. You shoulda heard his voice, he was so damn excited. I was happy for him, too. Honestly, I was. But somewhere deep inside me, I was bleeding. I couldn't help feeling like my life was doomed and I had only myself to thank or something. I'd been a Giant once. I coulda been in that video. *Shit, you think The Refrigerator's got some fresh dance moves? You ain't never seen Roy Simmons cut a rug. I coulda been in that video. I coulda been a major star.* How had I lost it all so fast?

Jimmy flew out to Pasadena and watched the Giants beat the Broncos to win the Championship. This time I wasn't there to ask him for some coke. I wasn't part of that world anymore. I'd been cast aside and forgotten.

12

I DECIDED TO start over and ended up moving back north, where I took a room at the YMCA in downtown Newark. I liked it there 'cause the building was full of dealers and that made it easy for me to snort up and freebase. It was like a private little hotel for druggies, my own little cocaine community. The only problem was that Roz refused to visit me there even though she lived close by. She hated that place so much that she made a personal pact with herself to never set foot in there. She wasn't the only one. Even though I was practically down the street from many of my former teammates and hordes of my own relatives, I kept such a low profile that I might as well have been living on the other side of the world.

Around this point, my old friend Dr. Goldberg tried to help me out once again. Totally unaware that I was a raging alcoholic, he helped me get a job at a liquor store in Livingston. I became the assistant manager, making $15 an hour. I ordered bottles, set up displays, kept inventory, and so forth. I was also responsible for closing up the store, which naturally meant that a lot of bottles made their way into a box at the end of the night. And the box made its way into the back seat of the cab that took me home. I had a fully stocked bar at my place.

During this phase of my life I was so far gone on drugs and alcohol that I nearly killed myself a couple of times over. A man can do himself some serious damage when he's up all night every night downing quarts of top-shelf liquor: *Courvoisier, Rémy Martin, and Korbel Extra Dry Champagne. Tanqueray gin, Taylor port, and Blue Nun.* I was drinking so much that I frequently forgot to eat. Between the coke and the drinking,

I nearly collapsed in my seedy little room at the Y. I was running real hard and real fast away from something—but what? I was lost.

I guess I wasn't ready to go like that 'cause at one point I knew I was in such a bad way that I walked across the street to the hospital and put myself at their mercy. They admitted me and kept me for three or four days. They pumped fluids into me 'cause I was on the verge of yellow jaundice.

None of my colleagues at the liquor store ever noticed the missing bottles. There was so much dissension within that company! All the managers were trying to cutthroat each other. Last thing they cared about was inventory. They left that all up to me. Damn fools.

I ended up transferring to another outlet for the liquor chain in Newark. It was closer to where I now lived, but I hated that damn place. Smack dab in the middle of the ghetto. And wouldn't you know it? I found out that certain products were ordered in abundance to cater to particular regions. For instance, there hadn't been any malt liquor at the Livingston store. But in Newark the shelves were stocked up tight with 40-ounce bottles of Colt 45, Crazy Horse, Brick House, St. Ide's, Black Bull, Black Belt, Black Ice, and Black Label. The key word here was "black'"—as in, *a selection of liquors to keep black people numb.*

I hated working that store. The manager was a crook who treated the customers like shit, took whatever he wanted, and fixed the receipts so he could make off with funds. I mean, sure, I stole liquor, too. But I made sure to smile real polite and say my "pleases" and "thank-yous," I never treated anyone badly. I lasted two months at that liquor store.

❖

SOMEWHERE IN ALL this, I met a guy named Chris at Murphy's, which had become my almost-every-night gay bar hangout. This guy was small and neat, a high-yellow-toned African American who could almost have passed himself off as a white man with a suntan. He had a neat little trimmed mustache and always wore Armani suits. He did administrative work and apparently was real good at it; that boy told me he could type 60 words a minute. Not bad for a guy who'd never crossed paths with Mavis Beacon! Chris's ex-lover had put him out. I never got to the bottom of that story. But I let him stay with me after we'd met a few times. I had to sneak him into my room each night 'cause the Y had an absolute no visitors policy.

Now, this should give you a pretty clear idea about the kind of moods I was prone to around this time: One night Chris and I went out to a club and he was drinking up a storm, but for once I didn't feel like staying. I told him, "Look, man. I'm going home. You coming with me or not?" Home being my tiny little room at the YMCA. That was home for both of us just then.

Chris said, "No, no, I'll be home later." He was acting real glib, like he was staying at the Ritz-Carlton or someplace fine where he could just saunter in and out whenever he wanted. He was definitely not clear on the circumstances we were operating under. I said, "Hell with that, man. You don't come home now, I ain't gonna be able to get you in the damn door." Which was partially true—like I said, the Y *did* have a policy.

But there was another layer to all this, and that's the fact that I get jealous real easily. Jealous like I'd been with Joe. Chris wasn't much, but he was all I had back then. I'd be damned if he was gonna pick up guys and get his piece on while I waited around at home like an old nanny. That shit was just *not* gonna happen.

I tried to be reasonable. I told him to be home by 12:30 and I left Murphy's. I went straight home and sat around, waiting and waiting. Kept myself from looking at the clock for hours by sheer force of will until finally I couldn't cut it anymore. I glanced over at the digital on the wall. One A.M. No Chris.

That's when I sort of lost control.

I took all that bitch's Armani suits outta the closet, along with all his beautiful tailored shirts and his lovely silk ties. Administrative work? Damn, that couldn't have paid much. Chris obviously wasn't well off—he sure as hell didn't have his own place to crash at. Those suits must have been what he plowed all his money into. His prized possessions. The illusion of affluence. Chris was a poseur. A pretender. He withheld his true self from people. Hell, I was aware of that; it takes one to know one. Maybe this attack on him was really all about an attack on myself, I don't know. But I threw everything into a big pile in the center of the room and tried to light them on fire. They wouldn't burn, which only got me angrier.

So I gathered up the whole pile and took the elevator down to the street level. Went out to the corner, where I doused his whole fucking wardrobe with hairspray and tried again. They burned this time, all right. Oh *man* did they motherfucking *burn*!

Lucky for me nobody was around in the street to see me doing this. So I walked off into the night with this huge-ass smile on my face and went back up the elevator of my building. When I got to my room, I looked out my window and watched the fire department show up. They started scrambling around to put out the fire. Who would've thought eight Italian suits would cause such a goddamn blaze?

Eventually I heard a knock at the door and I opened it. In walked Chris with this drunken, huge-ass smile on his face. He was having the night of his life. Poor stupid sonovabitch. I guess he saw some kinda expression on my face or something cause almost immediately he said, "What's wrong? What happened?" And I had to tell him at that point. Which was kinda weird. Hearing me tell what I'd done was like listening to somebody else's voice coming out of my very own head. I think that's the first time in my life that I ever suspected that I might have something mentally wrong with me. What kind of a man would do what I'd just done? I told him I'd burned his motherfucking clothes.

Chris did not take the news well. He started blubbering. "No, man. No, Roy. Please. You didn't—aw, shit! Tell me you didn't do that! Why? Why?" He ran to the closet door and threw it open. No suits, no shirts, no ties, no nothing. "WHY WOULD YOU DO THAT?!?"

I didn't have an answer for him and that's when I started to feel real bad. Chris actually started to cry, and when he did he looked real small, like a child who'd just lost his best friend. He sat there on the edge of the bed and rocked back and forth, holding his sides, poor man. Part of me felt this incredible guilt, this horrible, gut-wrenching sorrow and revulsion over what I'd done. But all I did was stand there and watch him cry.

Finally, after a long while, he got hold of himself. Calmed down and looked at me, very clear-headed. Not even angry. He said, "I can't believe you would *do* this to me." Like I said, I felt bad. I mean really, *really* bad. I really wanted Chris's suits to come back. Somehow I hoped they would just *reappear.* But it never happens like that. What's gone is gone.

The next day, Chris was gone, too.

❖

MY MONEY FINALLY started dwindling down from *very little* to *practically nothing.* I got so poor I had to leave the Y, even. Ended up moving in with an old fraternity brother who lived ten minutes away in a place called the Colonnade Apartments deep in the heart of downtown Newark. Not the most pleasant place to be under most circumstances, but as I soon found out, it had excellent perks.

I'd met this fraternity brother at a popular club. His name was James and he was a retired schoolteacher who'd started working at a local hospital. And through this man, I was introduced to something I never really knew existed before: a working gay community.

James brought me around to meet all his friends and I sure as hell was impressed. These were professional people who kept really nice apartments, enjoyed good food, and upheld a high standard of living. They were office managers and corporate supervisors and professional educators and financial officers. On the outside, they appeared to be straight. On the inside, they were all as queer as a two-dollar bill.

In this community, everybody knew everybody else. They helped each other out wherever they could. They traded professional services, referrals, and skills too for help painting their apartment or shifts in the neighborhood watch group. They genuinely loved and valued each other. They loved and valued *me.* I tell you, this was a major eye opener for me. I'd never seen anything like it. This was the first time I began to feel pride about being gay.

A few of the guys I was introduced to made passes at me, but that's as far as it went. I was flattered. One of my friends was a gay man named David who came from Beverly Hills. David took a shine to me early on. He was very well-respected in this group—he was kinda the leader of the pack. So I became well-respected, too. It wasn't all that hard to win their admiration, actually. I guess some folks would be surprised at how many gay folks actually turn out to be hardcore sports fans. The fact that I'd once played pro ball gave me a sort of celebrity which I didn't deny.

I still got high, I still got drunk. In spite of the grounding influence of my new gay friends, I still slept with whoever, whenever, for whatever reason. As far as the crack was concerned, I used to stand in line at the project across the street from our apartment, a building that was boarded up and condemned and scheduled for demolition. There were people living inside who had a system set up. They sent a runner out and took money from the next person waiting on line. The runner took the money deep into the bowels of the building and came back with crack. I think everybody in the neighborhood knew what was going on. I'm pretty sure the cops even knew what was going on. I didn't care. I stood right out in the open anyway and waited my turn.

Looking back, after all I'd been through, you'd think I would've learned. But that's assuming you're dealing with a calm, logical, rational person. None of these terms can describe me back then. None of these terms can describe an addict. An addict will walk thirty-five miles in his bare feet over broken glass to get one hit. An addict will sell her own infant to lay her hands on some really good shit; hell, she'll sell her kid just to lay her hands on some *medium-grade* shit. Addiction is a form of hopelessness. It's that black hole that fills up your spirit when you've lost all faith—faith in God, faith in your fellow man, faith in yourself. When you've fallen into the deepest depths of that hole, you'll cling to anything at all that feels safe and firm, even the things you know will eventually destroy you. The crack pipe. The vial. The bottle. The spike. You might as well not even be human anymore. A stumbling, moaning zombie from one of those old B-movie horror films has more life in him than an addict at his worst. They smell better, too.

Then one night I was walking through that lot and I took myself upstairs to a room where I was sure I could score some rocks. I bought some shit and went back downstairs. As I was coming outta the building I heard this voice say, "Stop right there. Gimme your fucking drugs."

The first thought that went through my head was, *What's he talking 'bout, "gimme your fucking drugs?" Is this motherfucker crazy?*

I was about to say something out loud when the guy put a gun to my head and pulled the trigger. I heard the hammer go click. And my heart stopped. My body went stiff. I couldn't breathe. I thought, *Am I dead? Is this what it feels like to be dead? I didn't even hear the explosion.*

Next thing I knew, I was alone. All I heard was footsteps running away in the dark. And suddenly I realized I was alive. I could still move. Something had happened and the bastard was getting away. Which is when I started to chase his ass down.

For a guy who abused himself the way I did, I was still pretty fast. Fast and big. I caught up with that sonovabitch in the parking lot of the project and I jumped on his motherfucking ass, tore the gun outta his hand, and started beating him in the head with it. All the while I heard somebody screaming and cursing. Then I realized that somebody was me.

"Motherfucker, motherfucker, fucking motherfucker!" *WHAP! WHAP! WHAP!* "Trying to rob my ass?! And for what? Huh? For *what*?!?" *WHAP! WHAP! WHAP!* "For a piece a motherfucking fucked-up crack?!" *WHAP! WHAP! WHAP!* "Piece a fucking god-damned rock cocaine?!?!" *WHAP! WHAP! WHAP!*

I took the gun and put it to his head like he'd done to me. The bastard screamed, "No! No! No!" I jammed the barrel into his ear and pulled the motherfucking trigger. Click! Guess it hadn't been a misfire after all: asshole didn't have any goddamn bullets in his gun. He was probably so stoned out he'd forgot to load it. I beat him up some more and left the parking lot real fast.

I walked home in a trance. I couldn't believe what had happened. I couldn't believe I'd been robbed, almost killed. I still had the fucking gun in my hand. I'm walking around downtown Newark in the middle of the street with this fucking gun in my hand and a pocket full of money and crack cocaine. I was a police officer's dream—I knew it, and I just couldn't give a shit. I almost shot that guy. For the first time in my life, I almost wanted to be dead. Wanted to put an end to the insanity. Killing myself seemed the only way to accomplish that.

I couldn't figure out what to do next so I stopped by this club called Zanzibar where a friend of mine worked the door. You shoulda seen the eyes on him when I walked toward him. "Roy?" he said. "ROY?!?" I guess he saw the gun and all. I kept walking toward him.

"You know what fucking just happened to me?" I heard this voice say. Still couldn't recognize the sound of my own voice. "Some guy just tried to *rob* my ass! See?" This is the part where I held up the gun to make sure he could see it. My friend looked at it, all right. And he said this again: "Roy?!? Roy?!?"

"This is the goddamned gun I took off his motherfucking, crack-dealing black ass!"

"Okay, Roy. Okay."

"Fucker tried to shoot me."

"Okay. Okay. I got it."

"Look at this gun!"

"I see it. Are you okay?"

"Fucker tried to shoot me with this gun!"

"Roy, you need to go home."

"I almost got shot!"

"Go home, Roy. Go home!"

This sort of made sense to me. So I turned around and walked home.

Later on, when my roommate James got home, I told him what happened and showed him the gun, too, just so he'd believe me. He acted concerned when I was telling him the story. But the gun sort of changed his mood. He was like, "Roy, get that goddamn thing outta my house right now." I told him I would. But I didn't do it right away.

Turns out this was a good move 'cause a little later on I was walking down the street near the project when a guy came up to me and said, "Yo." I turned around and looked him right in the eye. After the whole shit deal with the dude and the gun and all that, I was in no mood to take shit from anyone. I said, "What?"

"Hear you've got something that belongs to a friend of mine."

"So fucking what? Do I know you, motherfucker?"

The guy backed up a step. I could see him reevaluating the situation.

He didn't look like he had the sand to get into anything. He wasn't the mastermind. He was just the messenger. "All I'm sayin' is that word a mouth is that you got a gun. Further word a mouth says that my friend wants the gun back. He's willing to pay for it."

"How much?"

"Dunno."

"How *much*?!"

"Yo, man. You wanna talk deal, you talk to my friend. I'm just— you know."

"Yeah. I know. You're just the messenger."

"That's right."

I went back to the project later on and brought the gun with me. I wasn't scared. I just walked right up to the same room I usually went to when I made my buys. Knocked on the door and somebody opened up. There was a whole bunch of people inside. Some were getting high, but most were already there. All activity stopped when I walked in the room. I took a moment to size everybody up, then I said, "I got something for somebody. I'm gonna pull it out real slow." And I did. I pulled out the gun. I announced it like that cause in a crack house you never know who's packing heat and who's jumpy. You never know who's gonna take offense at whatever and you can never say for sure that anybody's on your side. So I warned them first and played it real cool. Even then, you could see everybody watching the gun like it was about to go off in their faces.

I gave the gun back for $40 worth of rock, all of which was gone by the time I left the project that night. For better or worse, the whole stupid incident was over. Now maybe you think *that* finally would have been enough for me. Hell, for anybody. Oh no, sir. The worst was truly yet to come.

❖

THE LAST HARROWING experience I had in Newark was the time I went back to the projects after the gun incident, bought more crack, and was leaving the building, same as last time, when I got jumped with the gun. This time, however, as I was moving through the lot, I ran smack dab into this young fucking punk with a monstrous white pit bull with a spiked collar and some kinda industrial boat chain for a leash. Fat links of steel. The punk says to me, "Yo, man. I *know* you got drugs for me. Gimme *all* your fucking drugs or I'm gonna have this pit bull here bite your ass and chew it up."

Now, I had a few hundred dollars in my pocket at that precise moment. Plus I was wearing a gold necklace, a beautiful piece of jewelry. But all this kid wanted was the four, maybe five 20-rocks of crack I had on me. Which at the time seemed like a pretty fair price to pay in order to not get bit. Hell, I'd never seen a pit bull with a chest that big neither! I wasn't about to stand around and negotiate.

So I threw all the drugs on the ground and I said, "Here! Dammit! Take 'em! Take 'em all!" And just in the case that dog was hungry I turned right around and jumped on the back of a car that was parked nearby and stood on its motherfucking roof. The guy just bent right over liked he'd dropped a pen out of his pocket. Picked up the crack just as easy as you please, didn't say nothing about it. Then he and the pit bull started strolling along like they was just taking in the evening. I hauled ass back home.

❖

AFTER LIVING IN Newark, I moved out to Passaic, where things really began to bottom out. Once again, I moved into the Y, which was smaller but nicer than the one I'd stayed at in Newark. The administrators had more of a lock on what was going on in the place so there weren't any drugs around that I could see, and trust me! I looked!

The nicest part about living at the Passaic Y was the fact that it was right around the corner from my job. I worked as a supervisor at a Catholic Church shelter for runaways. I had no experience, but they felt my sports background would help me to connect with the kids. Needless to say, they knew nothing at all about my drug use.

I really loved that job. It made me feel responsible, like I was contributing something to the community. I dealt with people who were most definitely in need and I believe that we made a tremendous difference in their lives on a deeply personal level. For the first time in years I felt proud of myself. For the first time in years I felt like I was healing. Maybe helping those kids was a way of helping the little kid in me, I don't know. But I suddenly found myself smiling a lot. Suddenly, I had that old spring back in my step.

Unfortunately, I lasted only four months. Someone overheard me talking to a friend over the phone about ordering drugs and the administration called me into a conference room the next day, questioned me, and asked me to leave immediately.

Looking back, I think I sabotaged myself at that job. I can be dumb sometimes but I'm not stupid. There was no damn reason in the world to talk about drugs over the phone at work, no reason at all. It was almost as if I wanted to get caught. Then I'd have one more excuse to check out of reality and spend all day getting high again.

❖

BELIEVE IT OR not, I moved back in with Aunt Betty after calling her up and finding out that she was willing to give me another chance. And while I was living in Orange again I saw a help wanted ad in the *Newark Star-Ledger* for an intake clerk at the city bankruptcy court. The ad said *WANTED: people with good organizational and people skills.* I thought, *Hell, okay, let's try it again. Let's see if we can make something work this time. C'mon, Roy. Let's see if we can do it* right *this time.*

I got the job and soon found out that every piece of mail that came into the building where I worked had to pass through my hands. That was an awesome responsibility. I had to examine every envelope, package, flyer, and legal document we received, designate it for a particular judge or a department within the court system, stamp it, wrap it, and send it on its way.

Imagine! Me: on the side of the law for once. Who would've figured? I was sworn into my office and given a badge of the court. I was given—I still can't believe this—the largest office in the whole building and I was making about $45,000 a year. Suddenly I was a success! I even flirted with the idea of cleaning up my act for good, getting off the drugs, buying a house, settling down.

I was making friends again. I handled the mail for the chief clerk of the court. She was from Georgia, too, so we took an instant liking to one another. Her name was Cecilia. She was a workaholic and I liked that. If I managed to stay sober at a job I found out that I was a workaholic, too, deep down—I liked to get really *into* a job. But I don't think Cecilia ever figured out I was still doing cocaine. Mostly snorting it now. Sometimes I'd come to work and get nosebleeds from the bingeing I'd done the previous evening.

❖

IN TIME, I made more bad choices, like moving away with a new lover named Gerald. It was an impulsive decision. He'd had a bad spat with his former lover and one thing led to another. We got together and decided to give it a go out in Pennsylvania where he'd grown up. After all I'd been through by that point, I should have been able to see we weren't meant to last. My heart screamed at me that the whole affair was moving too quickly. But just like before, I was still looking for an anchor. In fact, I think I wanted an anchor in my life more than I wanted anything else in the world. I was willing to take crazy risks to get it. Three months after I went away with Gerald, I was right back in Jersey again.

❖

THE LATE '80s were an especially rough time for me. Suddenly there was a new word in everyone's vocabulary, a word that people I knew— gay men—were using all the time in conversation: AIDS.

By that point, AIDS was a full-fledged global epidemic. Back in the early '80s it started out being called the Gay Plague. Because it hit gay men so strongly, some scientists claimed the disease could wipe out the entire gay community within a few years. Holy Rollers even said that AIDS was God's retribution against the Sodomites for putting Adam and Steve above Adam and Eve, or some such shit.

'Course, as time went on, we found out so much more about the disease. Word started trickling down that it wasn't just a gay thing at all, but a virus that could strike anybody. It's primary victims were gay men, recipients of unscreened blood, crack babies, and intravenous drug users. I remember thinking, *Hell, man! Lucky me! I ain't no crack baby,*

I don't use needles, and I ain't never received bad blood. Only thing I gotta worry 'bout's one outta four—and them odds ain't bad! Besides, I usually wore condoms when I had sex. Usually, but not always.

I felt listlessness back then from having no direction in life. I wasn't able to hold down a good, nurturing relationship or a full-time job, and my addictions were at their peak. The whole damn world seemed like it was awash in cocaine. Whole blocks of time, months and months at a time, went by and I can't tell you with any degree of certainty what the hell I was doing. Except that I was doing drugs. Lots and lots of drugs.

Everybody I knew at the time was high on something, but in the middle of that craziness at least one of us got clean. Jimmy Hester climbed on board a flight bound for Houston one day to visit old friends and met a minister of God who, by pure chance, turned out to be his seatmate. Jimmy's soul was saved that day in mid-air as his plane awaited landing instructions in Texas. Right after that, he got sober. Looking back, I guess I could say that this was also *my* first step on the path to sobriety, but my journey would take much, much longer.

❖

IF THE '80s were my lowest point, the '90s at least saw the beginning of my truth-telling. Specifically, I was outted to my family by my younger cousin, Alisha, the same little girl whose kindergarten class I had visited back in my days with the New York Giants. She was twenty years old now and, like most women in the Simmons clan, stubborn as a mule. I had her over to my place one time and she was recalling the past, mostly the part about how her cousin Betty had always had such a big crush on Joe. And that's when I came right out and told her. It wasn't planned or anything like that. Looking back, it was easier than I'd ever imagined possible.

I said, "Joe's gay."

And she said, "Say what?"

I repeated, "Joe's gay."

"How do you know?"

"'Cause he was my lover." Just like that, it was done.

❖

I HAD NO idea what kinda repercussions that tiny little conversation was about to make in my life, however. If I did, I might never have outted myself to Alisha. She and Roz were really close—they used to do one another's hair. Shortly after I'd confided in Alisha, Roz called the house to find out where I was. By that point in our relationship, Roz had forgiven me for breaking off our engagement. The quality of her mercy, however, was about to be strained once more.

Roz asked Alisha where I was and what was going on and why, all of a sudden, was I not paying any attention to her? Was I seeing someone else? she asked. Alisha just told her flat out. "Roy's gay," she said.

"Gay? He's—what? He's what?"

"Gay," said Alisha. "He's bisexual. Just don't tell him I told you so." Roz was shocked.

Alisha told me later that she told Roz 'cause they were real close friends and Roz felt that I was playing her for a fool by sleeping with her again on the side. Alisha knew that I was acting wild and promiscuous and she felt that I could possibly do Roz some harm, emotionally if not physically. Hell, she was right. But I wasn't prepared for it to come out so fast; I didn't want Roz or *anybody* to know. But it doesn't work that way. Once you tell one person, the matter is outta your hands. Your secret goes wherever it goes and you just have to follow.

Roz called me up that night. "Why didn't you tell me?"

And I said, "Tell you what?"

"Why didn't you tell me about Joe?"

"What about Joe?"

"DON'T LIE TO ME!!!"

She just sort of exploded like that, outta nowhere, and all I could do was sit there staring at the phone with my mouth wide open. She didn't have to say anything else at that point. She knew, that was all. And I knew that she knew. The lies, the secrets, the sneaking around. It was all over with Roz.

"Why didn't you tell me?" She was crying. "Why did you make me find out like this?"

I made one last chance at playing the game. "Roz, what the hell are you talking about?"

"Don't," she said. "Don't. Alisha told me."

And just like that, my black ass was outted. Happy motherfucking New Year's to me.

Roz spoke a lot that night and I spoke very little. She had a lot of things she wanted to get off her chest, so I did what was right and just let her keep right on talking. Besides, when you got right down to it, I only had one thing to say to her anyway. Those two little words: *I'm sorry.* I kept repeating that over and over again. Didn't seem to help much. "Dammit, Roy! If I'd have known? I would have ended everything, right then and there. You took all my choices away from me. You had no right to do that."

I nodded. "Look, this is a horrible time for me. I can see you're completely—"

"You?!? What the hell you going on about you, you, you, *you*?!?! That's the problem with you, Roy! That's the whole damn problem right there! It's all about *you*. It's never about anybody else."

She dropped me back off at my house and I went inside with every intention in the world to fucking kill my cousin, Alisha. I wanted to wring her goddamn neck for telling Roz what she did. As it was, I chased her around the house when I got home, but she was nimble. I'd get near her and she'd pick things up off the coffee table—picture frames, table lamps, books, knickknacks, you name it—and throw them at me. I was temporarily insane with anger. "C'mere you little bitch!" Alisha picked up this little crystal thing that I'd got from an officemate one Christmas. Hauled back like it was a baseball and fucking threw at it at me. Line drive, straight up the center. Caught my shoulder and bounced the fuck off. Ugggghh. "What right?!?" she demanded. "What right did *you* have?!? Roz is a sweet person! She loved you and you did that to *her*?!?"

"I was gonna tell her," I said. "Dammit, I was gonna tell her." But we both stopped for a second when I said that; we both knew I was lying.

❖

So THAT's HOW it happened. No more hiding for me. Everything I'd worked so hard to keep in the closet for so long was now out in the open for everyone to see. I knew how things like that worked; my secret would get around. Alisha knew and she obviously wasn't so great at keeping things to herself. Roz knew and that woman couldn't lie to save her life. When someone asked her why she was so upset, and they were bound to, she'd have to tell them. I knew how it worked; word would get around. I'd lost everything and everyone: Sheila and Kara, my football career, my football friends, Joe, Kathy, my job, and the respect of my family. Now I'd even lost Roz, the one woman who'd stayed with me through it all, the one woman who was always there, even when times got rough.

My life was changed forever. There was nothing left for me in New Jersey, nothing left in Georgia. I'd burned every bridge I ever crossed in cities around the country. Bad move, in retrospect. 'Cause now I found myself in a position where I had to escape, to flee. Find someplace new and start over and maybe lead an openly gay life for a change, kill a few demons in the process. This is what I told myself I was up to, at any rate. But really, who knows? Maybe I was trying to liberate myself, maybe I was just running away one more time. In the end, the only thing that's clear to me is that I went to the bank, withdrew ten grand, and booked myself a flight on Delta Airlines. The next day I flew to San Francisco, gay capital of the world.

13

Turns out I was wrong when I said that I'd lost Roz. Hurt her, yes—I'd hurt her bad—and I hated myself for it. But true to form, Roz forgave me. In fact, she even drove me out to Newark Airport.

I sort of thought she offered to take me to the airport 'cause she wanted me on the next plane outta town. But then I saw the tears in her eyes as we got closer to my departure gate. She told me outta the blue, "Roy, I still love you." And I didn't know what to say to that. Stupid fucking me. I just sat there and stared out the window. I didn't want to make things any worse for her.

Before we parted, she kissed me on the cheek and held my face close to hers for a long, long time. She wasn't crying anymore, she was done with that by then. Now it looked more to me like she was trying to take a picture of my face, like she knew she was never gonna see it again. "Roy," she said, all clear and reasonable. "Don't do this. I don't think this is a good idea. You're running away from another problem. What will this accomplish? Stay here with me. Stay here with your family. We'll find a way, all of us, to deal with this together."

I shouldn't have refused an offer like that. Shoulda said yes and let my new life begin right there. But I wasn't ready to take control of my life. Crazy as it sounds, I preferred the chaos. Sometimes I think we're all of us like stones dropped into a big pool of water that's called life. It takes some of us longer than others to settle into a buoyancy that's comfortable. Me? My life has taught me I'm the heaviest stone that ever walked the face of the earth. I was still plunging straight down.

I hadn't touched bottom. Not yet. There was still open water beneath my feet.

"I gotta go," I said, and picked up my bag.

Roz just gave me that look. Sort of the same look that Grandma Lou used to give me. Roz and Grandma Lou had similar streaks in them. Quiet. Powerful. Direct. No apologies. Roz said, "Call me when you get there." And just like that, she turned and walked away.

❖

I KNEW SAN Francisco a little from my days playing ball. I planned to stay at the Hilton when I first arrived, but just a few blocks away from the hotel I saw a crowd of people hanging out on a street corner. It was the Tenderloin district. First class ticket to trouble. I told the limousine driver to please stop the car. At first he refused to do it.

"Sir," he said. "Excuse me, but . . . you don't want to get out of the car here."

"Yes, I do."

"No, sir. You don't. This is a very bad neighborhood."

"Don't tell me what to do, goddammit. I said stop the car." And he did.

You shoulda seen the look on all those faces when they saw big ol' me climbing outta the back of that polished limousine carrying my nice luggage. My eyes met a few different sets of eyes and the understanding that passed between us all was instantaneous and real.

Welcome to the party, man. Welcome to the jungle.

❖

I FOUND A hotel that was cheaper than the Hilton. Much, much cheaper. I put down a week's worth of rent, got to my room, took a shower, put on some cologne and fresh clothes. Just like that I was ready for the night. I locked the door behind me and went hunting.

First I stopped at a pay phone to call Roz like I promised. We didn't say much during that conversation. I think we were both still sort of in shock over my coming out. Roz said, "Be careful, Roy. Just be careful." I told her I would and I hung up the phone. Felt this twinge of guilt pulling at my gut, too, 'cause I knew that I'd just lied to her. Honestly? Careful was not something I was real interested in being that evening. I was interested in other things entirely.

I turned around, tapped a passerby on the shoulder, and said, "Excuse me, man. Where's the best gay club in town?" He told me to head to a place called the Blue & Gold.

I marched right up to the bar and downed a few cocktails fast, which attracted the attentions of the bald-headed, muscled-up bartender. He propped both his elbows on the bar, leaned in real close, and said, "What's up, man? How you doing?"

I said, "I'm doing pretty good right now. I just landed."

He smiled real big. "Is that so?"

We ended up sitting by the fireplace in his apartment up in the hills of Daly City. I drank champagne and we made out. Talk about moving fast! I hadn't even changed my watch over from Eastern Standard Time, and here I was already getting laid! I stayed the night. Took the BART train back to my hotel the next morning.

Me and that bald-headed bartender actually grew to be very fond of one another over the next few weeks. But he was clean and sober, never touched drugs at all, and that grew to be an inseparable barrier.

A little later that first week I called my aunt Betty, who was one of the only family members I'd told I was leaving. She knew I was gay by this point. Just like Roz, she didn't have much to say to me. And just like Roz, she told me to be careful. But what did I know about being careful?

A little later in my second month in San Francisco, I called up Sheila. She knew by that point. I don't know precisely how. But word had trickled down through family members up north, trickled all the way down to Savannah and the fiancée I'd left behind. Why'd I call her? I don't know. I guess I figured she had a right to know. I guess I figured she had a right to hear it from me.

"Why didn't you tell me?" she asked. Same question everyone had asked, but for Sheila the answer had to be different. "How could I? Baby, I was in love with you. How do you do that? That's really hard to do."

She said, "How do you *not* do it? You know what you never really understood, Roy? Just 'cause something's hard to do doesn't mean you shouldn't do it. Fact of the matter is, the only things in life *worth* doing are the things that seem so hard."

That's the last I heard from Sheila in what turned out to be a long, long time. It was a powerful note for her to leave me on and I wish I'd taken it more to heart. 'Cause there I was in a brand-new city starting a brand-new life. I had no job, no friends, no plans, and—very soon—no money.

But if I'd followed Sheila's advice, I probably would have figured out that what I also had ahead of me was no limits. I shoulda started building something new right there. New friends, new job, new life, new self-respect. In San Francisco, my sexual orientation couldn't hold me back. I shoulda left the past behind and embraced the empty future.

I didn't, 'cause there was still one more thing that wouldn't let me go—my Old Faithful Excuse: drugs.

❖

I LIVED ON welfare the first eight or nine months I was in San Francisco. The food stamps helped put food in my mouth but they also put crack in my pipe. Any city you go anywhere in these United States, the deal's always the same. Food stamp are drugs stamps. I've seen it all over America.

My luck started to pick up a little, though, when one day I was walking down the street and I heard this guy holler out my name.

"Roy!! Fucking Roy Simmons!!"

I whirled around and was like, "Who is that?"

"Roy! Roy! Over here!"

It was Leroy, an old friend of mine from Jacksonville. I'd met him and his best friend Nate when I played for the Bulls. They were two old navy buddies, and Lord, were they cute! Nate and I actually became quite close back in Jacksonville. We weren't really committed to one another and Nate kinda wanted me a bit more than I wanted him. Even so, I had great memories of him and Leroy. I remembered right then that they had both grown up in San Francisco, and seeing Leroy in the street like that sure was a balm for my soul!

Leroy ran up and hugged me right there in the street. "What in God's name are you doing here?" Leroy asked. So I filled him in real fast about coming out and leaving the East and not playing football anymore and that kind of thing. You would have thought I'd hit this motherfucker with a brick.

Then, out of the blue, he said: "Nate's here," with this sort of even tone in his voice.

"You're kidding me, man! Hey. Can we go see him?"

If I hadn't been so excited about seeing him, I might have noticed that Leroy's tone had turned somber. I still probably wouldn't have been able to figure out what was going on inside him, but I definitely would have noticed that something had changed.

"Sure," Leroy said. "Let's go right now."

❖

MY OLD LOVER Nate. Such a weird-ass, beautiful man. He was 6'3" with dark skin and a huge mustache, and he was very hairy. I'd tickle him and he'd holler and squeal and kick and say, "Nooooo, Roy! No, no, nooooooo!" Nate was a very funny, witty man.

When I walked through the front door of his apartment he nearly had a heart attack. Man, was he overjoyed to see me! But I almost had myself a heart attack, too. He'd lost so much weight. I looked at Nate and thought, *What the hell happened to him?* He wasn't just thin, he was gaunt. And all that hair I'd loved so much was still there, but it looked thinner. Less luxurious. Same thing with his skin. It looked sort of the way I remembered it, but underneath there was this *other* thing, this ugly color, purplish and ashy, maybe, like his whole body was bruised beneath the brown. Everything Nate did—every tiny little movement, every breath he took into his body—seemed to take a lot more effort than it used to, like maybe he was suffering from arthritis or the flu cramps or something.

What the hell is going on?

I was like, "Ooooooh, damn, Nate. What's wrong with you?"

He looked me in the eyes and tried on a little smile. "I have AIDS, Roy."

Oh my God.

I ended up moving in with Nate for a while.

❖

WHY DIDN'T I go get tested for AIDS? I don't know. It doesn't make sense to me now, looking back. 'Course, not much of my behavior from back then makes a whole lot of sense to me now, truth be told. I guess I thought I was lucky or impervious or bulletproof or some such shit. I should have gone and gotten tested, I know.

I guess you could also say I had other distractions at the time. After all, I'd just come outta the closet and just moved my ass to San Francisco. It's a high like no one on this planet's ever known, lest they been there. You're running flat out for months at a time—meeting new people, partying like a mad man, doing drugs, doing each other. When you're moving that fast, nobody stops to take their own blood pressure. It was all gonna start catching up with me, though. Hooooo, maybe Roz was right. Maybe I *was* just running away from one problem to the next. Sounds as good a theory as any to me. Anybody running as fast as I was had to be one of two things: real desperate to get somewhere new, or real desperate to get away from something old.

I had my first urban altercation in San Fran around the time I met up with Nate again. Hooooo, it was God trying to tell me what was what. *Slow down, Roy. Slow down, you're moving too fast, taking too many risks. You keep up like this and you gonna end up face down in some alley somewhere with your boots stripped off.*

How right God almost was.

❖

ONE TIME I was out buying crack and this guy in an alley made the very bad mistake of selling me some fake shit. When I got back to my apartment and took a look at what I had in my hand, I coulda put my fist through the wall. I coulda brought the whole roof down with the force of my mind. I was so motherfucking angry, I headed right back to the street. That motherfucker zoomed me good, but one good zoom deserves another. I came up with a simple plan: track his ass down, grab hold of his skull, and beat it on the pavement.

I found his ass, all right. He was in an alley not far from the alley where he'd zoomed me. I started to approach him, all stealthy-like, but he saw me coming and pulled out a knife. I was like, *Oh Lord, here we go. . .*

I didn't back down—that's how far gone I was at that point in my life. My hatred and my irritability over having been fucked with got the better of my common sense. This bitch started swinging away with his blade, slashing and sticking at anything that moved, which was mostly me. I ripped off my shirt and wrapped it around one hand to protect the flesh. Then I started swinging back at him with my shirt-wrapped fist, like I was some kind of mad-ass matador. My attacker wasn't all that good on the draw. I was still real big and real fast. Hell, I was the same Roy Simmons that used to beat all the other guys on the track team running the 110 in Converse sneakers. I was careful—real careful—then I stepped in close. Got the motherfucker in a clinch and twisted the knife from this hand. He screamed—I don't know why. I think he was just upset. Then I reversed the knife blade in my hand and started stabbing him. He screamed again and again. This time I knew the reason. I stabbed that bitch maybe a half dozen times.

It was weird feeling that knife blade going into another human being. At first there was a little bit of resistance, like when the blade broke through a muscle wall or something. But once it was in, hooooooo, it was in! There was a hot jet of blood and the blade would start to wiggle like it was alive. The dude started screaming real loud, but I hit him over the head a few times with my fist to cool his ass out. And then I stuck him some more.

It was over real fast. The dude was lying there on the floor of the alley, not moving a muscle. *Did I kill him? Is he dead?* That thought ran through my head like an audio loop. It didn't take long for me to decide that I didn't care. I hauled my ass out of that alley and left his sorry self to bleed. Took the knife with me, too. In the back of my mind I was thinking: *fingerprints.*

So there I was, all battered up and rumpled, with a knife in my hand and somebody else's blood all over me, walking through the streets of San Francisco. Eventually, I made it down into the government area and found a building with a nice high first-story window sill where I stuck the knife after I'd wiped it clean. Figured nobody would find it there. Then I went back to the place I shared with Nate.

I kept my ear to the ground for weeks but I never heard of a crack dealer turning up dead in an alley. Maybe the guy walked away from the whole thing, after all, I don't know. Nowadays, I'd like to think that's the way it happened. After that incident, though, I started carrying my own knife around with me, just in case. It folded up real nice and safe and I kept it in my back pocket for an easy draw.

❖

I WAS DEVELOPING a rough reputation around town. Events like the knifing were a good reason for that. The knifing wasn't the only fight I got into. I was irritable back then. My temper went off over practically anything. Somebody who stepped on my foot accidentally in a club might easily have found himself picked up by the lapels of his jacket and thrown across the room, grunting to say *excuse me*. I was big, I was strong, I was hopped up on drugs, I was frequently drunk, and I was always unpredictable. Basically, people learned pretty quick not to fuck with me.

I learned something from these dark days, though. I learned that tough people are really the ones who are softest inside. All that hard edge they put up on the outside is nothing but a crude mask, sort of like a short man wearing elevator shoes. Back then Roy Simmons wasn't the Sugar Bear any more. The Sugar Bear was gone. Roy Simmons was acting like something else entirely—a rabid Grizzly Bear, perhaps. Whatever kind of animal it was, it was motherfucking lethal. And scared.

The personality switch worked, too. People stopped coming up to me and fucking with my high; they learned to leave me alone to talk with the demons and monsters in my head, which was exactly how I preferred it just then. No, it wasn't such a good thing in the long run. At that point in my life, I desperately needed to be part of a working, upstanding community, a community like I'd found with James and David and the Colonnade group out in Newark. In San Fran, I wasn't part of some tie-wearing, white-collar sect of society. Hooooo, no! I was an outlaw living in an outlaw's world. And an outlaw's world never stops being dangerous.

❖

I DIDN'T STAY with Nate for long, so I was right back out on the streets again, living in dingy little hotel rooms that I could barely afford. There wasn't much difference back then between me and any other motherfucker you might see drinking or getting stoned hanging out on a street corner. Except that sometimes I did my drinking and getting stoned alone in my hotel room. And every once in a while I'd try to better myself by getting a job.

For a while I tried to find work with the Glide Memorial Methodist Church, but they acted like they knew I was some kinda addict. I guess it wasn't that hard to tell, looking back on it. So I started to attend meetings through Glide. I hit NA and AA a few times, but it wasn't really a serious effort. Hoooooo, I wasn't ready for Step One, let alone Step Twelve.

I'd say, "Yes. Hello. My name is Roy and I admit that I'm an addict." And everyone else would say, "Hi, Roy," just like they said to everyone else in the group. Difference was that I was lying. I wasn't lying that I was an addict, I was lying about *admitting* I was an addict. 'Cause inside I was really thinking, "Man, I'll say anything to get a job with these people. Any old shit at all."

Pretty soon I ran outta money. My mother wired me some and Western Roslyn wired me some, too. And it helped. *Lord*, did it help! Generally speaking, I had enough money to keep me from shoplifting. 'Course, there were also times when I didn't.

I shoplifted all the time here and there, and yes, it's true what they say. Crack addicts *will* shoplift in order to buy—surprise, surprise—more crack. I've heard that some people shoplift just for kicks and I've heard it so much that I guess it must be true. Wasn't like that with me, though. With me it was about the drugs, pure and simple.

The first time I got caught was when I went into a Walgreen's and grabbed me two clothes irons in boxes. Don't ask me why I grabbed clothes irons. Things like this make a lot more sense when you're on the pipe. In my mind, the clothes irons were somehow equal to rock and that was all there was to it. I tucked the damn things under my arm and headed toward the door.

Now there was this one bitch at one of the counters who'd been giving me the eye ever since I walked into the damn place. She knew I was up to no good and I *knew* that she knew I was up to no good. Still, I was determined. I had made up my mind to leave that motherfucking store with those irons in hand no matter what. 'Course, all this got real ugly when she stepped in front of me on my way out the door and said, "Sir, I need you to put those down."

I was like, "Put *what* down, bitch?" Not the best way to make friends, I admit. And she was like—you could see it registered with her now that I was outta my fucking mind and probably dangerous. She got all drawn up the way people do when they're about to jump into battle. Her body got all stiff and her face sort of curled back into an animal snarl and her eyes crossed for a second like she was gathering strength.

She said to me, "Sir! Put them down and leave or I'll call the police!" Well, I responded to that by just pushing her ass outta the way and heading straight for the door. But wouldn't you know it? She'd called the police already. Before I knew it I was lying facedown on the ground screaming, "Hellllp! Hellllp! Hellllp!" while these pissed off cops tried to kick me in the balls.

They took me downtown and booked me and I stayed there overnight. The next day I was released on my own recognizance.

❖

JIMMY FLEW UP from Los Angeles to visit me in the spring of 1990. I guess he'd been sober for about a year right around that point, though I didn't know it at the time. That part would come later. He was still working for Beverly Johnson and still working his ass off to try and conquer the world before he hit thirty. He'd planned to stay with me at my place but that idea didn't last long. I'd moved seven times in the past five months and my current digs were a welfare hotel where the tenants were lolling around in the hallways all strung out. They'd piss on the walls and puke on the floors of the common area. It was a mess. My own personal space wasn't much better. I had gay porn magazines lying around all over the place and garbage that I hadn't taken out for God only knows how long.

Jimmy walked around the room on his toes, like he was afraid he was going to stick to something. He had this face on him like he'd just swallowed a cockroach. When he found this big dildo I kept around just for special occasions, he blew the fuck up and said, "No way. That's it. I'm outta here." He found a hotel that was more to his liking.

Later on after he got settled and we met up for lunch. Jimmy had some rather pointed questions for me.

"Roy, what the fuck's going on here?!"

"What're you talking about?"

"What am I *talking* about? Look at you! Look at the way you're living! Are you out of your damn mind?"

"Jimmy, look—I think I know what you're saying. But there's no reason to worry. Really."

"I'm not worried so much as I'm angry, Roy."

"Angry?"

"Yeah. That you could respect yourself so little. You're obviously out of control."

The conversation went on like this throughout lunch. We didn't make much headway.

Later on we took a walk down Market Street. It was a beautiful day, the kind that San Francisco's famous for. We talked some more and Jimmy laid some more heavy shit at my doorstep. He told me first of all that he was sober, and I gotta tell you, this was news to me. I couldn't imagine Jimmy Hester being off drugs. I mean, of all people, right? He also told me that one of the reasons he'd come up to San Fran was to help me get sober, too. Which I sort of took the wrong way.

"Look, Jimmy," I said. "You've done something good with your life, it works for you and I'm happy. But what gives you the right to come up here and tell me how to live mine, huh? Congratulations on your sobriety and all. I think that's great. But I'm cool, man. I'm doing fucking swell. So that's the end of that story, okay?"

We walked along in silence, and then Jimmy said:

"Roy, there's something else you should know."

"Oh yeah? What's that."

"I'm gay."

Which made me want to laugh right out loud. In fact, I said, "Hooooooo, *child*! I know that you're *gay*. Shit, I *always* knew you were gay." This was news to Jimmy. He'd just admitted it to himself a little while back, so the fact that I knew kinda took him aback.

"You *knew* I was *gay*?!"

"'Course, Jimmy. Hell, man. I'm gay, too."

"You *are*? I *knew* it! I mean, I always kinda *thought* you were gay . . . wow."

And that's how we told each other. Just two old friends walking down the street in San Francisco. We'd come a long way. But we were only just beginning.

14

WHEN MY FRIENDSHIP with Jimmy began, I was clearly the older brother and he was clearly the young man searching for guidance and a firm moral hand. Now the tables had turned. Jimmy had his sharp tongue, his youth, and his new-found sobriety. How could I compete against that? My age and relative experience had long since played themselves out, and my coked-out head was no match for this kid who was now on his way to conquering the entertainment business single-handedly.

Our relationship took itself to a new level that week. Now we were like the Odd Couple. We weren't lovers—we never would be. But all the same, we loved and hated each other in equal measure. We bitched at each other over the tiniest little details and stomped away from each other in frustration as often as not. Still do, by the way.

Jimmy told me he'd been gay all his life, but he didn't really know how to accept it until recently. This was something that I understood, of course. He told me he had a thing for straight guys and I nodded. Then he told me he'd once done ménage-à-trois with a running back from the Chicago Bears, which perked my ears up, I can tell you that.

Then he started asking me the kinds of questions only Jimmy could ask, the kinds of questions he'd spent years crazy to hear the answers for. "Which of the Giants had the biggest dick? What was so-and-so's ass like? You gotta tell me, Roy! Please! You gotta tell me!" I knew, of course. And yes, I was telling.

"How could you *stand* being in the same locker room with Odis

McKinney?!? I mean, how the fuck could you *stand* it?" Finally, I had a friend I could talk about anything with.

Later on that week, our relationship soured all of a sudden. Jimmy picked me up in his rental car and I brought along a bottle of Korbel Extra Dry, which was my preferred potion at the time. Looking back, it wasn't the coolest thing in the world to do to a friend coming up on the one-year anniversary of his sobriety. In fact, given the fact that it was also illegal to drive around with an open container of liquor in the car, it was also pretty fucking stupid. To fucking crucify the matter, it dashed Jimmy's hopes of getting me sober into tiny little pieces. And Jimmy was not shy about telling me how angry and disappointed he was.

"Roy, stop. I don't want you drinking in my car."

"Fuck you, when did you become such a prude?"

"Roy, I'm serious. Get rid of the bottle. I do *not* want you *drinking* in my motherfucking *car*!"

"If the bottle goes, I go."

Jimmy decided he could live without both of us, so he pulled the car over and waited in silence while I got out, cursing up a blue streak. I looked over my shoulder just as Jimmy pulled out, and I saw his little car disappear down the street. Then I realized he'd dropped me off right in the middle of the goddamn Cinco de Mayo parade. Which turned out to be a blessing in disguise, 'cause I could walk around drinking my bottle without anyone really bothering me.

❖

LATER ON, JIMMY went over to visit my lover Nate behind my back. (I'd introduced them to one another when I was still playing for Jacksonville and Jimmy came down to visit once.) While Jimmy was there, Nate collapsed in his apartment—his AIDS was taking its toll—and he needed to get to a hospital fast. Jimmy helped him down the stairs and into his rental car. He drove him over to the emergency room and stayed with him for a while.

During all that time, Nate filled Jimmy in on my latest and wildest behaviors. "Look, Jimmy," he said. "It's like this. Roy sort of lost his head a little when he first got here, but—deep down he's still the same beautiful guy he was back in Florida. He's still so generous, you know? I swear to you, he'd give a total stranger the shirt off his back without having to be asked. We're all trying to keep an eye on him and calm him down a little. I think it's working." Nate started coughing so hard right then that he nearly collapsed in the passenger seat.

At the end of his vacation, Jimmy came around to my room again to say good-bye. It was not a pleasant occasion. He knocked several times but I refused to come to the door. I didn't want to be bothered. It was easier to just sit there and smoke more crack. When I got high, nothing mattered at all—not Jimmy, not sobriety, not God, not my friends. I listened to Jimmy's steps finally start back down the hallway and I thought to myself, *Thank God that little bitch is gone!*

Jimmy went back to L.A. very concerned about me, and I went back to my old ways of debauchery and depravity.

❖

I STARTED DRESSING up in drag, just for kicks. I had this friend named Jiggett who'd once won the pageant for Miss Gay San Francisco, and she knew all the tricks of the trade—wigs, makeup, the tissue-padding you wear to make curves, and how to hide your dick. Shoes were hard to come by, since I have a size 16 foot. I eventually chose to wear sneakers with stockings instead of heels.

We went to the Halloween party at the Blue & Gold, and lemme tell you! Such a pageant it was! I remember thinking, *Now I understand why guys do this shit, it's so liberating!* Just me and Jiggett sashaying our way down the street, wiggling our asses here and wiggling our titties there. The ultimate way to let yourself go, man.

This was right about the time that Magic Johnson announced he had the AIDS virus, and the news hit me hard. It shocked and confused me. First of all, it was like, *Magic is gay?!?* Then it was sort of like, *But the man's married, isn't he?!?* Which led to *Right, okay, but I was almost married, too, so what's the difference?*

Then there was a whole bunch of other question that kept popping into my mind. Questions like: *What kinda men did Magic like? Did he go for queens or did he like to get himself some straight dick? How did he pull it off all those years? Did he keep himself secret like I did? What the hell's going on with the world if a guy like Magic Johnson's got HIV?* 'Course, the one thought I didn't have at the time would've been the most important: *If Magic can get it, then* anyone *can . . .*

But despite all that, I never got tested for HIV. Call it hubris, call it stupidity. Call it major, *major* denial. Frankly, you can call it anything you damn well please. I really can't say anything except, "You're right." It was stupid. I'd spent years and years dancing on the edge of the razor. Sooner or later, I was bound to get cut.

❖

Tyrone called me up during my second year in San Francisco. He was living in Savannah at the time. I'd introduced him to the whole gay community down there and he'd made it his home. He knew all my old friends—his friends were *my* friends. It was summertime when he called, and summertime in Savannah can be *hot*! But he told me:

"Roy, something's wrong, man."

"What's the problem?"

"It's Gerald, man. He's sick or something. It's a hundred and five degrees down here, he's walking around with a jacket and thick, heavy pants on."

My mind flashed back to one of the last times I'd seen Gerald, in 1987. Even back then, even before I'd come out, I had the occasional hankering to visit San Francisco, and I told Gerald this one time. I told him we should take a trip to the coast and visit the city together. We could hit all the clubs and drink champagne and it'd be just like old times, man. It'd be just like old times . . .

He made a face and sort of turned his head away. He didn't answer me, so I said, "What's wrong?"

"I don't know, man. I just don't feel like myself these days."

I put my hand on his and said, "Hey, man. That's not like you. Come on. It'll be fun. Just you and me. We deserve a vacation."

But he wouldn't do it, man. No way, nohow. He was adamant. And I remember thinking, even if it was just a moment, *Does Gerald have the virus?* I remember thinking the same thing I thought when I heard Magic had AIDS. I thought, *What the hell's the world coming to?*

❖

NOT LONG AFTER that, Tyrone called me to say that Gerald had died of AIDS. I dropped the phone when I heard the news. Gerald and I hadn't spoken since that time back in 1987. My old friend, who'd once brought such joy to my life. A person who accepted people for who they were no matter where they came from, what they enjoyed, or what they were about. How we'd laughed it up in Home Ec class! How we'd laughed it up *period*, man! And now—just like that—he was gone, through no fault of his own. How many of us had been infected before we'd ever even heard about the damned virus? Wiped clean from the earth.

About four years later I went back to Savannah and I stopped by Gerald's house to visit his mother and express my condolences. She answered the door and just stood there, stone-faced, while I rattled off some *How are yous?* and *I'm so sorrys.*

She slapped me in the face hard enough to make my ears ring. And then she demanded, "Why the fuck are you here? Coming 'round after it don't make no difference! Why weren't you there for him back then, when he was dying?"

I had no motherfucking answer to this question.

❖

I DIDN'T STAY long at Gerald's house, but I was there long enough to learn that he'd been furious at the whole world right up until the end. Apparently he thought that life had dealt him a bad hand and he didn't mind letting everyone know it. I remember thinking, *No, couldn't be. That's not the Gerald I knew.* But of course, people can change, especially toward the end.

The Gerald I knew was lucky. Impervious. Bulletproof. *Just like me.* But he'd died. He'd gotten AIDS and he'd died. Just like so many people I was hearing about. And maybe just like . . .

No.

I visited Big Cat a few hours after stopping by Gerald's house and told her how Gerald's mother had slapped me. Well, she picked up the phone right then and called Gerald's mother right up, and said, "Goddammit, who the fuck you think you are, bitch?! Don't you ever slap my nephew again or I'll run right over to your house and beat your ass blue, you hear me?!?" Big Cat. Still looking out for me after all those years.

A little later on, Nate died of AIDS in a San Francisco hospital. I wasn't there for him when he passed; I heard it through the grapevine. Lord knows, I didn't have the strength to deal with a reality like that. The devil was on me, now. He was smack on my back with his claws dug in deep and he was holding on real tight.

❖

JIMMY DIDN'T HOLD a grudge for long. He came back to San Fran almost a year later and offered to introduce me to the woman I'd heard so much about, the famous Ms. Beverly Johnson.

Beverly was in town for a celebration of African-American entertainers and was looking forward to meeting me. Jimmy had told her all about me. What he didn't tell me was that he'd also told her how concerned he was over my behavior. He also didn't tell me that the two of them had set up this little conspiracy to see if they could get me clean and sober. So basically I found myself smack dab in the middle of an AA-type conspiracy.

I remember going straight to Beverly's dressing room at the Hilton, where I'd told myself I was gonna stay that first week I landed in San Fran. She was a beautiful woman, just unbelievably beautiful. "Roy, Jimmy's told me so many stories, I feel like I know you already. Why don't you and I become very close friends?" And just like that, she took me by the arm and we were off on a whirlwind tour of San Francisco like I'd never seen it.

I have to be the only addict in the world who ever found himself riding around his own crack-infested neighborhood in a sharp limousine while dressed in a gorgeous tuxedo. Suddenly I was on the inside looking out, quite a change from the way I'd been living for the past two years.

Crackheads don't usually get the chance to hang out with the likes of the world's first black supermodel, the mayor of San Francisco, the governor of California, Danny Glover, and Chaka Khan. But then, I guess most crack addicts Can't say they once played pro football with the likes of Lawrence Taylor and John Riggins. Fact of the matter is, most crack addicts can't say much of anything except for, "Gimme another hit from that pipe." Which is pretty much what I'd sunk to by this point.

Beverly and Jimmy's plan had begun to take root. Here I was laughing it up and having a grand old time with Chaka-damn-Khan. That woman has the cutest little freckles! I'm out there swapping war stories with movie stars and players, and nobody but *nobody* stopped me at any time throughout the course of the evening to say, "Hey, Roy! Where the hell's your crack pipe?"

To these good people, I was something altogether different, see? I was one of them, a celebrity. In their eyes I was accomplished and successful. I had wit, charm, intelligence, and style. I had experiences that set me apart from most everyone else. So, with all that going for me, why the hell couldn't I pull my ass outta the gutter?

A tiny seed of hope was planted inside my head that night. Jimmy planted it and Beverly watered it. If that seed was allowed to grow, Lord knows what kinda tree it might become. Maybe a maple, or a grand, sweeping oak. Maybe a whole *forest* of oaks for that matter. Who the hell knew?

It was all just wishful thinking, though. The moment Beverly and Jimmy pulled outta town, that old voice popped right back into my head again, saying, *You thought you could get away from me? You thought you really* wanted *to get away from me—is that what you thought? You're not witty and intelligent and accomplished and successful. You're a fucked up, cracked out, good-for-nothing fag. Everything you ever touched in your whole damn life has come to ruin. Get used to it, Roy. You're ain't going nowhere.*

Oh, how the mighty had fallen. And how impossible it seemed for the mighty to get up.

❖

I RAN OUTTA money one night not long after Bev and Jimmy came to town. I'd already been behind in my rent, and now the landlord swooped in and kicked me outta my apartment. I had no place to go and nothing to eat, so I wandered the streets, homeless, sleeping wherever I could, wherever I felt it was safe enough to grab a few winks. Then I realized I could improve my situation dramatically if I prostituted myself. So I did, anywhere from two to five times a week.

I still remember the first guy I did. He wasn't bad-looking, not at all. In fact, it almost seemed kinda fun, like we were meeting each other at a bar and hooking up for the first time with maybe a future ahead of us, a friendship on the rise, and maybe even love, you know? It was exciting like that. I was deluding myself, of course. In reality the guy wanted me for one thing and one thing only.

"Yo, man. Here's the deal. Suck my dick and I'll give you some cocaine."

Most of the time guys would pick me up in and around the peep shows and the adult-magazine stores. Sometimes I got $15, sometimes I got $20, but usually never more than that. The most I ever got for a single engagement was $100, and that was 'cause the guy was a traveling businessman—you could tell by the way he talked and dressed. He was well-heeled, looking for some excitement, and probably didn't know any better.

Sometimes these guys had drugs on them and that would get factored in with the payment. In fact, a typical scenario for me was this: I'd meet some guy at the peep show and we'd strike up deal. He'd give me a hit from his pipe just to make sure the deal was sealed. Then we'd go inside and grab a booth together and close the curtain. I'd kneel down and suck the guy's dick while he watched some old black and white porno movie. Then he'd pay me a ten and a five and that was it, the gig was over. Next customer, please.

'Course, there were variations. Sometimes the customer dropped me two tens instead of fifteen and that was always appreciated. Sometimes we did the deed in a back alley somewhere or in the men's room of a club. Sometimes I was the sucker, other times I was the suckee. Regardless of what happened, it was all about survival. It certainly didn't do a whole lot for my self-esteem. Before I knew it, I think my mind sort of became unhinged.

One night, for instance, I woke up alone in this dilapidated hotel room—don't ask me whose it was and don't ask me how I got there. I couldn't tell you if I tried. I know it was about ten o'clock in the evening, 'cause I remember looking at the clock on the nightstand a few times. The window was open and there was a cool breeze blowing over my body. Weren't no curtains on the windows, so I could see the full moon up in the sky, looking down on me like this pale blue eye. I felt fear, I know that for sure, and maybe that's the only thing I knew at that particular moment. I felt fear like I'd never felt before in my entire goddamn life.

Maybe I was high at that point. Maybe I wasn't. Things had gotten so I couldn't even tell the difference anymore. But I remember looking over at the wall. The moonlight fell against it like a curtain of cold light and I saw writing everywhere—dark blue cursive script with no spacing between the words. The characters were all tilted backwards and spidery, like the Devil himself had written a poem to me and left it right where I could see it, out in the open across the whole motherfucking wall.

I have no idea what those words said. They were written a language I couldn't understand. But instinct told me they wasn't saying nothing like, CONGRATULATIONS, ROY SIMMONS! YOU JUST WON THE MOTHERFUCKING LOTTERY!!! If anything, those damn words spelled out my doom. They were some kinda message from beyond, that's what I thought at the time. A message from beyond that said, END IT. YOU KNOW YOU WANT TO. END IT NOW.

I guess some part of me still wasn't ready, 'cause the last thing I remember about seeing those letters written on the wall was this high-pitched voice screaming fucking bloody murder. My own voice. Then the feeling of my own legs carrying me outta bed, across the room, straight to the door, which I ripped right open, practically ripped off its old rusty hinges. Then down the tilted corridor, leaping over the bodies of junked-out, stoned-out crackhead fools. Down the flights of step, my bare feet thumping WHUMP! WHUMP! WHUMP! Into the lobby with the one neon light burned out and the guy behind the counter, head back in his chair, feet up, mouth wide open and aimed at the ceiling like he was a corpse propped up in the seat.

I was still screaming when I blasted out the front doors of the damned hotel from hell. Still screaming as I ran down the street, the moon overhead now, following me wherever I went. Relentless.

And where did I go? I have no idea. I don't think I'll ever quite remember what happened after that. Lord help me. I don't want to.

❖

NOT LONG AFTER that I spent five months in jail for shoplifting. They locked me up in San Bruno, down the peninsula from San Francisco. I don't remember the incident that landed me in prison. They fingerprinted me and took away every little personal thing I had on me. Then they strip-searched me and had some intake clerk look up with my ass while I spread my cheeks and bent over. I remember getting a grungy set of clothes and paper shoes to walk around in. It was humiliating.

I never called my mother or my family or anybody, really, to tell them where I was. I was way too embarrassed. What would I have said to them? *I fucked up again.* I was an addict, I was a loser, and I'd pretty much betrayed everyone I ever loved. But at least I hadn't been a convict. Now I was. Roz knew, eventually; I called her. Apart from that, though, I had no contact with the outside world.

So I settled in for a little while. I never told anybody that I'd played professional ball. Jesus, why in the world would I do that? That was none of their business. And eventually I figured that if I was gonna stick around for five months, I might as well make the best of it. I studied up on all the little things that the Califonia Penal System had to offer and began to take advantage of everything I could.

I went to NA meetings and AA meetings, the library, and church. I ended up taking a culinary class and actually won a scholarship from the jail to attend culinary school in San Francisco when I got out. I thought, *Maybe that's what I'll do. I'll get outta here and study to become a chef. Open my own restaurant. Some place cool like the Front Row where all my friends can come and we can have us a grand ol' time. Just like the old days. Just like we used to . . .*

For a second there I was right back in Miss Blake's class serving baked chicken and collard greens to Mr. Otis J. Brock. All I needed was a glass of good old-fashioned Georgia sweet tea to seal the deal. I gotta tell you, though, they don't know a damn thing about sweet tea in the California penal system.

I could have lived on the gay inmates' tier but I chose not to. I figured prison life was bad enough without being branded a fag. Who I liked to sleep with was nobody's fucking business but my own. That was my opinion and I stuck to it, even though that led to fighting the administration. I won out after a lot of letter writing. The guards put me in with the rest of the inmates and I felt a great deal of motherfucking satisfaction.

I got a job working in the kitchen, and that was cool. I dug the white uniforms and the camaraderie I had with the other inmates on my shift. My cellmate and I got along well even though I had the top bunk. Being a little on the claustrophobic side, I spent many a night without sleep 'cause I was real, real close to hyperventilating due to the close proximity to the ceiling. And I made a few friends. No lovers. Just friends. Yes, there were some nice-looking guys all around me—and some of them were bad-ass built, too. Nothing to do in prison but pump fucking weights and groom, right? But it wasn't worth the risk to start nothing with nobody. I kept my head down and kept to my business.

Sometimes—oh hell, lot of times—I found myself giving myself a pep talk. *Roy, this ain't you, man. This ain't what you're about. Don't worry about it, dude—you're down, but you ain't out. Not yet, you ain't. Your ass was not made to rot away behind some fucking cell door. Your ass was made for some different purpose altogether. You may not know exactly what the fuck that purpose is just yet, but you don't have to. Eventually, you'll figure it out. Just keep your shit together and get through this, that's all you gotta do. Don't have to love it, just gotta get through it.*

In the five months I was in prison I saw no visitors, and that was just fine with me. Didn't want any. At that point, I was too embarrassed to look anybody I knew directly in the eye.

❖

I DIDN'T DO any drugs in prison but I drank me some Pruno, which I have to say was not the best idea in the world. Pruno is this godawful prison wine you could make from regular food supplies. You take ten oranges plus a can of fruit cocktail and tossed them in a Ziploc bag. Then you mash the shit outta the bag, add water, wrap the bag in a towel and toss it on top of the radiator to heat it. This sparks up the fermentation. Now you gotta wait 48 hours.

While you're waiting, the bag'll start to swell up like a beach ball. It starts to smell all yeasty, like bread dough. When that happens, it means it's ready for the next step. You add some ketchup packets and about 50 sugar cubes and mix that all up real good. Then you put it back on the radiator again, this time for 72 hours. If you don't have a radiator, you can maybe run the bag under hot water in your sink for about half an hour once a day. Either way is fine. After three days, you strain off all the fruit pulp and that's it. It's to drink.

Lord did that shit smell bad! But it gave you a buzz all right. Fucked you right the fuck up, but hey. Beggars can't be no choosers.

❖

I WROTE POEMS in prison—never wrote a goddamn poem before in my life. I drew a lot of pictures, too, even though I can't draw for shit. I wrote a lot of letters to Roz and she wrote back with words of strong encouragement. *Keep the faith, Roy. I know it must be tough, but I'm praying for you.* Bless that woman's heart. 'Course, it was a whole lot easier keeping the faith when she sent a money order along with her letter.

Time was I put on 25, maybe 30 pounds. I coulda used it back then. I guess the weight mostly came from my job in the kitchen. Lot of times I just ate whatever I wanted, and sometimes I made up a whole buncha extra triple-decker sandwiches and hamburgers, which I'd hide in my clothes and smuggle back to the cells where I'd sell them. Totally illegal, but that's what I did. I'd guess I ate about as much as I sold—it got so my clothes didn't even fit me when it came time for me to leave.

And leave that motherfucking place I did. With two weeks left to go in my sentence, San Bruno remanded me to a residential treatment center called Project 90. And that's where the hard work began.

❖

THEY GOT THE term Project 90 from the fact that you went to 90 substance abuse meetings in 90 days, plus the two weeks I had left in my sentence. According to the program, I lived on the property for the first 30 days. After that I got shipped out to the houses at the off-site location. On some nights we had dinner and then a meeting with a Project 90 alumnus who'd made it on the outside world. Those were always kind of inspiring. It was especially critical for me to get into the swing of things, since I was technically on probation. One more screwup for me and I was motherfucking back in jail.

Therapy at the project was pretty much the same as the therapy I'd always had. The process required total goddamn honesty. I think I fulfilled that, but I never told anyone about my sexuality. Or the rape. Again, I figured it was nobody's business but my own, see? If someone asked me if I was gay or straight, I wasn't about to lie to them. And if someone just out-and-out pegged me for a gay man, hell, I wasn't about to protest. But who I liked to sleep with was still something I considered my business and my business alone. I wasn't ready to take that next, big step.

At least this time, though . . . when I admitted I was an addict, I know I meant it.

15

I GOT INVOLVED with the Pilgrim Baptist Church in San Mateo while I was still in the treatment center, and it turned out to be one of the best things that ever happened to me. This wasn't no poor church full of poor black people like I'd grown up with back in Savannah, no sir! This place was the house of worship for the black bourgeoisie. They had money to burn. For all that, though, they were the most beautiful-spirited people I think I ever met in my life.

There was *always* something to do at Pilgrim Baptist. These folks didn't know the meaning of the word "rest" unless you meant the spiritual rest they found in the arms of Jesus Christ. We held bake sales to draw in new parishioners. There were dances and raffles and bingo nights and music shows. I got involved in several different choirs at the same time, including the men's choir, the mass choir, and the inspirational choir. I went to NA meetings, and even became the head of a singles ministry. I got people to start bringing pot luck dishes to the ministry meetings so we could always look forward to a nice little buffet. Folks loved the idea!

I'm not sure if they knew I was gay. I know they knew I was a reforming convict and that was enough for me. Like I'd done in prison, like I'd done ever since I hit the West Coast, I kept my sexuality to myself. Sure, everyone back east knew. But at the time, that was more than enough for me. I was finally living clean out west, and that took up just about as much energy as I was capable of giving right then.

Things started going so well that I invited Roz out to visit me while I was still in Project 90. She stayed at the Holiday Inn Express in San

Mateo and I got a pass from the treatment center so I could spend time with her in the evenings. It was good to see that woman again!

We had the most beautiful time together, did everything that San Francisco has to offer. Took time to tour the Castro district. Went down to the bay and had dinner in Ghirardelli Square. One afternoon over Alcatraz, I saw the biggest, most inspiring rainbow I'd ever seen. I just wanted to cry. With Roz at my side and the past feeling like it was all behind me, I kept thinking to myself, *Now? Can I start living now, God? I don't want to sink much lower than I already have. Ain't it time I deserved something good in my life? Ain't it time, Lord? Please?*

We went back to Roz's hotel room, which she'd made comfortable with all sorts of scented candles and sachets. And then we made love. It was Roz's choice—she asked me and I said yes. I asked her, "Baby, are you sure?" And she said, "Roy, I wouldn't have it any other way." We made sure to use a condom. I remember falling asleep that night and thinking, *Wow. So this is what it feels like to be human again.*

I proposed to her again the next day. "Roz, honey, I gotta know. I want to do this. I think this time it's right. Will you marry me?" She didn't say anything for a long, long time. So I said, "Baby? Did you hear me?"

And she said, "I heard you, Roy. I just—married?"

"Sure! Why the hell not? It's so simple out here. We hop in the car, haul ass out to Vegas, and get it done. I want to, Roz. I really want to. You're the only person in my life who's loved me more than I ever loved myself. And I've never stopped loving you for that, Roz. This makes sense to me."

She thought it over for a few moments and said, "I have to ask my mother first." This was *not* the answer I'd been expecting to hear! I said, "Your *mother*?! I don't want to marry your *mother*, I want to marry *you*! Your *mother* ain't in the damn *equation*!"

But she held firm. I could see it hurt her to do it, too. Not that that made the moment any easier for me, you understand. But she said, "Roy, listen to me. You're not stable yet. You're in a drug rehabilitation program. You got no money, you can barely take care of yourself. How the hell you gonna take care of me if you can't even take care of yourself?"

I just stood there blinking at her. "You want me to take care of you?"

She looked at me like I was maybe the kindest, sweetest, stupidest man on earth. "Roy," she said. "I'm a woman. Of *course* I want my man to take care of me." All this time and I still hadn't gotten the basics of relationships through my head. Roz loved me enough to turn down my second proposal for marriage. This time she could clearly see it was for her own good as well as for mine.

❖

Now, MARRIAGE AT that particular moment might sound rash to some, but to me it made perfect sense. I'd come so far in the treatment center and the church. I'd been in *jail* and I'd weathered that out. I felt the best I'd felt in all my years. I was ready to ditch all the lies, the deception, the sneaking around—put that all behind me and start over fresh. My lust for men was subdued at the time so I thought that at last I'd be committed to Roz. Call it the influence of the church, call it the result of getting clean, I honestly can't tell you the reason behind it. But my libido had dissipated so much that I was barely sure if I'd ever really felt it at all. What I wanted was a partner, simple as that—someone to love and who could love me back.

Plus, I was ready for God to restore my sanity. I'm not quite sure when that yearning hit me but it was there. I was raised in a good home with God-fearing people but hadn't really given it a thought for a long time. Now, it was like everything the folks were saying at the Pilgrim Baptist Church was finally starting to make sense. God saves. God heals. God wants you to come back to him. He forgives even the worst transgressions. I began to give myself over to God more and more. Suddenly I felt as if I really had made a turn for the better. I prayed every day and I kept attending church services. I sang my heart out in the choirs. And every word I uttered in every song seemed to root me deeper and deeper in my love and gratefulness and passion for the power of the Almighty. I was convinced it was God who helped me stay in the treatment center for the full 90 days and it was God who helped me become a model resident.

Project 90 offered me a job as a house manager when I got outta the program, so I had a job when I was through; I hit the ground running. They made me responsible for eight clients. I conducted house meetings and had my own living space, a loft right there in the building. I felt responsible. I felt productive. I was making money. I was living again. And all this was thanks to God, as well. I'm not saying I didn't have my rough days here and there. But I'm telling you I stayed sober. I'm telling you I played the part of Jacob and wrestled my demon. I pinned that bastard to the mat and won the match.

It's true what they say—sometimes God works in mysterious ways. Sometimes he sees that you're not paying much attention to him so he does whatever he's gotta do to bring you back around. He'll stick your butt in a hospital bed or stuff you in a jail cell, maybe. Or he'll take the life of someone close to you, just to give you a little perspective. Maybe he'll take all your material goods, everything you own in the world, and throw them in the ocean just so you can learn once and for all that nothing in this world floats but hope. Sooner or later you're gonna start to listen to him—and *that* is *everything*.

God became my compass through times of storm and the rudder who guided my ship through rough waters. He became light for my eyes in dark places—a firm path to walk when the rocks have torn my feet—drink when I'm thirsty, and food when I'm hungry. God spoke to me at this time in my life. He spoke to me often, in a loud, clear voice. For once in my life, I was listening.

I'd met a man named Thomas at the treatment center. He came in about five days after I arrived and was admitted to the program as an alcoholic. He worked as a technician for a company that manufactured home entertainment centers and we were assigned to room together. At first I thought, *Here we go*. Knowing, of course, that living with someone is always difficult, *me* living with someone is always *tremendously* difficult. And me living with someone while I was trying to reform myself was gonna be pretty much next to *impossible*. But wouldn't you know it? Thomas and I clicked.

He was a real sweet man. He wasn't gay, but anybody might've guessed that he was. Fact of the matter was, Thomas was straight but real unlucky at love. He'd had a girlfriend break his heart a long, long time ago and that sort of put him off relationships for probably the rest of his life. I have to admit, before long, I had a little crush on him.

Thomas had grown up in the San Francisco area, not far from Stanford University, where his grandfather had worked in some important capacity. His family was *very* well off. His mother owned a mansion; Thomas had grown up there under the supervision of a nanny and a maid. He even introduced me once to the nanny who'd raised him.

Thomas and I stayed in touch for a while during my time working at the treatment center as a house manager. We went to meetings together and attended the Project 90 Alumni Night. I think we both knew at that point that we'd found a good friend in each other and we cherished that. It was all the more important 'cause we both knew where the other had come from, meaning the Project and addiction and our histories and all that.

Well, I was not destined to stay at Project 90 for long. All that abstinence from sex finally took its toll. While I was working as a house manager, I went out to a club one night—not for drinks, just for the ambiance—and I met this great-looking man. We hit it off, traded phone numbers, and started talking on the phone off and on—nothing more than that. A couple of times I invited him to come to church with me, and he did. He got along just fine with everyone in the parish. It was nice. It was easy. It was fun. It was the best relationship I'd had in a long, long time.

We were just two people looking to make each other's acquaintance in an easygoing sort of way. Then one Sunday he called up and said, "Hey, why don't I come over?" Which sounded like a great idea to me. So I gave him the address and he came around and we had sex; it was simple as that.

Looking back, I wish I'd chosen to find a hotel. But I shouldn't have had to do that, even. Yes, I had clients living directly downstairs from me, but my loft had a private entrance, and anyway, it was none of anyone's business who I had over so long as I wasn't drinking or doing drugs. That's the way I looked at it.

Turns out that one of my downstairs clients was this nosy motherfucker named Vince. He came up to my apartment for one reason or another and snooped around until he saw me fucking this man in my bedroom. Like I said, Vince was nosy, but he also had the hots for me. I would've taken him up on that urge, too, if I didn't have a solid rule in my life at the time to keep from mixing business with pleasure. He was also my client.

To make a long story short, jealous Vince told my manager that I had a guy upstairs with me. Now technically this wasn't against the rules for a house manager, but as you might imagine it was strongly discouraged. Worse than that, though, I'd never officially declared my homosexuality to the administrators of Project 90. So here I was outed again.

When my manager called and asked me to come to his office for a talk, I hit the roof.

"Simmons, we have this report from Vincent here that you had a naked man over at your place."

"I don't know what Vincent is talking about. I had a guest over, yes, but he wasn't naked." I felt it only appropriate to lie about having sex with my friend since, the way I saw it, Vincent shouldn't have walked into my bedroom in the first place.

"I'm sure you know how the Project feels about guests in people's apartments regardless of whether they're naked or not."

I sure as hell did. Which was almost exactly the same moment as I put two and two together and figured, *Hell. If I can't have friends over to my place whenever I want to, this isn't recovery. This is some kinda lockdown. I'd be better off back in the outside world.*

My manager and I spent the rest of that meeting going over the official Project 90 rules for clients and house managers. Then we had a frank discussion about the rules that *weren't* written down, the rules that were sort of implied between the lines. I could have fried Vincent's ass by making a case over what he'd been doing up in my apartment in the first place, but I chose not to.

My manager kept talking and I kept nodding my head and saying things like, "Uh-huh. Okay. I understand. Sure." It was a great performance in the role of the compliant employee. But really? I was five or six miles away in the downtown streets of San Francisco, looking for an apartment of my own. Maybe that was too grand an aspiration to have, considering I'd only been sober for a comparatively short amount of time. But the notion of having a relapse never entered my mind. Or—who am I kidding?—maybe that's what attracted me to the situation with Vince in the first place. If the Lord truly works in mysterious ways, then I have to tell you from firsthand experience, addiction does, too. Two or three weeks after that incident, I resigned from Project 90. That same day I found myself trolling the streets of San Fran with an APARTMENTS FOR RENT flyer in my hand. I was fulfilling that very same vision.

❖

As it turned out, Thomas was looking for a place, too, so we decided to become roommates once more. By pooling our money we were able to rent this sweet-ass apartment! It had stained-glass windows. Chandeliers in every room. A garage plus a huge backyard with lemon trees and rose gardens. The area had everything we could have wanted in terms of amenities. A farmer's market was 200 feet from our front door. We were even gonna have us a deck right off the back door with a huge hot tub on it. This place was my goddamn heaven!

'Course, all this stuff cost money so I got a job in a marketing research firm at $12 an hour. It wasn't nearly enough, so I took a second job as a social services supervisor at $15 an hour; I worked with six mentally ill or otherwise disabled people. That second job kept my feet firmly rooted in the therapeutic community. I worked with three caseworker counselors who were technically my subordinates in a gorgeous five-bedroom house up in the hills above San Mateo. Mostly, I functioned as the team nutritionist; I cooked well-balanced meals for the clients and staff. It was a heavy schedule what with the two jobs and all. Most days I worked 13 or 14 hours a day. Plus I was still attending the alumni dinner and meeting at Project 90 every Thursday night, and AA meetings nearly every other day at either Pilgrim Baptist or the Martin Luther King Center. I was crazy busy, but I was happy. I was tired most of the time, but I could sleep pretty well at night knowing that my damn life had started to turn itself around.

Then I got hit with a big fucking white envelope in my mailbox one day and that sent me through the goddamn roof. The letter was from the San Mateo child support office. But really you could say that it was a letter from Sheila.

Now granted, I'd been an absentee dad to Kara. And even if I had been present, my addict's ways and crazed lifestyle probably would have hurt and confused her terribly. I didn't have any formal arrangement with Sheila about sending money for Kara's well-being. It was catch as catch can, and most of the time—I'll be honest—I was a bad father. I deserved to be taken to task on that. But I'll say this much in my defense: after I got outta Program 90, I really was trying very hard to do the right thing. It was the first time in a long time that I'd picked up the phone and started reconnecting with friends and family back east, let alone reconnecting with them while I was sober.

I'd spent whole years interacting with my loved ones on autopilot. Who the hell knows what you're saying and thinking when you're high on drugs? I accept responsibility for all my actions; I had no one to blame but myself. I just wished Sheila had called me first to tell me, "Roy, this is what I've elected to do." Maybe we could have worked s omething out.

My conversations with Sheila had tended to follow the same old routine over the course of several years. I'd call her up whacked out like a zombie on crack or reefer or liquor or all three. We'd go through the motions of having a "talk," but pretty soon Sheila'd just start repeating the same old thing. "Roy, that's nice. Now send the money." I guess money was the only thing she thought I could provide for my daughter at that point. The truth hurts. She was right.

Sheila was one of the first people I called when I got back on my feet after leaving jail and the treatment center. I told her my intentions straight up. Wanted Kara to know that I was her daddy. Wanted her to know that I'd be coming out to see her at some point. Wanted her to know that I loved her and I'd *always* loved her, even if I'd made some big mistakes in my life. Sheila'd said she understood all that. She sounded to me like she meant it, too.

She never said, "Let's try and work something out." She never said,

"I understand your predicament and let's see if we can handle this just between ourselves." Never even tried to talk about it. Talking hadn't ever gotten us very far, however, if the truth be told. She went straight ahead and put her grievances in writing. I had to appear in court and have the judicial system basically crawl over every inch of my life until they decided what I was good for: about $400 a month, as it turns out. Basically all the money I was making from my market research job.

❖

STILL, THINGS KEPT on looking up. Jimmy sent money so that I was able to visit him out in L.A. for a little while. In many ways, Jimmy became my inspiration for so many things. He was gay and he was out; he was living his life with bravery and dignity and a constant sense of adventure. Why couldn't I? Jimmy was off drugs and alcohol, too. He'd battled his demons and beaten them into submission.

"Does it get easy after a while?" I asked him. "Come on. It's gotta get easy."

He just looked at me and shook his head. "No, Roy. It doesn't get easy. Sometimes it even gets harder. But the rewards sure keep getting bigger." That sounded awfully good to me.

Not long after that Jimmy called me up all excited. "Roy! Man, do I have an opportunity for you! You're gonna love this. How would you like a free trip to New York and tickets to the premiere of Whitney Houston's new film?" To which I responded, "What's the catch?"

The catch was this: Jimmy had been in touch with Lillian Smith, the senior producer of the Phil Donahue show. Apparently they were interested in doing a show about WHAT IF YOU FOUND OUT THAT THE GUY YOU WENT TO THE PROM WITH WAS GAY AND HE NEVER TOLD YOU? Lillian mentioned the show to Jimmy, who told her that one of his oldest and dearest friends in the world was a guy who used to be an offensive lineman for both the Giants and the Washington Redskins. So Lillian said, "I want him."

"This show is perfect for you, Roy," Jimmy said. "I think that part of your problem is that you've never come clean with everybody all at once. You've been very guarded with your sharing."

To say the least, I was a little apprehensive. I was like, "Hooooo, oh *God*, Jimmy. I don't know . . ."

Jimmy kept urging me to do it. "Roy, if you don't start the process of freeing yourself, you don't stand a chance at real happiness and sobriety. You've got to make this a mission. The Donahue show can help."

I thought it over and thought it over. Man, it was the toughest decision of my life. Coming out on national fucking television? Back then Phil Donahue was the goddamn Oprah Winfrey of the talk show circuit. This wasn't gonna be some quiet little sideshow, this was gonna be the motherfucking main event. I didn't want to go into it lightly. However, as scared as I was about outing myself to the world, part of me felt this confusing urge to dive right in. A deep need to take responsibility for my life in a bold way. Oddly, the offer to do the Donahue show came at a time in my life when I believe I needed it most.

Finally I called Jimmy back and said, "Okay. I'll do the show if Thomas can come, too."

"Roy, I don't know if they're gonna be all right flying two people out, two people's expenses, that's a lot to ask."

"Thomas comes too or I don't do the show."

And just like that, I was booked.

The whole idea of the show was this: three gay men would form the panel. They'd sit right out in the open at the top of the show and introduce themselves. Then, one by one, the women they'd once dated would come out—not knowing what the show was about—and introduce themselves. The men would then reveal their sexuality both to their former girlfriends and to the world in general for the first time, in front of the live TV audience. Talk about pressure!

'Course, the next question from the *Donahue* producers was, *Who's Roy gonna tell?* There were many to chose from, of course. So Jimmy got back on the phone and started calling around.

The first and maybe most natural choice was Sheila. I'd had a child by her, after all, and she certainly hadn't known I was gay when that happened. By this point, though, Sheila and I were fighting like dogs. She was the last person on earth who would step up to take part in the show. Plus she didn't really fit the show's agenda 'cause she already knew

I was gay since I'd told her over the phone, just after Alisha outed me to Roz. I still remember that conversation, too:

"Sheila? It's Roy." Dead silence on the other line. "Hello, Roy," she said. Flat. I could tell by the way she spoke those two little words that she'd already equated hearing from me with trouble on the way.

"Sheila . . . I have something to tell you." I couldn't believe I was doing it. After all this time, where would I begin? What would I say? How would I defend myself? *Could* I defend myself? *You have no right to defend yourself after everything you've done to her. To Kara. To everybody.*

Sheila said, "What is it, Roy?" She sounded exasperated, like she was beyond the end of her rope. The tone of her voice hurt me, especially at that particular moment. But of course, I knew she was right. Part of me *was* a spoiled child, the part of me that wanted everything in the world without sacrificing anything: I wanted to be gay and have a wife and kids; a football player and a crack addict; at one with God and an alcoholic. *Oh, Sheila,* I wanted to say. *Sheila, baby, please forgive me.*

But instead all I said was, "I'm gay." Just like that. The line was silent for a very long time. When Sheila finally spoke, there was disbelief. Then the sort of revulsion that comes when you think someone's telling you a bad joke. Next came the sharp intakes of breath that signaled she'd realized I wasn't kidding, I was telling the truth. Then the confusion, then the anger. Finally came a whole bunch of questions. *Who did you sleep with? When did you start? Why didn't you tell me? All through school? You bastard! How could you?* After that, there was nothing but tears and curses and the final, haunting click as she hung up the phone and the buzz of the long, dead line down to Savannah droned softly in my ear.

No, asking Sheila was not an option I was willing to entertain. But Jimmy insisted. He thought that having Sheila on the show would make for a great segment. He urged me to call her. I was like, "Hell, no. Fuck that. I ain't gonna call her, *you* call her." So Jimmy did.

❖

SHEILA AND JIMMY had actually stayed in touch with each other over the years. He rang her up and at first they talked, mostly about old times and people they still had in common. Jimmy wasn't calling to reminisce, though. He asked Sheila if she'd want to appear on the Donahue show and her answer—to put it mildly—was no. So Jimmy called Roz next and got pretty much the same answer. "Hell, no, Jimmy. Are you outta your goddamn mind?!?" He didn't give up. He just kept going right on down the phone tree, calling women I'd known. He called Nigeria, but she was married by that point, and no, the idea of putting herself on TV in that position didn't sound appealing on account of the new life she'd built with her husband. Then he called Kathy, the beautiful white tomboy I used to see way back when I was still living in Jersey. She was still living in the New York metropolitan area. We hadn't spoken to one another in years.

Jimmy said, "Kathy, look. I'm guessing you haven't seen Sugar Bear in quite some time." This was true; Kathy and I had sort of lost touch. So Jimmy put the situation to her in the most therapeutic terms: "Kathy, I was wondering something. Did you by any chance know that Roy's gay?"

No, she most certainly did not. In fact, the news took her by complete surprise. So Jimmy went this route: "Look, I'll understand if you have very strong feelings about this. But Roy's going through a tough time right now and he could really use our help. Nobody else will stand with him when he makes this announcement public. Will you do it? Will you be on the show with him?"

Kathy said that she would. God bless that woman! Jimmy said he'd have the producers send a limousine around to pick her up on the day of the show and that was that, we were booked on *Donahue*. Now all I needed to do was tell my family and friends what they should prepare themselves for.

16

Roz called me up before I left California and begged me not to do the show. She said, "Roy, please understand this from my point of view. All my relatives watch that show and they know who you are. They know our history. Isn't it bad enough that *I* lived through the whole damn embarrassment of not knowing who you really are? Do you have to drag all my friends and relations through this shit, too?"

I'd hurt Roz again and again, but this time I had no choice but to act honestly, even if that was going to embarrass her. To be truthful, it was going to embarrass me, too, but I saw the show as a healthy, necessary step for me to take. Frankly, I was scared to death about the whole thing; my feet kept getting colder and colder every day. But I kinda felt this was a good sign. Coming out was *supposed* to feel tense, wasn't it? I thought: *For years I've felt tons of pressure pressing down on my shoulders. Just think how relieved I'll feel when I put that weight aside and walk upright into the world for the very first time.*

Thomas and I arrived in New York City late at night. The next day a car picked us up at our hotel and drove us to the NBC Studios where *Donahue* was taped. My life in the closet was about to be over and I'd never felt so terrified.

Although the news that a former pro football player is gay was a bombshell to everyone, I wasn't the first NFL player to come out of the closet. The first was David Kopay, a running back and special teams ace from Southern California who played for the 49ers, New Orleans, the Redskins, Detroit, and Green Bay. Kopay played pro ball from '64 to '72. He officially stepped out of the closet in '75, and followed up with a book called *The David Kopay Story* in 1977. Surprisingly, I'd never heard of David Kopay. Didn't even know the man existed until Jimmy told me about him. Back when I was playing, I was preoccupied with keeping my homosexuality a secret. Never mind my suspicions about other players being gay or the rumors that went around about players' sexuality. For all practical purposes, I felt completely alone in the NFL. I thought I was the only gay man in pro football.

The big question on everybody's minds is always this: Are other players in the NFL gay? My answer today is an unequivocal *yes*. Kopay, for instance, was real honest about the affair he carried on with another Redskins player, an all-pro tight end by the name of Jerry Smith. In fact, the relationship these two men had is something of a sports legend. They were lovers for years, and both managed to keep their sexuality under wraps while leading their teams to fantastic playing seasons. An assistant general manager of the Redskins also officially came out a few years after the team. So I guess there's gays both on and off the field and in the front offices of the NFL.

'Course, when you really think about it, all this is truly common sense. Gays have always been present in all walks of life. Why should American football be any different? Why should *any* part of modern-day America be any different? Every book I've ever read lists the world homosexual population as somewhere between six and ten percent of the whole. If the NFL is viewed as a subsection of the overall population, that means that six to ten percent of all professional football players are gay, too.

❖

THIS IS HOW Phil Donahue introduced me to the world: "If you're into sports, you will recognize our next guest, the highly regarded Roy Simmons. Let me tell you about Roy. He was an offensive guard and . . . ah, where'd you play in college, Roy?"

Lord, it was hot under those studio lights. I was sitting there dressed in my best tan suit with my chin tucked into my neck and a big ol' smile plastered on my face. I could feel my hands shaking a little, so I locked them together into a sort of big fist and left them in my lap to kinda calm down or something. I hoped I looked cool and calm and collected. But inside, I was a motherfucking ball of nerves.

"I played for Georgia Tech in Atlanta."

Donahue nodded and leaned in a little bit. He could do that real well. He'd lean right on in and it was like he was saying, *Just for a second, forget that the whole world's watching. It's just you and me here—we're keeping it real—and, anyway—hell—ain't we pals?* Donahue leaned in real close to me and chuckled like I'd just told him a good joke. He said: "And I bet you were something in college, too, weren't you?"

"Yes, sir. I was."

He turned back to the audience and suddenly it was like he was a carnival barker all over again. "Roy Simmons was a New York Giant from 1979 to 1985 . . ."

Damn, he got it wrong, I was only with the Giants till '82 and then I was a Redskin till '84 and then—"and he's coming here today to tell you that he is now . . . and always has been . . . gay!"

Dead silence. You coulda heard a pin drop in that studio. Donahue played it up real well, too. He turned around with a mock look of surprise as if he was just then noticing the dumbfounded expressions throughout the audience. Then he gave this little smile that sort of said, *Hah! Got 'em just where I want 'em!* and he went in for the kill. He was quite the showman, that Phil Donahue was.

"Are you surprised?" he asked the audience. And nobody but nobody said a word. Then Donahue turned back to me and said in that same *ain't-we-pals?* tone of voice, "Well. You've got 'em in the sports bars now, kid."

Donahue went on to introduce the other two guests, a guy named Barry who'd come outta the closet seven or eight years ago, and another guy who was an actor and a playwright named David Drake who performed a one-man show he'd written called *The Night Larry Kramer Kissed Me*. Then he turned back to me. "Roy, let's start with you out of respect for your size. You don't mind if I call you 'sir,' do you?" The audience kinda chuckled. "Now the woman who's coming out here, her name is Kathy and she's white, right? Was her family okay with that?

Or did her folks say, 'Hi, Roy. Come on in and have a ham sandwich?!'"
Like I said, that Phil Donahue was quite the showman.

I told him how Kathy's race never made one bit of difference to me. I
told him that I found her attractive 'cause she had a good heart, a heart
that matched mine, and that was all that mattered to me when I was
with somebody. *Gay or straight never made a bit of difference to me. What's
in a person's heart means everything. I didn't always return that love to my
partners completely but their good-heartedness meant everything to me.*

Donahue said, "How long's it been since you've seen Kathy?"

"About five years." Which is what Jimmy and I and Kathy had figured
out. Five long years. Imagine what Kathy would think if she'd known
the full truth. Hell, never mind I was gay. What if she'd known I was
a crackhead? A peep show prostitute? A violent criminal? And so on?
How could anyone make sense of the reckless life that I'd led?

"Well, she's here. Right now. And she knows about you. Any idea
how she found out?"

"Yes," I said. *Jimmy.*

"Well, let's bring her out then. Ladies and gentlemen, say hello to
Kathy!"

You know what's funny? Once again, my whole body went numb.

❖

LORD, THAT WOMAN hadn't changed a bit! She was still so beautiful!
I stood up and gave her a great big hug when she walked into my arms.
And it was like all the time that had come between us—all the *every-
thing* that had come between us—melted away in just a few seconds.
We sat back down and the show continued.

Donahue asked Kathy questions about how she was raised and what
her values had been growing up. Kathy was cool as a cucumber. She
said that she was brought up in a household with nine brothers and
sisters. They were taught to love and respect one another. They were
not taught prejudice and homophobia.

Yeah, girl! That's my Kathy. Go on!

Then Donahue said, "So how did you find out?" Meaning about
me, I guess. And Kathy said, "Through another one of his girlfriends.

Another one told another one and so on and so forth until eventually I heard about it, too."

Hell, this was news to me. But then I guess maybe Roz had let it slip. Or Nigeria.

Or one of my relatives. As it turns out, Kathy had known for years, even if—like she told Donahue—she hadn't really believed it.

Donahue looked confused. "Uh, Roy? How many women did you date back then, Roy?"

"Huh. Uh . . . several."

"So you were a real gandy dancer then, weren't you?" I'd never heard that term before. But Donahue continued. "So, how can we put this? I guess it's safe to say you were walking down both sides of the street, right?"

"Yes. Yes, I was."

"All your life you were doing this?"

Oh, you poor man, Mr. Phil Donahue. You don't know the motherfucking half of it.

At little after that, Donahue did something that surprised me. He said, "Roy, here you are. You've stepped forward on the highly regarded *Donahue* show—" he paused for a second to let the audience have their laugh"—and you've come here to say *what*, Roy? *What*? Do you want to say, '*I'm gay and I'm proud?*' Or do you want to say, '*This is who I am?*' Or is it, '*I'm really bi-sexual*,' or '*It's none of your business?*' Which is it, Roy? Please tell me, I'm curious."

Even though I'd known for weeks I was going on the show, this question still caught me off guard. It was just too big to answer all at once. Where should I begin? With Travis? With Wayne? With Stick or Gerald or that sailor—the first man I was ever with, at the Flex Club? Should I tell them about all the times I wanted to hurt myself because of everything I was doing to Roz, to Sheila, to Kathy, to my family? To me? Should I tell them about my daughter and all the regrets I had? The way I honestly wished I could turn back time and erase drugs from my life? The way I wished I could play in the Super Bowl one more time? Where do you begin when someone asks you, *What's your life about, anyway?* If you'd gone through everything I'd gone through, done all the things I did, where do you begin to explain to the world what happened?

I wasn't easy, but I gave it a try. "I came here to say that today I'm the same Roy Simmons that I was years ago. Same heart, same speech, same personality. I'm just a little more knowledgeable about my sexuality and what's going on in my life. Before, I couldn't accept the idea of myself, the feelings I was experiencing. But now I'm older. I'm able to put it together. I can deal with it more. I'm involved in a lot of church activities and social functions, I'm working with the youth a lot. Today I can look at myself for who I really am and be proud. I don't need to be in the closet any more."

The audience applauded that. I had to bite my lip to keep from crying. *They understand! They really understand me!* There! I'd said it out loud for the whole world to hear. My sexuality was no longer a secret. My *soul* was no longer a secret. I'd never have to hide who I was anymore. Here I was being cheered on by an audience for the first time since I left professional football. My heart started thumping the same as it did when I'd run out through the locker room tunnels into that stadium jam-packed with 75,000 wild fans. In that moment, I felt a sensation I hadn't felt in years. I felt pride.

Phil turned to Kathy and said, "Kathy?" Like he was saying, *Ma'am, is this true?* Kathy took a long look at me and a little smile crept up on her face. I knew that smile real well. Hell, there was a time I looked forward to seeing it every day of my life.

"He's the same Sugar Bear," Kathy said. "I'm sure he is. He's the most lovable man in the world and he'd do anything for anybody." I thought: *Anybody but myself, girl. Anybody but my goddamn self.* Right then, I wanted to kiss her. Like Roz and so many others who'd loved the best parts of me, in the end Kathy was able to see the love I had inside me, the love that existed even through all the craziness.

❖

SOMEWHERE IN THE middle of the show a young man phoned the studio and Phil took the call. I didn't know it at the time, but all throughout the broadcast they were flashing a sign across my chest that said 1–800-FON-PHIL. The phone line opened up and this young man said to the whole studio audience, "Um. I'm gay, and I just recently got engaged. And I want to know . . . how am I supposed to tell her?"

Donahue looked like he'd been hit on the head with a brick. "Um . . ." he said. "Ahhhh. Huuuhhmmmmm. Ahhhhhhh . . ." The question was serious and real and it had caught him completely off guard. So he cut to a commercial. When the show came back on the air, the caller was gone and nobody'd ever answered his question. We just kept right on going.

The other two guests talked mostly about how difficult it was for them to come out of the closet, and the discrimination they'd felt throughout their younger years. Although I, too, had grown up closeted, I didn't relate much to what they described. I'd always been popular in high school. Nobody ever picked on me. I was captain of the football team. If I told people I wanted to fuck men, sure, I would have been crucified just like anybody else. But if I went about my business and did what I wanted and other people ignored what I thought I'd put right up under their noses, then it was *their* decision, not mine. And they chose to ignore it. That's the way I started looking at things that day on the show.

It took me by surprise that Donahue was so sympathetic. In the middle of the show, he shocked me by saying, "Let's try to understand what gays are up against here. Let's be honest. Those people who are fearful of gays in a very real way have the support and backing of organized religion. The Catholic Church is legitimizing homophobia. You cannot say you hate the sin and love the sinner without inevitably bringing prejudice against the so-called sinner. And you have the Joint Chiefs of Staff—we don't know exactly how many uphold this, but a few have been outspoken—against gays in the military. You have a lot of teenage high school boys going out, beating up queers—and they're not even sure why. Oh, we'd better get a hold of this! Oh, *boy*, we'd better get a hold of *this*!"

Naturally, the audience had questions. Donahue scrambled over to each person and offered his mike. The first woman said, "Roy? Would you be with a woman now? And if you were, would you tell them you're bisexual?"

"Yes, I would be with a woman. I would also state my sexuality." Meaning openly.

The next woman said, "Roy, do you still date women now? If so, how do they handle the situation?"

"At present, I'm not dating anyone. I have very good friends. I'm more involved with the church now, and . . . I'm in a lot of organizations . . ." I sort of blanked out here. My mind was screaming, *Like San Bruno Prison and Project 90 and rehab and AA and NA!* "Uh . . . I just have friends at the present day." Whew.

Then a guy in the audience with jet-black hair that had a white streak over one eye stood up. "Important point, if I may. I agreed with Mayor Ed Koch's bill back in 1980 that said you cannot discriminate against gays for employment, housing, and so forth. But at the same time, the Board of Education sponsored gay programs for first graders and kindergartners! First graders and kindergartners! I think that's inappropriate. I say: if you people want to come out of the closet? Welcome. Society welcomes you. But keep away from my kids and our children. I'm willing to respect *your* rights so long as you—"

Donahue cut him off. "What do you think will happen to your kids if they attend these programs, sir?" Too late. Or was it? By this point the audience was up in arms. The guy with the black hair shouted, "By the way! I think I speak for large amounts of people out there!" But Phil pulled the microphone back. "I do, too! So what do you think will *happen* to them?!"

The black-haired guy was now clearly perturbed. He grabbed the microphone back and said, "Muslim! Catholic! or Jewish! These beliefs should be respected, just as yours should! By the way, I disagree with gay-bashing. I think anyone bashing for someone being gay should be prosecuted to the fullest extent of the law—"

Phil grabbed the mike again. "Your suggestion that gays can't be trusted with children is a bashing all its own!" The black-haired guy pulled back. "I didn't say that! I'm saying a man with a gay lifestyle isn't reflecting *my* lifestyle. I'm saying I want to work with you guys and I want to respect you, make sure no one harasses you. If there's gay-bashing going on, I'm on your side one hundred percent! But I'm *also* saying please don't come near a kindergarten classroom. Are you educating these first graders? Or ramming a political agenda down their throat?!"

The audience went wild.

Barry, my fellow guest, rebutted the black-haired man. "Didn't you *hear* the caller from before? He didn't know how to *tell* her! That's *exactly* what we're talking about! If that little boy had known from *childhood* that he was a boy who liked other *boys* . . . just think of all the *pain* he'd be saving this girl *right now!*"

The man looked stupefied. Barry pushed further.

"If we don't get education into the system in time to say to kids, "Hey, this happens often. This is a way people love each other, and what's really wrong with *that?*" Just think of what that could do!"

The black-haired guy started sputtering. "My position is that you are educating these first graders and ramming a political agenda down their—" But Barry stopped him. "Don't you see? It's education. The same as telling people fifty years ago that African-Americans aren't bad. It's nothing more than education. And while we're on the subject, this *lifestyle* of mine is not a *choice!*" He made these little ticky motions in the air with his fingers to indicate *quote, unquote: choice.* "Any more than the color of my eyes. What I'm saying is that gays are here. Start dealing with us. If we take care of it in the early years, it can go better on everybody."

After the show, Donahue came up to me and pulled me into a dark corner of the hallway so we could speak in private. He said, "Good show! Good show, good show." His head was bobbing over and over again and he was kinda talking real fast. "Glad to have you here. Really. It took a lot of courage to do this." And just like that somebody grabbed his arm and whisked him away. Honestly? I could never really tell whether he cared about the things we'd been talking about or not. Part of me wants to believe that he did. But part of me also believes that he was sort of just fanning the flames of the conversation the whole time, pitting both sides against the other, supporting no one but the heat of the fire. I didn't have any illusions that his first obligation was to his ratings. In the end, though, I suppose it doesn't really matter. I'd got what I wanted. I'd come out to the world. For me, the horizon was all brand-new.

Thomas and I were driven back to our hotel by another limousine and we had something to eat there, Courtesy of NBC. I was ecstatic. I was thrilled. I was proud. I was exhausted. We flew back to San Francisco the next day.

All along I'd imagined the impact the show would have on everyone I knew, but suddenly it seemed like the whole world was trying to get in touch with me. I was overwhelmed. The Donahue show forwarded hundred of letters to me and then there were the phone calls coming in from my ex-teammates. Kent Hill. Eddie Lee Ivery. Lucious Sanford. Don Bessilieu. Doug Van Horn. J. T. Turner. And they all asked me the same damn thing. "Sugar Bear! have you lost your mind? You been drinking one too many cocktails or *what*?!" None of them congratulated me or said, "Hey, man, that took a lot of guts. Good for you."

My brother Gary had his own strange experience. "I was outside play-ing football with some friends at my cousin Mark's house. I guess I was eighteen years old at the time. In the middle of the game I remembered that Roy's program was on, so I grabbed everybody on my team and dragged them inside and put them in front of the TV set and turned it on. The picture and the sound came up at the same time that that guy, Phil Donahue, said, '. . . that he is now and always has been gay.' After that, all I remember is someone hitting me on the arm and saying, 'Yo, man. Your brother's a fag.'"

Gary was so embarrassed for me and my entire family. "I was in shock. I started saying things to my friends like, 'No! No, it can't be! I *lived* with him! I *saw* him with girls, girls, *girls*! He's gotta be doing this for the money or something. This is bullshit!'"

For a while, the attention felt really, really nice. I'd done something honorable at last. And receiving that kind of love from so many people, most of them strangers, made me feel like I'd felt way back when: on top of the world. I was walking on air. I even called up Roz and begged her to forgive me, which she did.

❖

ABOUT A MONTH later everything was still going fine. I was sober, I was back in the good graces of the church, and I was well on my way to a brand-new life as an openly gay man. But around this time, I showed up at choir practice one day to find it had been cancelled without anyone notifying me. I found the church doors locked. I sat down on the steps of that church and listened—really listened—to all the noise I was surprised to find thundering away inside my head. *You think you've won? You think going on some TV show and whining about how gay you are was a good thing? Stupid motherfucker. You ain't fooling nobody with this act—sobriety and honesty and forgiveness. Please. Roy, you ain't meant to be nothing but a complete fuck-up so far as this world is concerned. Better get yourself out there in the streets again and get some crack. Better get high. You know it's gonna happen sooner or later.*

How could I go off the deep end again so fast? How could I slip back into the low life and sink so deep that I'd empty out my apartment of all my belongings—all of Thomas's belongings—all for crack? All for nothing? Hell—it was easy. Once a junkie, always a junkie. I got up from the steps of the church and brushed little bits of crushed granite off the seat of my pants. Then I went out to get high.

17

I'D FOUND THE Donahue show to be a liberating experience, sure I had. But it also made me feel like a glacier. Glaciers are famous for moving real slow. Sometimes those big sheets of ice take years to move a matter of inches. Even so, those inches are crucial because glaciers build up tensions over the years. One day the glacier gives a tiny wiggle and all of a sudden it sparks an avalanche that could bury a whole continent.

The Donahue show was like that for me, one tiny little moment in my life—a movement of inches, nothing more. The repercussions, however, were staggering, violent—strong enough to set off whole earthquakes and shatter the landscape of my mind for miles around. The layout of my thoughts would never be the same.

I guess the truth of the matter was that I hadn't taken time out after the show to deal with the upheaval of my soul. I ignored it, instead. I kept myself busy every minute of every hour of every day, hopping around town. Work, choir practice, meetings, sleep. More work, more choir practice, dinner with friends, more meetings, more work, more sleep. I was running away from trouble again, only this time, I wasn't running away to San Francisco or Newark or Florida or D.C. I'd refined the process considerably and now I was running away inside my own damn head.

I kept myself so busy that my day-to-day thoughts were loud enough to drown out even the sound of the avalanche going off inside my mind. Sitting down on those church steps just before my relapse was the first time in a very *long* time that I'd honestly tuned in to all that awful sound.

Mostly the noise was a chorus of voices from my past. People blaming me for hurting them. People saying they didn't love me anymore.

One voice above the rest was all too familiar to me. It was the second voice, the one that lay beneath all the others, the one that said it knew my soul like no one else. The one that said it always spoke the truth. *Shit, Roy. You know you ain't made for sobriety. Ain't you suffered enough lately? Huh? All this coming-out shit and smiling at people and telling them how blessed you feel having finally told the truth, when you know the only thing on your mind right now is throwing a sharp one and going off on a tear. Just like the old days. Just like you used to . . .*

It *had* been a difficult time for me. I felt all sorts of pressure building up inside me, like someone was pumping hot air into my lungs, air that was all balled up inside now, building up enough force to explode inside me and tear me to pieces. All of a sudden I wanted a hit from a crack pipe so bad that the fingers of both my hands had curled themselves into fists. The hands that had maybe taken the life of a man in a back alley of San Francisco not two years ago pressed its manicured fingernails into the flesh of both my palms and made little tiny crescent-shaped furrows.

I'm telling myself, *Don't do this, Roy, don't do this! You've come so far.* Not far enough. *What do I do now? Jesus Christ, oh God, help me. What do I do now? Do what you always do. Run, motherfucker! Run!*

I didn't run, not at first, at any rate. I headed over to my friend Gladys's house instead. She lived two blocks from the church in a lovely old house. I have a lot of good memories being in that house. Lately, I'd spent whole weeks there. In some ways Gladys had taken over Big Cat's role in my life. Like Cat, Gladys loved to cook; Sunday dinners were her specialty. She'd have everybody we knew over and we'd watch movies, tell jokes, play cards, and laugh until our bellies hurt. I think that deep down, Gladys wanted to be my lover. She always told me how she couldn't wrap her head around the fact that I was gay. "Roy," she'd say, "are you sure? Are you really *sure?*" She'd taken to reading books on homosexuality with the hope of figuring out the root of it in me. I think she had some crazy idea that it could be removed with the proper surgery or something. In a way, her belief was sort of pitiful. It was also one of the dearest things I'd ever seen anybody do for me.

I was one block away from Gladys's house when I made a wrong turn on purpose. Or did I? Who can say what power guides an addict back on the trail of addiction? I'll give you a clue: the addict can't. Not unless he's committed his entire soul to finding the answer to that question. In the end, it doesn't matter to the telling of this story. Suffice it to say, I don't know what came over me, but I knew there was this convenience store down the wrong-turn way, a little place where they sold cold beer out of the refrigerators and drugs around the back of the building. The place was a neighborhood legend. Bunches of guys used to sit around that place right out in the open, drinking and getting high.

I also knew that one of the guys who usually hung out in front of the convenience store was this dude I knew from church, an ex-basketball player named Delamis, six feet and seven inches of pure, black sexy. Delamis had a deep voice and this cute little raggedy-ass beard. I'd always wanted him and I'm pretty sure he knew it. This time, when I saw him hanging out in front of that convenience store, I knew the reason why I'd made that wrong turn in the first place. Delamis knew all the dealers who worked on the block. A plan formed in my head. Thomas had gone outta town on a week-long business trip to L.A. I had the apartment all to myself. So the first thing I'd do, I'd buy some crack. *Not for me*, I thought, *oh hell no, I'm in recovery. We'll get it for Delamis. Help him chill out and enjoy the evening a bit more.*

Step Two of the plan: we'd pick up some beer. Again, not for me, of course. *GAWD no! An addict? In recovery? Drinking beer? Hell, no, that sort of thing's not gonna happen here. I'm completely in control. And besides, I'm not thirsty. I intend to stay sober!* Lie number two. Next we'd go back to my apartment, where Delamis would get all fucked up. And when he was good and ready—final step of the plan—I'd have him. I'd have that motherfucker any which way I wanted him. Lie number three.

If you take nothing else away from this story of mine, remember this: nobody on earth can lie to themselves like an addict.

Nothing happened according to plan. First of all, Delamis knew what I wanted before I even opened my mouth. That kinda threw me off a bit. I thought I'd have to spend a few minutes sweet-talking him, but no, I guess he wanted this thing as much as I did, because he was around the corner in a flash to pick up the crack. I picked up the beer, and ten minutes later we're back at my apartment, where he's loaded the pipe, puffing away on the shit like he's a goddamn chimney. Meanwhile I'm down on my knees, sucking his dick and loving every second of it.

He offered me some of his beer and you know what? I *was* a little thirsty. So I told myself I'd just take a little swig, just a tiny one. Wasn't really cheating at all, you know, just a little swig. And after the first swig, I figured that another one would only be appropriate. After all, I'd *invited* Delamis over to my place for a drink and here I was the only one not indulging in a beverage. How rude. So I grabbed a beer and drank it down fast. Then I grabbed another and started in on that when suddenly I noticed Delamis outta the corner of one eye. He was loading up the pipe again, getting ready for another hit. Which is when I heard my own voice say, "Gimme that fucking pipe over here." And that, as they say, was that.

Later on that night I know I tried to fuck Delamis's tall, lanky body. For some reason, though, I couldn't get it up. It was embarrassing. Delamis just laughed and told me not to worry about it. I don't think he was the sort of guy who really liked getting fucked, anyway. Having his dick sucked was one thing, getting fucked was something else entirely. We spent the rest of the evening getting royally high, and Delamis left the next morning.

I finally made my way over to Gladys's place just after that. I don't think she suspected a thing. Real hard-core addicts can hide the effects of their addictions even from themselves. And that's what I was by that point—all over again, I was an addict. I told Gladys I needed to borrow her car and she gave it to me. A woman in love with you usually has no problem letting you borrow her car. I drove around the neighborhood, telling myself I was just looking for some*thing* to do. I knew better than that, of course. I was looking for some*body* to do. I was also looking for more crack.

I spotted a girl I knew hanging out on a street corner, the daughter of a preacher from another church. She had some shit on her so we sat in the car and smoked it up. Then she turned to me and said, "Hey, man. If you like *this* shit, I got a friend named Mike who's got the real fucking deal."

"Oh yeah? Where's he at?"

"East Palo Alto. Lives in a fucking Winnebago. You gotta meet him, you'll love him."

"I ain't never been out to East Palo Alto."

"Then I guess it's time we went, motherfucker!"

Who could refuse an invitation like that?

You pretty much know the rest of the story. Like I said, we went out to Mike's place and he and I clicked. Next thing you know it was me and him in the back of the Winnebago with the music playing nice and loud. Mike knew the deal. I got down on my knees and sucked his dick while he smoked crack. He handed me the pipe and there I was smoking crack, too. We smoked up his whole damn supply before we got the idea to drop the preacher's daughter off back at her apartment and go out looking for his friends so we could buy some more crack and keep right on smoking.

By this time, my funds were running low. My two-day binge had drained my account. When I binged it wasn't all that uncommon for me to blow through four, five, maybe six grand in two days. Maybe lose a watch or a ring or some other nice piece of jewelry in the process. Then came the same old routine of writing checks I knew were gonna bounce, coming up with lies, coming up with alibis, begging for loans, pleading for people to understand. Hell, I didn't want to put myself through all that shit again. *Why on earth should I put myself through all that shit? I'm Roy fucking Simmons. I played football in the goddamn NFL!*

So it was back to my beautiful apartment with the stained-glass windows and the chandelier instead. My gorgeous Garden of Eden. My home—my home and *Thomas's* home. Then it was good-bye furniture, good-bye appliances, good-bye to Thomas's priceless grandfather clock. After that? Say hello to the Golden Gate Bridge.

❖

A FEW DAYS later I got outta the hospital and tried to get back to some kinda normal routine. Fat chance with that. I knew Thomas was gonna hit the fucking roof when he got back from L.A, and I was in no position whatsoever to do anything but beg for his forgiveness. I was pretty sure he'd kill me when he saw me, so I moved in with a guy I knew from church, a fellow N.A. member named Jimmy who was also a sometime lover. Jimmy had this real nice apartment down in Mountain View.

I didn't see Thomas for the next three weeks. During that time I called him up and tried to explain what had happened. I really tried to apologize, but he wouldn't have it. He just kept saying the same thing over and over again. "How could you, Roy? Oh my God, how *could* you?!"

"Thomas, I don't know. I honestly—Jesus, I'm sorry. I don't know."

"Okay, just tell me this. Where's my stuff. How can I get my stuff back?"

"Thomas . . . I don't think you can, man . . ."

"How could you, Roy? How *could* you?!" We never made any headway in that conversation.

❖

THREE WEEKS AFTER I sold all our stuff, I was in the middle of mass choir practice at the San Mateo Baptist Church when the doors to the cathedral exploded open and Thomas stormed in. He looked a mess! Clothes all rumpled, hair messed up. His eyes were red and crazy and rolling around like billiard balls in his skull. His face had swollen up all pink and ruddy from drinking. He must've had a relapse, poor man. He saw me standing among the other choir members and pointed. "You!" he said. "I wanna talk to you, goddammit!" He was so angry he was crying.

It was a totally embarrassing moment, but Jimmy saved the day by playing it cool and acting fast. "Stay here, I'll handle this," and he slipped out of line. Grabbed Thomas by the arm and hauled him outside, where the two of them apparently had words. I have no idea what Jimmy said to Thomas, but somehow he calmed him down. Thomas left the church grounds and that's the last I ever saw of him.

❖

My time with Jimmy didn't last very long. Like every other lover I'd been with, our relationship started to spin out of orbit after a couple of months. He wanted to control me. Wanted to know who I was out with, what I was doing, was I still doing drugs, was I still following the 12 Steps. We got to arguing so much that I thought seriously about killing him a few times. I left his place in Mountain View after a few months and that's the last I saw of him, too.

By this point I'd come to the sad realization that I was a fucked-up person living a fucked-up life and nothing I could ever do would change that. There wasn't a 12 Step program on earth that could give me back the Sheila that I once loved or my daughter's childhood. There wasn't a Sinner's Prayer in the entire biblical canon that could give me back my football career. And even if I somehow managed to get sober—even if I managed to come to terms with the fact that so many prime opportunities in my life had been squandered on self-indulgences—none of that would actually repair the damage I'd done to my family, my friends, my lovers, and my colleagues. I was exhausted. Finished. I honestly started planning to jump off another bridge. This time, though, I'd be a man and finish the job.

Which one should it be? New York City has some fine bridges. The Brooklyn Bridge, the Queensboro Bridge, or the Verrazano. There's the Manhattan Bridge, the Whitestone Bridge, the Williamsburg Bridge, too. But really—what did it matter? From that high up, I'd heard that a man hits the water at 75 miles per hour. A hard way to go. There's pain involved. Pain I felt I deserved.

❖

All that thinking about New York must've put the proper energy out into the universe, 'cause a few days later my phone rang. It was my brother Gary, who could tell that something was wrong with me. Gary's a bulldog, man. He's never backed down in the face of anyone's problems and he wasn't about to start with mine. He'd been on the phone with Jimmy Hester, who'd expressed his doubts about my current state of sobriety and sanity. Gary'd taken that data and used it to put two and two together. My long periods of silence and my emotional upheavals whenever I *did* talk to family members were telling. Plus, I'd confided the whole incident of selling Thomas's possessions to Jimmy Hester. Jimmy'd turned right around and told my family, which had them terrified for me. "Roy," Gary said. "You gotta come home *now.* Everybody's worried. Enough with the running. We want you to come home."

"Home," I said. "What do you mean? I *am* home." I flinched cause it sounded like a bullshit answer even to me. Gary wasn't having it. "Home is *here*, Roy. Home is back east, where your *family* is. Whatever's going on with you, we'll deal with it together, as a family. But we can't start the process till you come back to us."

Little by little, he made me come 'round. *Home. Yes. With my family. Yes. With Momma and Ricky and LaTwan and Aunt Betty. The people who love me. My family.* I was starting to see it. Me: back east. Yes. I could do that. Sure I could. Start over. Only one little problem left, though: I didn't have a dime to my name. So naturally I called Jimmy Hester.

❖

I HAD CALLED Jimmy up about a week after the whole deal with the Winnebago. I needed a lifeline, someone I could talk to on a deep and personal level about all the shit that had happened. I told Jimmy the whole story about the relapse and how I sold all of my stuff plus Thomas's stuff, and he didn't say a word throughout the whole damn thing. Just a massive amount of silence. When I finally got to the end of my tale, I heard myself laugh nervously and I said, "Honest, Jimmy, I was gonna do it, too. I was gonna throw myself off that goddamn bridge, man. Ain't that crazy?"

A little tiny beat went by. Then Jimmy said—real quietly, "You should have."

"What?" I couldn't believe my ears.

"You *should* have jumped off that bridge, Roy! You should go out right *now* and throw yourself off that goddamn bridge! How could you have done this to Thomas? How could you have done this to yourself? I have nothing more to say to you. What good does it do? Nothing ever gets through to you, does it?" And just like that he'd hung up the phone.

So here I was in the position of having to ask Jimmy for money. I didn't have much pride left at this point, but what little I had, I swallowed. I got him on the phone and said, "I really need your help here, Jimmy. I gotta get outta here, I'm just *so* fucked up. Gotta head back east and get into rehab. Will you help me? Please. Say that you'll help me."

All the while I've got this image in my head of the thirteen-year-old kid sitting on a stool at The Front Row bar with that crazy handheld electronic football game. *Breeeee breeeeee! Skreeeee skreeeeee skreeeeee! Bee doop! Bo deep!* Whatever happened to that little kid? Whatever happened to me?

Jimmy listened to me rant for a little while longer. He chose to stay silent. When I was finally out of breath all he said was, "Stay by the phone. I'll call you back." And just like that he hung up again.

This time he called right back. "Roy, I can help you outta this but you have to do exactly what I say, do you understand me? No deviations."

"No deviations," I said. My heart was fluttering inside my chest. "I understand. No deviations."

"My friend Lloyd is a flight attendant for Continental. He's staying in San Francisco tonight between flights. I want you to stay with him at his hotel this evening, just to keep you safe. Lloyd has a plane ticket for you to fly back to Newark tomorrow."

"Jimmy, I don't know how to thank you—"

"Enough, Roy. Get your shit together." *Click.*

❖

I FLEW INTO Newark and caught a bus to New York's Penn Station. From there I took the Long Island Rail road out to Amityville where my mother and my brother Gary were waiting. I remember walking up the front porch steps of my mother's house. She and Gary were standing there like some kind of receiving line at a funeral parlor. It wasn't the homecoming I'd imagined. In fact, it felt more like someone had died. Namely me.

They hugged me and kissed me and didn't say much of anything at all. Then they led me inside the house and gave me a glass of sweet tea, just like I used to drink growing up with Grandma Lou down in Savannah. My mother asked me how I was feeling, and I summoned up all kinds of cheerfulness for her benefit. "Oh fine, you know! I'm really, really good." You should have seen the way she looked at me. Horrified. Furious. Hurt. Betrayed. I saw that look on her face and that was it. The jig was up.

I broke down and cried. I cried for the pain I felt over everything I'd done and I cried for the fact that I didn't know who I was anymore. The Horse was gone, Sugar Bear was gone, even the man I'd known as Roy Simmons was gone, too. I was thirty-six years old going on ten. Suddenly I was goddamn certain that if I'd stayed out west I would've died, and not died easily. I would've gone hard, kicking and screaming and whoring and smoking and drinking. I cried for all the wrong turns I'd made on the road of my life and for all the people I'd left back at so many different crossroads, the ones I hadn't had enough strength of will to ask, *Will you join me on this journey?* So I'd walked alone—miles and miles and miles I'd walked alone. And I cried for that, too. I cried for myself.

Gary and Mama just stood there in the kitchen, watching me. It was an awkward moment, the first of many between us. Finally I couldn't take it anymore. I raised my head and wiped tears from my eyes. I looked at Gary then I looked at Mama and then I looked back at Gary again. "I'm sorry," I said. 'Cause it was all I could think of to say. "I'm really, really sorry." Gary shook his head. He took in a deep breath like he was extremely disappointed in me and said, "Man, your ability to bullshit people is running at an all-time high."

We discussed treatment centers. Some of the places I looked into insisted that you commit to their regimes. The one I found most attractive—a place called Apple Treatment Center in Wainscott, New York—demanded that you give them two years of your life. Shit, I was already thirty-six years old. In two more years I'd be thirty-eight. Two years after that I'd be forty. My daughter Kara would be seventeen years old. I'd be out of pro football for nearly a decade at that point.

I finally talked it over with Gary and Mama. I said, "I don't know. This Apple place looks great but . . . two years? Two years is such a long time, you know what I'm saying?" Again, they looked at me contemptuously. Then Gary said, real slowly, "Two years ain't nothing when you consider you shoulda been dead by now." He was right, of course. I knew it. I could *feel* it. I decided to check into Apple.

I entered treatment in April of 1993. The first stop was an intake program at Hempstead Hospital, where I figured that getting sober wasn't going to be so bad after all. They fed me so well at that hospital I felt like I was right back in the football players' cafeteria at Georgia Tech.

My first day at Apple, I attended the nightly seven o'clock meeting. We went around the circle introducing ourselves and stating what we were in treatment for. When it came my turn, I stood up in front all these brand-new faces and said this:

"My name is Roy Simmons. Hi. Uh, my drugs of choice are cocaine. Alcohol. Reefer. Ah . . . beer and champagne. I guess that's alcohol, right? Crack. Which is cocaine. Sort of. Ha. Huh. I guess you could say I got an addictive personality. I mean, when something gets its hooks in me, it *really* gets its hooks in me. I love having sex, too. I guess you could say I'm addicted to that. Sex is kind of a drug. Oh! Hobbies! I love football, tennis, playing cards. I play a mean game of Spades, so—if any of you are interested . . . theater. I love theater. Love opera. I'm from Savannah, did I tell you that? Right. From Savannah and . . . oh! I have a little girl. Her name is Kara. She lives in Savannah, too, and she's thirteen years old right now. I think. Hang on, lemme see. Eleven, twelve, thirteen . . . right. thirteen years old and her name is Kara. And she's the cutest, man, she's just so beautiful. I haven't actually seen her since she was, ah, lemme see. Maybe one year old. It's complicated. Her mother isn't real happy with me right now. We had this thing. Ah. But anyway. Is that good? Is that right? I think that's it. Ah. Okay. I'm gonna sit down now."

There it was again. Why was everybody looking at me like that?

❖

EVERYONE IN THE treatment center was there for alcohol or drugs or both. We were there to learn about the effects the drugs we'd been using had had on our bodies, our minds, and our ability to navigate our way through our own decision-making process. We were also there to learn how to start living our lives without drugs in our decision-making process. When you're an addict, that's a tougher job than most people might imagine.

'Cause when you're an addict, it's like everything you do in life is really being done by another person. This other person is a daring criminal. He's kidnapped you and stuffed you away in a dark corner of your own house. You're bound and gagged so you can't hardly move, can't blink an eye, can't make a sound. All you can do most of the time is watch in horror while your kidnapper assumes your identity and opens the front door of your house and invites all sorts of people whom you would never normally associate with to step inside. Sometimes you struggle against the ropes that hold you. Maybe even one time you break free of your bonds and run around your house like a madman screaming for help, screaming for all these bad people—these degenerates, these *users*—to get out! Just get the fuck out! "This is my house, goddammit!" you scream. "My house! So you get the fuck out!"

It never lasts. The kidnapper's too strong. He's always able to hit you over the head again and knock you out cold. Tie you back up again—this time making the knots even *stronger*, the coils around your chest and throat and pinning your arms even *tighter*—and stuff you back in that corner. When you come to again, you're groggy and your head hurts and you're wondering what the hell just happened. Did you really break free for those precious few moments? Or was it all just a dream? A blip on the radar screen. A flash of sunlight breaking through the constant curtain of black clouds hanging in the sky.

Addiction can only be understood by an addict. 'Cause an addict knows the truth of his own behavior. He'd sell a baby to get another hit. He'd fuck his own mother to get another drink. He'd cut off his brother's arm and feed it to him to snort one more line. He'd cut off his own foot and eat *it* just to shoot up once more.

Everyone I met in Apple was an addict. And if I thought *my* life was fucked up, I was in for one goddamn hell of a big surprise. One girl I met had been in the facility for seven months when she was granted her first pass to go home and visit her family. Her drug of choice was crack, and she'd been clean the whole seven months, but something about going home proved too much for her, I guess. She relapsed. In the middle of a highly delusional state, she began to have auditory hallucinations which she assumed were the voice of the Devil, and the Devil was telling her to kill her own baby. Which she did. She beat it to death with her own two hands. After she came down off the drug, she'd plunged into a catatonic state for a little while. Getting her back to reality was apparently no easy trick. But here she was, sitting in the circle, attending the nightly meeting like any other addict hoping to reform. It gave me chills to think of what this woman had done. It gave me chills to think that she still held out hope for having any kind of normal life at all.

One guy in the group had robbed his own grandmother blind of everything she owned. He took thousands and thousands of dollars worth of priceless family jewels—diamond rings and heirloom necklaces that had been with his folks for generations. When his grandmother confronted him with the theft, he beat her within an inch of her life. This was an elderly woman, maybe seventy-five years old. Apparently she cried like a little girl while her grandson did his dirty work. But here he was, sitting in the circle, attending the nightly meeting. Another addict hoping to reform.

I looked at this man and thought, *I been there, man. I been there, too. Poor Thomas. Poor Sheila. Poor Roz and Jimmy and Joe and Kathy and Nigeria and Ray and Gerald and Travis. Poor everybody.*

Most of all, what I learned at Apple was this: you can never say never to a person on a drug. You can never say never to the thing that's driving a person to *use* a drug. You can never hope to recover until you get to know the person buried deep inside you, the one who's cowering in pain. Deeply wounded. Afraid to come outside. And you can never alleviate that person's pain without a tremendous amount of upheaval on the surface of what you consider to be your life right now—the life you lead in the moment. The life that you lead as an addict.

My work at Apple was like opening a great big door that had stood locked for many years. The door was thick and tough to move. But I turned the key and I shoved it open. Not much, just a crack. Just enough to squeeze through. After that, I began the long, dark journey down the corridor that led straight to the core of myself. I found a lot of demons waiting in that dark center, and each one of them scared me within an inch of my life. There was comfort, however, in knowing that each one of them was a part of me. Mine to create, which I did long ago, and mine to destroy, which I set about doing.

After eighteen months at Apple, the treatment center offered me a position as a substance abuse counselor. It was an honor to be asked and a big decision, one which would change my whole life if I chose to accept the job. By that point, I was sure that I wanted to give back and that I could give back. But the responsibility that came with this job—the responsibility of having other people's lives in my hands—was massive. I wondered if I was ready for it. Eventually, I decided I was. I accepted the position at Apple and set to work.

Mostly I did family counseling, and I loved my job. It was so reward-ing to bring people who loved each other together once more despite all the pain and rifts that drugs had caused them. I also spent a fair amount of time working with the Department of Motor Vehicles to get my clients' driver's licenses back. A fair amount of the people I worked with had logged over 125 traffic tickets before their addiction landed them at Apple. That kind of red-tape tangle takes a long, long time to unravel.

Everything was going well. I worked that job until 1997 and I worked it with incredible commitment and a great deal of success. I helped a lot of people get their lives sorted out, helped them get a brand-new start, where before they had faced a dead end.

Then I relapsed again. I wish I could say there was some major event that pushed me back over the edge, but I don't want to lie to you. Addiction doesn't always work that way. Sometimes it creeps back into your life for no good reason at all and takes control again. Commands you again. Shrinks everything around you—family, friends, job, hob-bies, world events, local news, your future, your past, and even your present—makes them grow smaller and smaller until finally they're nothing more than a microscopic speck unworthy of your attention.

I started getting high once a week and going to work. Surprisingly, no one seemed to notice, but yes, I felt guilty. Oh *Lord*! I felt so *very* guilty. But I guess I didn't feel guilty enough to stop what I was doing. No, no! If there's one thing I've always been good at, it's living a lie. And one more time I dragged that lie right up to the feet of my loved ones. This time, though, I wasn't going to get a second chance.

18

M Y WAKE-UP CALL rang in 1997. I was working at Apple, smoking crack once more. That was just the beginning, however. The strain of being in recovery, the strain of being *sober* triggered some sort of reaction in me, and once again I was having lots of sex. Nothing serious, nothing lasting. It was all about getting off. Getting off was one of the few healthy pleasures I felt I had left, so I pursued it. I pursued it with gusto.

Something was wrong, though. I'd been experiencing all these minor ailments that kept recurring. A sore throat here, an ear infection there. Once the ear infection went away, the sore throat came back again. Sometimes I started running a mild fever for no apparent reason. Other times my joints began to ache a bit like I had a tiny case of the flu. I brushed it all off. My schedule was jam-packed and I figured this was what you get when you run yourself ragged. Plus, I was conscious of the fact that I wasn't so young anymore. Forty years old now. I still felt good, still felt strong for the most part. But the bloom was definitely off the lily.

I was spending a lot of time running around from one damn doctor to the next: ophthalmologists, pulmonologists, cardiologists, even a podiatrist. I had a whole team of doctors trying to fight each ailment individually, until finally my primary care physician, Dr. Anreder, convinced me to take a comprehensive physical, just to make sure everything was all right. A few days fter the physical, he asked me to come to his office in Westhampton Beach one afternoon in October of 1997. I knew right away the news was bad. I could hear it in his voice over the phone. "I want to speak with you about the test results, Roy. Come in and see me."

"What is it? What's wrong?"

"You'd better come in and see me."

When I got to his office, the nurse put me in an examination room and I hopped up on the table. Dr. Anreder didn't keep me waiting long. He walked in a few minutes later, closed the door behind him, and looked me in the eye. "Roy, your test results are back and you're HIV positive." I was shocked, but at the same time, how could I be surprised? Given all the reckless sex I'd had—on drugs, off drugs—why should I have ever expected to escape that damned virus. In fact, the news hit me in such a way that it almost felt—I don't know. Fair.

I guess I went into shock right there 'cause I don't really remember much that was said after that.

❖

GERALD HAD DIED. Nate had died. By that point—1997—I was also aware of many, many other people I knew who'd been killed off by AIDS. Hell, at one point a few years earlier it seemed like the phone was ringing every other day. *So-and-so just died, did you hear? So-and-so just got his blood work back and he's positive. So-and-so's been looking awfully bad these days, I'm worried. So-and-so's just left to go back home and be with his family—I think this is the end.* Quite a thing to live most of your life in fear. Yet I never got tested myself. I suppose I already knew deep down that I was positive. Just one more piece of my life that I chose to avoid facing directly.

My mind raced with all sorts of questions. *Who gave it to me? When did it happen? How do I tell my family, my friends?* The question that haunted me more than any other haunted me more than every other, though was: *How do I tell Roz?* All of these questions boiled down to the same goddamn answer. *I have no fucking idea at all.*

❖

IT WAS THE week after Thanksgiving. Roz was having a pretty hectic time 'cause one of her coworkers, a woman she cared about, had been in a pretty serious car accident and was laid up in a Pennsylvania hospital. True to her form, Roz took a few trips to see this woman and comfort her. When I finally caught up with her, she was physically tired and emotionally exhausted from the trip to Pennsy and caring for her friend. Still, she gave me every bit of attention she had left.

When we sat down, I think I actually kept my voice calm. I told her I'd had some blood work done and that something had come up, some sort of problem.

"What do you mean, what sort of problem?" I could hear in her voice how scared she suddenly was.

"Roz . . ." I couldn't say anything else. All of a sudden my throat felt clogged, as if somebody'd packed it with cotton. "Roz . . ."

"What is it? *What is it?!*" She'd already gone into some sort of shock. The strain was killing her. Hadn't I put her through enough hell? "I'm HIV positive."

Roz stared at me for what felt like a long time. Her mouth was open slightly and she'd brought her hand to her face. This was by far the most frightening news I'd ever had to share with her.

She sat frozen in place for a long time. Silent. I didn't know whether she was about to cry or scream. In the end, she did something even worse. She did neither. Just sat there and *digested* what I'd told her over the course of several minutes. "Well," she said quietly. Still not moving. Her hand still floating there by her mouth. "I guess I should go and get tested."

As it turned out, she was fine. Had I infected her, I'm certain that I would have actually killed myself. I wouldn't have been able to live with that reality. That's how much I loved Roz.

Next I went down the list and told everyone in my family who I thought should hear the news from me personally. This part was tough, since it meant exposing myself more and more, confiding in people. Letting them in on what felt like my dirty little secret. I told my cousin Genie and I told my cousin Betty; they were both tremendously helpful. They held me while I cried. I didn't know how to tell my mother, so I saved her for last. I called her up about a month after I'd heard the news myself and used the phone 'cause I couldn't bear to tell her to her face.

My mother has made a career outta keeping her emotions under wraps. She won't shed a tear in public, won't ever let anybody catch her upset—she keeps all that tied down and lets it out behind closed doors instead. Wasn't no different on this occasion, too. I told her about the test results and she said nothing for a long time. I thought the line was dead. Then she said, "Take care of yourself, son." A little after that we hung up the phone, and that was it.

It may sound like a cold reaction. Emotionally disconnected. But I knew what she was doing. She was waiting to get off the line so she could fall apart in private. She'd never wanted any of us kids to see how much she cared, how vulnerable she was. In the hard world she'd grown up in, that sort of reaction to bad news was a luxury no one had ever been able to afford. Picturing my mother home alone crying her eyes out over me broke my heart.

After a few months had gone by, the only person left to tell was my old friend Jimmy Hester. Despite how good Jimmy'd been to me over the years, he wasn't family, so I decided to wait and tell him the news last. Not telling Jimmy allowed me to keep my problem within the Simmons family and that's the way I wanted it. I wanted the circle to stay closed until all my relatives had had more time to adjust to the circumstances. Hell, I wanted more time for *me* to adjust to the circumstances.

Still, after all Jimmy'd done for me, I felt he truly deserved to know and I was wracking my brain for a way to tell him in the appropriate time and the appropriate place. I finally decided I would have to tell him in person. So I called him up at his office in Manhattan. He was working for a songwriter at the time and I told him I'd like to come in and see him, have lunch, talk about a few things. Jimmy was like, "Sure. Come on in tomorrow."

When I got to his office, Jimmy was swamped with work. He came out into the reception area and apologized. "Roy, I'm so sorry. Things are crazy. Just gimme ten minutes." Half an hour later he popped his head in again and said, "Really. Sorry. Just gimme another ten minutes." And just like that he was gone again. An hour later, he still hadn't shown up. I couldn't stand the wait, it was making me crazy, sending me into a panic all over again. So I left.

On the way home, I bumped into an old friend from some forgotten crack house or other—after a while they all tend to look the same. But I knew this guy and that was my dumb luck. Volatile emotions and crackhead friends do not mix. We wound up in a crack house in East Harlem. Two days later, I still hadn't left the place. I was minus a few rings and some other jewelry worth about $1,500, and that's when it dawned on me: I'd missed lunch with Jimmy and I'd missed a day's work at Apple. My whole life was back in the toilet. I needed an alibi and I needed one fast or I was gonna lose my damn job. So I called an ambulance and told them I was having chest pains. I said I needed to go to the hospital.

They came all right, real fast. Loaded me into the back of the ambulance, gave me oxygen through this tiny little mask, and strapped a blood pressure cuff to my arm. The paramedic riding along side of me in the back of the ambulance kept asking me all sorts of questions. "Mr. Simmons, how you doing? How does your chest feel? Can you follow my finger with your eyes, Mr. Simmons? Good. Can you do me a favor and breathe in real deep? Can you do that? Good. Okay, I just want you to relax now. Your blood pressure's normal and we're on our way to the hospital. You're in good hands."

"Which hospital you taking me to?"

"The closest hospital, Mr. Simmons is—"

"Fuck taking me to the closest hospital, bitch!"

"Excuse me?!"

"Don't you take me to no hospital in fucking Harlem. You take my ass to Beth Israel, hear me?"

"Mr. Simmons!"

"Beth Israel. I got a cousin there who's head nurse in one of the wards." Which was true, and I knew I'd need her help to get all the paperwork filled out properly so I could convince Apple I'd missed work because I'd been hospitalized.

"Mr. Simmons, if you're having chest pains, sir—"

"Just do it!"

❖

MY COUSIN WAS on shift when I arrived, and just as I'd planned, she made sure I got admitted fast, took care of all the red tape for me. The hospital kept me overnight for observation. I called both Apple and Jimmy to tell them what had happened. "Man, I'm so sorry I disappeared. I'm at Beth Israel. I started having chest pains and one thing led to another. Think I blacked out and somehow I wound up here." Everything was going according to plan.

But it all turned to shit when my whole family rushed into the emergency room. Jimmy rushed in, too; he was so upset to hear what had happened to me. He felt guilty about making me wait in his office and he didn't know how the hell I'd wound up at Beth Israel almost two days later. Seeing me there in that hospital bed really upset him and I started to feel real bad about deceiving him and everybody else. I basically lied to everyone I knew to keep them from finding out I was still smoking crack.

Right then one of the ward nurses walked into the emergency room. She was a middle-aged black woman and she was staring down at her clipboard with an incredibly disapproving look on her face. She sort of looked up and stopped in her tracks when she saw all these people hanging out around me.

"Mr. Simmons," she said, "how are you feeling?"

You should have seen my performance. I let my head flop back on the pillow like I was too weak to hold it up properly and gave her my weakest, most pitiful smile. "Fine," I said. Barely a breath, barely a whisper. "I'm feeling . . . much better now . . . thank you."

This woman wasn't buying it. No, not at all. She looked me right in the eye and said, "That's nice," but the tone of her voice was even. Too even. "Mr. Simmons," she said. "May I talk freely with you? I mean in front of everyone here."

"Yes . . . course . . . these people are . . . my family."

She smiled a smile that wasn't a smile at all. "That's good, Mr. Simmons. That's very nice. They look like a fine bunch. Now. If you don't mind my saying so." She held up the clipboard and waved it back and forth for emphasis. "I've looked over your blood work. The chemical analysis is very clear. And Mr. Simmons, I have to say: as an HIV positive individual, you should know better than to use large quantities of cocaine. You're just asking for trouble. Your immune system is very delicate, Mr. Simmons, and crack cocaine will kill you."

Performance over. I couldn't believe what that woman had just gone and done. Some of the people in that room didn't know I had HIV. But they knew it now. None of the people in that room knew I'd relapsed. They knew it now, though. And none of the people in that room had probably ever suspected I was such a low-down, dirty liar, but they knew that now, too. An all-time new low for me.

❖

LYING IN THAT hospital bed with everyone I loved surrounding me in a tight circle of shock, anger, frustration, and pain, a revelation came to me in that moment. That revelation told me: *I caused all this, I'm responsible for this mess. It didn't just happen out of the blue, it happened as a result of my actions, the things I chose to do and not to do all along the road of my life.*

That was a humbling thought. *What the hell was I thinking?*

Lying there in that bed, I didn't feel like Roy Simmons, professional offensive lineman. I didn't feel like Roy Simmons, the little boy, the neighborhood angel who used to help old people run errands to the market and mow lawns for fifty cents under the hot summer Savannah sun. No, I remember feeling like someone else entirely. Suddenly I was Roy Simmons, all over again, not 40 years old this time, but eleven. I'd gone over to Travis and Ellen's house to clean for them. Ellen'd left to go to town—she'd tousled my hair affectionately in that way she had and told me the money was up on the dresser in the bedroom. I could hear Travis's heavy breathing rattling away from inside. I could smell the gin. He was lying in darkness, cool and flaccid like a snake in its den. He'd drawn the curtains to keep anyone from seeing him do what he wanted to do.

Suddenly I was *this* Roy Simmons, the same little boy who got bumped from behind—it was no accident. The same little boy who answered Travis's call to enter the bedroom because he was an adult and I trusted him. The same little boy who he turned around and bent over the bed, pants down around his ankles, fists crushing the duvet into balls of fabric. Arms spread. Legs spread. The same little boy who felt the sting down there and bit his own lips to keep from screaming till he drew his own blood, a gushing taste of hot, coppery water in his mouth.

I was Roy Simmons. Again. The same Roy Simmons who'd felt the numbness creep over him as he walked home in the dark. Passed Grandma Lou watching her professional wrestling on the couch with her bottle of malt liquor. The same Roy Simmons who hid his bloody drawers in the hamper so that no one would know. And kept hiding. And kept hiding. And hiding and hiding until hiding became a habit, then a trait, then the basis of who I was. Who I would become. My personality. My spirit.

Lying there in that hospital bed, surrounded by my family—I stopped running. Stopped hiding. I had no choice. There was nowhere left to go anymore.

❖

MY DOCTORS STARTED me on HIV medication, a huge galaxy of pills called a "cocktail." This newly discovered formula of drugs prolonged the lives of people with AIDS, and for that I was grateful. But the medication made me nauseous. Some of the pills in that galaxy were enormous. They looked like they'd been made for horses. I experimented with everything I could to get them down my throat in the morning. Orange juice, apple juice, grapefruit juice, milk—nothing did the trick. I finally settled on washing the pills down with water. What the hell, it didn't cost me anything.

I stayed at Apple for about a month after the incident at the hospital. I took a risk and told some of my coworkers that I was HIV positive. It wasn't as hard as I thought it would be, in most cases. In a drug treatment center, such things are not unheard of. I was even shocked one time when one of my work mates listened very carefully to what I had to say and then nodded quietly. "So am I, Roy," he said. "So am I."

I made some real progress in the fight against my disease and my addiction my second time around. Then I relapsed again. And Apple fired me.

Unbelievably, Apple took me back *again*, though. Guess I wasn't the only counselor who'd had a relapse. It's sort of an occupational hazard within the therapeutic community. Apple even had a special six-month program for counselors who'd fallen off the wagon, only this time, in order to reclaim my job, I had to go stand up in front of the entire house the first night I got back and admit what I'd done wrong.

"Hi. My name is Roy Simmons. Ah . . . some of you know me already, some of you are new faces to me so—hi. Ah . . . I was a counselor here for eighteen months. In fact I see some of my clients here tonight. Hey, Shanda. Bobby. Scott. Tanisha. One of my clients even did well enough in her recovery to become a counselor—how you doing, Henry? Ahm . . . okay. So. I had this problem. I started—I started . . . I . . . Jesus . . ."

I couldn't say it, not in front of all these people. But that's the gig when they take you back. You gotta swallow your pride and go through the whole damn thing all over again. The shame and the guilt was like—oh my God. I just wanted to crawl under my chair, curl up into a little ball, and die.

And I was still using. Goddammit, that's the worst part of it all. After all this, I was still using the goddamn crack.

❖

How was I able to keep it up? Real simple. Experience. That's what it boils down to. Cold, hard addict's experience. I'd been smoking crack every day even while my HIV dictated that I see my doctors on a routine basis. They never suspected a thing. We only got tested if one of the counselors thought we *looked* like we were high. But a cold, hard addict like me is a veteran actor in that famous vaudeville show titled *Look, World! I'm Sober!* I'd earned myself some serious acting chops playing that role, I can tell you that. From the moment I set a foot in my physician's office to the moment I left, I was playing my most famous scene again. I was brilliant in the role of Sober Roy.

I knew enough about medications from my days in pro football to ask my doctors all sorts of highly informed questions about side effects, boosting one drug's effects with another, masking symptoms, and the extent to which a doctor would go before pulling back from the brink and muttering to himself about opening himself up to a medical malpractice suit. I'd fake symptoms and fake them well—I did it properly, there was research involved—to have grounds for requesting powerful pain killers from one doctor, which I mixed with the Prozac prescribed by another. Hell, I played doctors against one another: my pulmonologist against my primary care physician, my PCP against my dermatologist. *So-and-so said I should ask you for Prednizone. He said to give me the larger dosage and a brand name—no generics, no samples.* Then I'd put on my best innocent face and say something like, *Gee, do you think that might help me? So-and-so sounded really confident, and I* am *in a lot of discomfort here.*

Basically, whatever high I wasn't getting off the streets I was getting through the good old American health care system. And best of all, my insurance paid for it! This in itself is a perfect example of why addicts want to stay addicted. When you can play the system like that, why on earth go back to living a normal life where you have to sit around waiting for your boss to finally move on up so you can take over? How could you sit around listlessly knowing that the next guy who passes by your door probably wants nothing more than to take a crap on you and make you holler uncle? *Of course* an addict wants to stay addicted. I'd just brought the American Medical Association to its knees and here I was about to lie to my boss so I could qualify under Workers' Comp and get paid for not going in to work. That's a fucking great high!

Dealing with the folks at Apple was no problem. I had to tell my boss I was HIV positive and under a doctor's care in order for him to understand why I was handing him all these notes that said, "*Roy Simmons is far too weak to come to work at the moment. For the foreseeable future, he will be immensely ill and in aggressive treatment for his disease. Please begin whatever paperwork is necessary to place him in your company's Workers' Comp program, and by all means call my office immediately if you have any questions.*" But by the time they wondered if maybe something fishy was going on, I was bouncing back and forth to every crack house in Bay shore, Amityville, Bayside, and Bridgehampton. I had disability checks coming in and I could cash them real quick at any liquor store. I was ready to rock once more.

And rock I did. But in the spring of 1999 I made another attempt at getting sober and signed myself into a treatment center out in Central Islip. Jimmy drove out to Long Island for a visit and picked me up to go shopping in the Hamptons. True to form, generous Jimmy made a supermarket run and paid for everything. When we got back to Central Islip, all my cupboards and my refrigerator were full. I don't think I've ever felt that domestically tranquil in my entire life.

Jimmy said he was real proud of all the progress I'd made in my recovery. On his way out the door of my place, he paused in the threshold and said, "Roy, I know that things have been really rough for you. But I just wanted you to know—you're an inspiration to me. I know how far you've come and I know what kind of battles you've fought. If I can ever be of any help to you at all, I want you to know—you can call me any time. It doesn't matter where I am or what time it is. I'll drop whatever I'm doing and come to help you."

If the poor man only knew. I said, "Thank you, Jimmy. That's great. I'm so lucky to have a friend like you." Later that year Jimmy called me up with a job offer. It was December and the holiday crush was on and his office needed an extra set of hands to do odd jobs like stuffing Christmas bags and running errands. "If you want a little extra money," Jimmy said, "I could sure use the help." Now, how could I turn down an offer like that? "Absolutely," I said. "Let's make it happen." And just like that, I went to work again.

One day when the job was almost finished, Jimmy took me to a party at his boss's penthouse where I met Maer Roshan, the senior editor of *New York* magazine, and one of their top writers, Lisa DePaulo. I was very shy about the whole thing but Jimmy wasn't. He took me by the arm and dragged me across the room to meet them. True to form, Jimmy'd already put together his presentation in his head. "Guys! *Guys!!* This is my friend *Roy Simmons*. He used to play pro football. Wait till you hear *his* story." And just like that I was the life of the party. We talked about the best ideas for telling my story. *A movie? Studio, independent, or TV? A book?* I learned a lot about the way the publishing industry works. Jimmy and I were hits.

We were getting on so well that the next day he let me borrow his brand-new $100,000 S-500 Mercedes. The idea was for me to pick up my mother and bring her into the city to see Jimmy—they hadn't seen each other in years. Then my mother and I would drive the car out to Jersey so we could attend the funeral of Roz's mother. It was a simple plan that only took us a few minutes to hammer out. Then Jimmy gave me the keys to the car, along with $40, and he said, "Gas it up and get it washed. It's on me." This turned out to be a very big mistake.

❖

PICK UP MY mother in Amityville. Bring her into New York City. Quick reunion/shopping trip with Jimmy. Wave fond good-byes. Back out to Jersey. Funeral. Make sure to hug Roz, she needs you right now. Back out to Amityville. Drop off mama. Take the car back into the city. Meet Jimmy at his place to hand over the keys. Do that with a smile. Make sure to say thank you. Jimmy's been a good friend and we've been getting along lately. This is a good thing.

The whole plan was locked into my head and everything was going fine that morning. I was up early and dressed for the day. I had a good breakfast and just the right amount of coffee. All I had to do was gas up the car and get it washed. The $40 Jimmy gave me was lying on my kitchen table and I remember staring at it for a long time, like it was about to get up on its own two legs and say something important. But it never did. So I walked toward the kitchen table real slowly and picked it up. Then I headed out the front door.

I headed toward Amityville, hit a gas station, and filled up the tank. Then I got back out on the highway and found a car wash. I was in the middle of the second rinse cycle when a *beeeeeep!* went off in the car and I jumped. For a few moments after that, I couldn't figure out what the sound was. It beeped again: *beeeeeeep! beeeeeeeeep!* It sounded like a phone. Which is when I figured out: that's exactly what it was. Jimmy'd had a car phone installed with two-way speakers mounted right on the dashboard of the Mercedes. I didn't know how to pick the thing up. But apparently I didn't have to bother. Jimmy had set the protocols on the phone so it automatically picked up after three rings. This whole discovery took me a little while and caused me considerable turmoil.

It was my mother on the phone. One second I was searching around, trying to find the beeping noise, the next her voice was flooding into the cabin of the Mercedes. I didn't have to move a muscle to talk to her. Whatever I said, she'd hear me. The whole thing made me a little nervous. Every time I said a word to my mother throughout this entire conversation, I had the unsettling feeling that I was talking to God.

"Roy?" "Roy?! This is your mother. Where are you? I'm all dressed and packed and ready to go."

Really, it was the weirdest thing talking to the windshield while the car moved slowly forward on a conveyor belt and the big sudsy wheels rubbed right up against the glass. "I'm on my way. I'm at the car wash. Just wanna make sure they do a nice job. I want them to clean out the interior."

"Oooh. Is it a nice car?"

"Yes, it is. You'll see. Just sit tight, okay? I'll be there soon."

"Okay, Roy. Thanks." She hung up the phone and the cabin of the Mercedes was suddenly silent again.

I really had every intention of going to pick her up. The car was all gassed up and it looked gorgeous thanks to the car wash. It *shone* like a new car. The leather seats smelled fresh and new, the way good leather seats should. I was dressed in my best black suit. I knew my mother would be dressed to the nines, looking beautiful. In a car like that, we'd almost look too good to attend a funeral. We'd almost look like I'd always dreamed we'd be. Rich. Affluent. Happy. Prosperous. All the things we'd never been in Savannah when I was growing up. All the things we'd set our sights on.

But the car wasn't mine. The suit was the only one I owned. It was all a lie, a terrible lie. I didn't have any money. I wasn't affluent. The $40 Jimmy'd given me was gone. I'd spent it all. The gas plus the car wash cost me 39 bucks and change. All I had left was two quarters, a dime, and some pennies lying in the dashboard change well. *Here I am again, grubbing for cash and living a lie,* I thought. And something about that irked me. Something about that just didn't seem right. In that moment—don't blink, cause you might've missed it—I was pulled right out of myself. Suddenly nothing was important anymore. Motes of dust in the wind. What does it matter? Who really cares? The next thing I was knew, I was making a right turn where I should have gone left to reach my mother's house. A slight detour, that's what I told myself. Just a tiny little side trip.

❖

OF COURSE I knew where to get good drugs in Amityville: Albany Avenue near the Sunrise Highway. I'd have to play it cool and work hard if I was gonna score without cash, though. About an hour later I was still cruising around when I saw this black guy in his late twenties standing on the corner with a do-rag on his head and his hands stuffed into the pockets of his baggy jeans, looking real innocent. Too innocent. You should have seen his expression when I stopped that Mercedes right there in front of him and powered down the passenger-side window. It took him a second to realize that no, this wasn't a dream. This was real. This might be his lucky day. He stepped up to the car and leaned in.

I grinned at him. "Whas up, man? How you doing today?"

"Cool, man. I'm cool."

"I can see that for myself. Well. Whachoo doing?"

"Aw, you know, man. Nothing."

"You wanna go for a ride in my car here? We can hang out for a bit."

That's all I needed to say, he knew the deal from there. It's all about eye contact, and that's exactly what I'd given him. He thought it over for a second or two. Then he said, "Sure, man. Okay." And just like that he opened the passenger door and slid right on in. He looked around the car like he'd just entered an alien's spaceship. "Nice ride, man."

"It is, isn't it? Where we going?"

"'Round the corner, make a left, and down one block. I got a source."

I gave him my last piece of jewelry, a gift from Roz, and he was able to get us a $50 piece of rock, which we took to a hotel and smoked all to hell before having sex. After that, we went back to the streets, found some more rock and some more friends. Then some booze and some music. Pretty soon the night took on a life of its own.

❖

THAT EVENING, JIMMY went out on an early blind date at a restaurant in Union Square. He got back to his loft at Broadway and East 4th Street in time to meet my mom and me according to the schedule we'd hammered out. As it was, he ended up pacing for over an hour until he finally got tired of checking his watch and picked up the phone to call my mother's cell phone.

"Hey, Norma. It's Jimmy. I just wanted to make sure everything's okay."

My mother started screaming at him. "No, it is *not* okay, Jimmy! Where the hell is Roy? I been calling him and calling him, he won't pick up the line." Jimmy knew right then that I'd stolen his car.

Before going down to the police station to file a report, he took a chance and called the built-in speakerphone on the dashboard of the Mercedes. I was in the car along with three of my newfound friends—all of them crack dealers—when the damn thing rang and startled the hell out of me again. My friends and I were having our own private little rolling crack party in the Mercedes, giggling up a storm and passing bottles of malt liquor back and forth while I tried to keep the car moving straight along the highway. It was a tough job.

The phone rang once—*beeeeeeeep!*—and one of my friends went, "Gaaaaaaaaaagh!" and made a face. Everybody started laughing hard enough to spit.

The phone rang twice and somebody said, "What the fuck is *that* shit?! Is that somebody's *phone*?!?" I said, "Yeah, man. Ain't that great? It's right in the goddamn dash."

"Well, turn it off, man. It's fucking up my high."

"I don't know how to turn it off." Which was true.

The phone rang three times and somebody said, "Shit, man, who is it? I'm seriously starting to take offense here." To which I said, "Oh, you know. It's nothing, I bet. Probably just some stupid telemarketer trying to sell something. Pass that damn pipe over here."

Right then, Jimmy's voice boomed through the cabin of the Mercedes like the voice of God himself. "ROY SIMMONS, YOU SONOVABITCH! BRING MY FUCKING CAR BACK RIGHT

NOW!" I'd forgotten the thing was set to pick up automatically after three rings.

One of my friends rolled his eyes and said, "Who the fuck is that?! Who the fuck *is* that?!?" To which I just shook my head and threw up my hands. I was starting to giggle. "That," I said, "is the man who owns this car." Pure laughter from that point forward. I took another hit from the pipe and promptly forgot all about Jimmy Hester. It was pretty easy to do once one of the dealers figured out how to disconnect the dashboard phone. From there on out, everything was blissfully silent.

19

I HELD ON to the Mercedes for about a week, during which time Jimmy tried calling the dashboard phone about every five minutes. I quickly learned to ignore the blinking light that told me there was an incoming call. With its automatic pick-up disconnected, the phone actually became a moot issue. Besides, I had a lot to concentrate on. I was chauffeuring my dealer friends and some of *their* friends all over Long Island. We zipped back and forth to different hotels, where I was given a crash course in the commerce of narcotics. I watched cocaine get distilled back down to its pure essence, then watched the essence get cut with fillers, parceled into packages, and readied for sale.

When all this got too boring, I'd go back out to Albany Avenue and pick up girls off the strip who were professional shoplifters. I'd drive them over to a Walgreens and wait in the parking lot while they boosted merchandise, then drive them around to locations where they could fence all the goods they'd stolen. All the cash they made got plowed back into buying more drugs, so the circle completed itself.

Jimmy went ahead and filed a report with the local police precinct in Manhattan, which is why I was driving down a side street one day and saw red, white, and blue roller lights in my rearview mirror. I heard the siren. *Shit.* The girl in my passenger seat at the time was a hustler—you could tell just by looking at her—and I knew she had drugs on her person, same as I did. *This is not a good situation.* I pulled over.

The girl started getting a little nervous. "Yo, man. I got rock on me."

"I know. So do I. Hold on a second." I was looking in the rearview mirror. The cop was on his radio, calling in the license plate. We only had a few seconds.

"Yo, man. This shit is wack! I can't be caught again, man, been caught too many motherfucking times already—"

"Shut up! Here." I tossed her my wrapped packages of crack. They landed in her lap. Her eyes got all wide and she started rocking back and forth with indignation. "Yo, yo, *yo*! Whachoo want me ta do with all this shit?"

"Hide it! Just fucking hide it!" I could see the cop starting to climb out of his car in the mirror. He'd be on us in a second.

"Where the fuck am I s'posed to hide this shit?!"

"Just do it!"

And she did. She lifted her skirt and pulled down her drawers and packed those drugs right into her pussy, neat as you please. Just in time, too. The cop approached my window, so I powered it down. I noticed how he kept his distance from the car. He stopped far enough away where he could bolt if he had to, and kept his hand resting on the butt of his gun, ready to draw. *Shit, he's not taking any chances. We got a problem here.*

"Mr. Simmons?"

"Yes?"

"Are you armed, sir?"

"What? Hell, no."

"May I see your hands, please." I put them up on the steering wheel. "Is the woman in the car with you armed?"

"Armed? No, no. Hey, look. What's this all about? I think there's been some kind of misunderstanding here."

"Sir, you're driving a stolen vehicle."

"Stolen? No. No, this car belongs to my friend Jimmy Hester. He knows I've got it. Ain't no big thing—"

The cop put out a hand like he was stopping traffic. "Mr. Simmons, keep your hands on the steering wheel, please. This car is reported stolen. When I tell you to, sir, I want you to slowly—*very slowly*—get out of the vehicle with your hands up."

"Listen. This is all a big misunderstanding. Tell Jimmy Hester I'm gonna bring the car back real soon. I'm just having it detailed." That's when I heard the screech of rubber tires locking to a halt and glanced up. In the rearview, I could see more flashing red lights—lots more. Four more police cars had shown up and blocked off the street behind me. Police officers got out. You could tell by the way they were moving that they were ready for anything. More cars pulled up. My mother and my aunt Rosetta got out of one car, my brother Gary got out of another. Right then I wanted to crawl under the car and have the girl drive all over me, back and forth, back and forth, until I was deader than a doornail.

"Mr. Simmons, sir, please get out of the car, now. Slowly. With your hands up."

"I want you to let the girl go."

"Please, sir—"

"She got nothing to do with this. I want you to let the girl go!"

They did. Thank God. And they never found the drugs. She played it off all innocent like I'd just swung around on Albany and picked her up for a ride. They didn't want her. They wanted me. And they got me, all right. They got me real good.

I called Jimmy from the police station to apologize, but he didn't want to speak to me. He made one thing clear to me: that he felt hurt for Roz more than anything else. That didn't make any sense to me until I recalled that Roz's mother had passed away. Mama and I had been all set to go to the funeral. The details were fuzzy in my head, like I was recalling scenes from somebody else's life.

"You're a sick man, Roy," Jimmy said. "Roz needed you at the wake and the funeral."

"Jimmy, I don't know what to say."

"I wouldn't listen, anyway. I'm done with you."

And it turns out he was. Jimmy Hester wouldn't speak to me again for over two years. His father drove him out to Long Island to pick up the Mercedes. He drove it all the way back to Manhattan with the windows open despite the December cold so he could air out the stench of my bingeing.

I don't know how to end this story. I'd like to tell you that I finally got my act together and started walking the straight and narrow like a good respectable person, but I didn't. Over the next two years I was arrested several times for drugs and shoplifting and too many other offenses to list. Hell, I continued to get high even while ducking in and out of treatment facilities. I continued to scare my family and friends half to death on several occasions, dropping out of sight from time to time, often for weeks at a stretch.

One time my brother Gary went looking for me. He works for a division of the DEA, so he asked the local police to keep an eye out for the car I was driving at the time, a white Mercury Cougar. They found the car, all right; some crackhead was driving it. The cops tried to impound the car but the crackhead said he owned it now. He had the title deed in his possession and my signature was right there on the bottom line. Apparently, I'd signed it over to him—I don't remember how or when. Knowing me, I probably gave him the car for two hundred dollars' worth of rock. One thing you can say about people who live close to crack—they sure as hell get some great deals on automobile purchases.

I'd like to tell you that I never got high again and never had an affair with a drag queen who stole my clothes iron for crack while we were both living at a sober house in Brentwood—me and clothes irons and crack apparently have some sort of twisted, undeniable relationship. I'd like to tell you that stuff never happened. But I can't. 'Cause I did. Just like I'd like to tell you how I never got arrested at a Sears department store for shoplifting almost a thousand dollars' worth of baby clothes from the children's department. Guilty as charged. I'd like to tell you that I learned to be responsible. That I held down a good job and made people proud of me. That I got myself under control and finally conquered my addiction and my loneliness, my suffering and my ability to make other people suffer. But I can't. If I told you I did, I'd be lying to you.

Eventually I got into a stretch where I was sober for a full year. I called up Jimmy to tell him the good news. We hadn't spoken since the incident with the car. He accepted my call—very generous of him, when I think about it—and I asked him to speak at my one year ceremony. Who better than Jimmy? He'd been sober for twelve years at that point.

He knew the gauntlet. After all we'd been through together, it seemed only fitting to have him speak on my behalf. Jimmy accepted the engagement, and showed up at my treatment group's Tuesday night meeting in a preschool classroom at a church in Lake Ronkonkoma. My mother and my aunt Rosetta were also there. We were a family again, just like old times.

Five minutes before the meeting, I got so nervous that I pulled Jimmy into a little kitchen by the classroom and closed the door behind him. I could see this made him nervous. His eyes got all wide and he started edging away from me. "What is it, Roy?"

"Well, see . . . it's like this . . ."

"What?! It's like *what*?!"

"Jimmy, look. I don't care what you tell these people. You're my friend and I invited you to speak today and I'm so glad you did. You can tell them anything you want about my football career, you can tell them how I tried to jump off a bridge in San Francisco, you can tell them about stealing your damn car. I don't care. Just please—please, Jimmy. Don't mention that . . . that . . ."

"That *what*?"

"Please don't mention that I'm gay or HIV positive." Jimmy recoiled as if he'd been slapped in the face. "You mean they don't *know*?!?" he howled. Well, of course they didn't. I hadn't told anyone. Remember, I'm really good at keeping secrets. At keeping secrets, I'm the best.

I wish I could end my story by saying I've embraced full disclosure. That I'm proud of who I am—my sexuality, my spirit, my soul. I wish I could say that I've had long talks with all my demons and we've amicably settled our disagreements. I wish I could tell you I'm finally, completely in control of myself. I can't.

Jimmy went up to the lectern that night and made his presentation. He had the crowd in stitches; he's a natural-born storyteller. Hearing him tell the tale of how I stole his car and drove it around searching for crack had everybody rolling in the aisles. When he was finished, though, he smiled a little—smiled like he was sad—and he said, "Roy and I have had an amazing journey together. I'm very proud of my friend. He's leaped a lot of high hurdles over the years and he's got a lot more ahead of him on the long track of life. I wish him the very best of luck with that, and if he ever needs me to lend a hand, I'll be there. I promise you that, Roy. I'll be there for you. We all will."

He paused and thought about it some. Then he said, "Unless you steal my car again. Touch my car one more time and I'll never speak to you for as long as you live." The crowd laughed so hard they were crying. So was I. It's good to have friends. It's good to know that you can stumble and fall many times in your life. If you have friends, though, someone will always be there to help you get back on your feet.

❖

In March of 2003, I went back to Atlanta to see my daughter, Kara, graduate from Morris Brown College. It was a bittersweet journey for me, since I'd missed her high school graduation—hell, I'd missed her entire life. My entire family gathered to witness the ceremony, which took place at the Morris Brown football stadium on a cold, damp day. Watching everyone fawn over Kara—my aunts and my uncles, my cousins and family friends—watching how they joked with Kara and poked fun at one another and laughed about old times they'd shared, that's when I realized the extent of the loss I'd suffered in life. I'd done some pretty twisted things in my days, but none of them was as horrible as the way I'd abandoned my daughter.

It was suddenly all so clear. Kara was my daughter, but I hadn't been her father. We barely knew each other. And all that weekend, every time I tried to tell her how pretty she was, or how proud of her I was, or how I wished—dear God I wished—that I'd been a different man for her, a better man, her sweet face took on this expression I can't describe. Part like she hated me. Part like she loved me. Part like she wished I would just disappear.

After the ceremony, as she walked off the field, I ran up to meet her by the mouth of the stadium tunnel that led to the outside world. I startled her by putting a bouquet of flowers in her hands, and kissed her while she blushed. "Hey!" someone called. "Turn around, you two, so I can get a picture of you." We did; we linked ourselves arm-in-arm like we were old friends posing for the ten-thousandth time. And just as the camera flashes began to pop off like strobe lights, just as my own smile started bursting forth from between my lips despite all the awkwardness I felt in that moment, just as the years of darkness and running blind seemed ready to dissolve into smoke and lift themselves up to the gray March sky, there was Sheila, twenty feet away. The little girl I'd fallen in love with in the third grade was standing right before me, staring me down with hard eyes, trying to keep her anger under control.

You cut your beautiful hair, I thought. And you look older—older like me—but Dear God, you're still so pretty. Sheila, you'll always be beautiful—and not just to me. You're beautiful no matter who sees you; beauty and love are the only things that survive, I know that now. And I'm sorry, Sheila. You'll never know how sorry I am.

She refused to come near me. The camera flashes kept popping. I kept smiling, my arm still linked with Kara's. Then I saw an old family friend from elementary school, a woman by the name of Debra Newton who is Kara's godmother. She worked her way over to Sheila and spoke in her ear. Sheila's eyes got even harder; she shook her head. Debra said something else and Sheila bit her lip. Her eyes were locked on mine. I have no idea what Debra said to her—I'll never figure this part out—but whatever she did must've done the trick. Sheila began to move toward us. She walked right up to Kara and I and stood before us, trying to stay calm.

"Roy . . ." she said.

Debra appeared again at her side. "Go on, Sheila. Give him a big hug." I don't know who reached out first, her or me. And no, it wasn't a big hug, more like a quick pat on the back. But it was enough. After all I'd done to deserve much less than that, it was enough.

Maybe now, I thought. *Maybe now my life can begin.*

EPILOGUE

IN OCTOBER OF 2002, a defensive linebacker named Esera Tuaolo shocked a lot of people by retiring somewhat early from pro football, at the age of thirty-four. Tuaolo, who'd played in Super Bowl XXXIII for the Atlanta Falcons, shocked even more people when he told them *why* he was retiring. "No one in the NFL knows who Esera Tuaolo is," he told HBO's Bernard Goldberg. "What they saw was an actor." Tuaolo then revealed that he is and always has been gay, after which he broke down and cried on national television.

A Samoan by birth, Tuaolo is 6'3" and 300 pounds. He just might be one of the biggest damn men you've ever seen walking down the street. They called him "Mr. Aloha." After nearly a decade of keeping his sexuality a secret from his teammates and family, he was emotionally exhausted. He'd finally heard one locker room gay joke too many. For a long time, he thought about suicide. The details of how he wanted to end his life don't matter. I knew all of Esera's story the moment I heard the first sentence; it was my story, too. I wept when I heard it.

Tuaolo was known as a rough drinker. Legend has it that he went out with some teammates one time and downed twenty shots of tequila. The other guys loved this, of course. They called him an animal and clapped him on the back. To them, Tuaolo was a king-high stud, a man who could destroy his opponents by launching his massive body at them at high speeds and punching through their lines like they were made of balsa wood. But he could still parade around in public with a beautiful young woman on his arm, smiling like his face was about to crack. "What I was really trying to do was erase the pain," Esera said.

Me, too, Esera. Me, too.

Tuaolo's career was a lot like mine—not especially noteworthy. He managed to play nine years in the NFL and that's no easy feat. But rather than admit that he was an average player, he's been quoted as saying that he deliberately played *under his potential*. Being a rising star, said Esera, would've attracted too much attention to his personal life. He suffered sleepless nights every time he successfully sacked an enemy quarterback. He'd lie in bed staring at the ceiling in mortal terror, wondering if now would be the moment when the spotlight turned on him and some nosy reporter would check into his background, put two and two together, and start a tabloid frenzy. Being a household name wasn't worth exposing himself. The NFL was never Tuaolo's dream. He'd just wanted the paycheck. With a good job, he could have a happy life, just like the rest of us. Only the life Tuaolo dreamed of was the life of a successful gay man.

When I heard that Tuaolo'd deliberately dampened his abilities to hide his sexuality, I found myself wondering all over again, *What would my career have been like if I'd been able to focus on it without the drugs, the alcohol, the lies, the deceptions? Yes, it was a paycheck for me, too, and a fine one at that. But it could have been so much more.*

The HBO special featured another guest, Tuaolo's teammate Sterling Sharpe, formerly of the Green Bay Packers, lately a member of ESPN's commentator team. Goldberg asked Sharpe, "What do you think would have happened if Esera had come out of the closet while he was still playing football?" Sharpe didn't take any time to think it over. He knew the answer as well as I did. He said, "He would have been eaten alive. He would have been hated for it."

Times have changed for the better, I think. Other NFL players eventually offered their opinions on Tuaolo's coming out. Todd Steussie had been Esera's teammate on the Vikings from '94 to '96; he admitted he'd known Tuaolo was gay for some time. "To me," he said in an interview, "what Esera does on his own time is his own business. I consider him a friend. I really don't see this as being such a big deal. To me, it's a non-issue." I see this sort of account as exemplifying the sharp division among players in the NFL on the issue of gay players. Steussie said he couldn't care less if his teammate was gay, while Sharpe noted that a player who came out of the closet on a Monday wouldn't find himself at practice with the rest of the team by Tuesday.

Craig Sauer had also played with Tuaolo on the Falcons. Sauer said he'd heard rumors about Esera's sex life and, being a devout Christian, took the bull by the horns and called his old teammate. He said, "Esera, I've been hearing a lot of things and I want to know the truth. Are you gay?" Tuaolo didn't say anything for a long moment. In his mind the jig was finally up. Finally he admitted that yes, it was true. He was.

Sauer listened to the news and made his choice. He said, "Okay. Here's the deal. You know I disagree with it—" *it* being Tuaolo's homosexuality, "—and I believe that God disagrees with it, too. But I love you like a brother. If you can handle me not agreeing with your lifestyle, we can be friends." Tuaolo says he appreciated Sauer's honesty. He found Sauer's terms acceptable and the two have reportedly remained friends to this day. Tuaolo thanked him, but Sauer shrugged it off. He said, "You've been running a long time, Esera. Now you don't have to run anymore. Not with me."

Tuaolo later summarized his coming out to a reporter from Outsports. com. "I retired because I wanted to be happy. I feel wonderful now, like I've taken off the costume I've been wearing all my life."

On November 30, 2003, six years after I was diagnosed with HIV, the *New York Times* broke the story that I, Roy Simmons, former offensive linebacker for the NFL, was infected. The article was written by Maureen Orth and was called "Out of the Locker Room, and the Closet." Ms. Orth did an excellent job of recounting my life. She somehow managed to summarize all my crazy years by saying, "To keep his furtive gay life a secret, [Simmons] had cultivated a reputation for being the life of the party. He constantly juggled deception and compartmentalization, while placating those of both sexes closest to him." Too true. But what she didn't add was that being the life of the party always comes at a heavy price. I didn't pay that tab. My family and friends did. You have to read between the lines of the *Times* article to figure that part out, but that's the awful truth of it.

It was the first and only time to date that a pro football player has come forward to admit he's HIV positive. That in itself was shocking news, but it's also the first time I publicly admitted to being raped as a child. The article recounted the incident I'd had with Travis, and then it said this: "Years later as an adult, [Simmons] tortured himself wondering—often while drunk or high on drugs—if he would have been straight if he had not been assaulted. He blamed himself and suffered from a diminished sense of self-worth and confusion over his sexual identity."

I remember having to sit down when I read those words. Because suddenly everything I'd ever done in my life seemed clear to me. *Diminished sense of self-worth. Confusion over my sexual identity.* When I read that article, I couldn't help but shake my head. *Is that all it was?* I thought. *Was the root of all my craziness really as simple—as clinical—as all that?*

Maybe. Maybe not. It didn't matter any more. The only thing that counted was that finally, at long last, I had no more secrets. My journey began in a one-story row house on a dirt road called Burroughs Street on the west side of Savannah. From there my path took many twists and turns though landscapes dark and wild. Now it ended here, with confession. A plea for redemption in what I guess is the world's most celebrated newspaper. Who would have guessed that a poor black child growing up like I did—*when* I did—could run so far in one lifetime?

News of the rape stunned everybody like a bomb blast. Most of my family members hadn't been privy to that particular piece of information; like I said, we hid things well back in the '60s. And Dr. Goldberg was quoted in the article as saying that even though I'd confided my secret to him back in the early '80s, he "hadn't understood the trauma associated" with my sexual assault. I believe him. He's a good man who tried to help me every moment I was in need.

But news of the rape particularly devastated the closest friend I have in this world. When he heard what the Neighbor had done to me all those years ago, Jimmy Hester was devastated. "My God, Roy!" he said. I could see in his eyes what I'd done to him, what I'd done to *everyone.* Withholding the truth from your loved ones can be as mortal a wound as a knife through the heart. I know that now. "Why didn't you *tell* me, Roy? Why didn't you tell *anyone?*"

I don't know, Jimmy, I honestly don't. All I can say is that sometimes the past is too painful to reveal.

You try and you try. You cry out for help in all the wrong ways when the words won't come out right. Maybe you drive away every living soul who's ever loved you—maybe you even drive *yourself* away, drive yourself crazy, drive yourself to drink. Whatever. You bury yourself while you're still alive, throwing anything you can on the open grave just to fill in the hole. You toss in drugs, you toss in shame—and secrets, and jail, and madness, and lies. But the hole never seems to fill. No matter what you pour into it, it's always there, gaping open. Dark. Endless. So you take off running, try to leave it behind. One more desperate bid to stop the pain, one more shot in the dark at redemption you can search for all your life, and never find . . .

I'm sorry, Jimmy. I'm sorry, Sheila. And Kara and Kathy and Mama and Gary and *everyone*. It doesn't matter. It never will. No matter how fast you are, sooner or later, we all stop running.

ACKNOWLEDGMENTS

FIRST AND FOREMOST, I would like to acknowledge Jesus—without Him I am nothing. To my daughter, Kara; my first love Sheila; and to Roz for standing by me. I apologize for all the pain I brought to your lives. To my mother, Norma Jean Simmons, brother Gary and Aunt Rosetta for all the many wonderful things you have done for me and for the rest of our family.

To Jimmy Hester—you are truly a friend. You believed in me since you were a kid, even though we've had our ups and downs over the years. Nothing stopped you from getting this book published. If anyone ever needs the impossible done, call Jimmy Hester.

Thank you to my editor, Don Weise, for believing in my story. To my publisher, Will Balliett, to the publicity team of Karen Auerbach and Blanca Oliviery, and everyone at Avalon. Thanks also to my lawyer, Barbara Burns . . . and to Bethann Hardison for all your guidance and wisdom that you so freely gave to this project.

There have been many more people involved in this project that I owe thanks to. Butch Woolfolk—thanks for jumping on the ship in the beginning. You're a great writer. Benoit Denizet-Lewis—what a talent! Good luck with your book. Steve Serby—we wanted you sooooo bad! Thanks for the fun lunches at the Dish (thank you Dish restaurant). To Flo Anthony, our star. My lovely, beautiful and very talented Maureen Orth. It all started with you—thank you, dear. We love you. And finally to my co-author Damon DiMarco—you did an extraordinary job. I'm incredibly appreciative of your collaboration with me.

Thanks to Lillian Smith, *The New York Times*, *HIV/PLUS* magazine, and all the media that believed in my story and helped give voice to those who are living with HIV, as well as those recovering from child sexual abuse and substance abuse.

To all the women who put up with men like me—no one should be treated so dishonestly. All of you living with HIV—keep your head to the sky and remember God is watching over you. To all addicts who are on the path to sobriety—ONE DAY AT A TIME. To all survivors of child sexual assault—you did nothing wrong and you are not alone. I'd also thank all the advocates fighting daily for those of us living with HIV and those of us who are rape survivors.

I want to thank everyone for their prayers—prayer is powerful. Thanks to Pastor Marcia Buckley of the Apostolic House of Prayer in Martha's Vineyard, Minister John Meade and all the saints—a very deep thank you for your prayers and friendship. Thanks to Dr. Roni DeLuz of the Martha's Vineyard Diet Detox for helping me get my health back on track—you're a beautiful angel.

I thank everyone who has forgiven me—the list is too long to name everyone, but I love and thank all of you. For those I didn't make amends with, I ask for your forgiveness. I thank all the men who have been honest about their sexual lives with their women partners. We who are infected with HIV can help slow the spread of the virus by being honest with our partners and practicing safer sex every time. We owe it to ourselves and our partners.

God Bless Everyone.